Oral Discipleship

And

Leadership Training

Oral Discipleship and Leadership Training

Copyright 2024 © Western Academic Publishers

Enoch Wan & John Ferch, Editors

Cover designed by Mark Benec

ISBN: 978-1-954692-29-9

Western Academic Publishers

Table of Contents

Chapter 1: Introduction

Enoch Wan

The Background of this Book

This book emerged from the Orality Track presentations at the Evangelical Missiological Society's annual meeting held at Dallas Theological Seminary, September 2023. Several papers from the previous year's meeting at Dallas International University were also selected. Presenters included seminary professors, trainers and consultants in the field of oral Bible translation, and missionaries. Of the papers presented in the Orality Track, only fourteen have been selected for inclusion in this volume.

The Purpose of this Book

Orality is a relative newcomer in the field of missiological studies, though it has a long history in mission practice. Therefore, available literature is limited. This volume is an effort to rectify the situation by making a small contribution.

The Readership of this Book

This book is written for Christian workers and orality practitioners. Teachers and trainers, such as Bible school and seminary teachers will find the collection of papers informative and inspiring.

Definition of Key Terms

Orality

"A preferred way to hear, process, remember, and communicate with the human voice as the primary medium. Orality includes multiple media, such as storytelling, poetry, music, visual arts, drama, and dance."[1]

Oral discipleship and leadership

Discipleship and leadership for those who are oral-preference learners and operating within oral contexts.

---

[1] Tom A. Steffen and William Bjoraker, *The Return of Oral Hermeneutics: As Good Today as It Was for the Hebrew Bible and First-Century Christianity* (Eugene: Wipf and Stock, 2020), 317.

The Organization of this Book

The collection of papers is divided into four parts. Part 1 provides a basic understanding of orality and addresses issues related to the principles and practice of orality. Part 2 deals with oral discipleship training, including case studies. Part 3 covers the "what" and "how" of oral leadership training. The conclusion by John Ferch is both an informative and inspiring read on orality.

Part 1: Basic Understanding

Chapter 2:
Visual and Narrative Theology: Designing for Reproducibility

Ray Neu

Abstract

Can a picture teach theology? Can a story become a teacher? Can spiritual transformation take place through group dynamics? Can we do hermeneutics without reading? Can all of this be done without reliance on literature? The answer to all these questions is a resounding "Yes!" Oral Pastor Training is flourishing across several countries in Africa. This chapter explores some of the methods and mechanics driving this phenomenon that extends even to the 7th and 8th generations!

Introduction

I would like to paint you a beautiful, large panoramic picture, but I'm not an artist, so I'll tell you some stories instead.

Somehow, we ended up in West Africa, in northern Ghana—I don't actually recall what led to that first trip, but I'll *never* forget it! Such was the impact *on me* that I would like to share some things I learned.

Brush Stroke: Orality Training

We went to offer a "Bible training for people who do not read." That was the message shared at the local market as various vendors and customers heard and carried this odd message back to their communities. First day, only about 30 people showed up, which was a significant disappointment as we had traveled for 2 ½ days to get there. The second day, 60 people showed up because the first curiosity seekers realized and spread the word that this really was *for them*, Bible training for those who did not read!

There was a tall, thin, well-dressed young man, sitting back *very* relaxed, as close to lying down as you can get and still be in a chair. My astute observation was that he was definitely there for the free lunches. He was quiet, not engaged much, and yet he sat in the front row. I decided that was to give his long legs space to recline. Nevertheless, we pressed on.

I was not fully aware at that time of the lessons I was beginning to learn, including a most valuable statement from Éla: "It is meaningless to make Christianity a religion of the written word in a civilization of the spoken word!"[1] My learning journey was just beginning. *I learned that there are various types of oral, visual, physical, and non-verbal communication.*

Brush Stroke: No Chalkboard

I had created a truly wonderful illustrative drawing which helped explain the usefulness of understanding and applying "Worldview" considerations into Orality Ministry. Normally, we would draw this out on a whiteboard, or a chalkboard, or if need be, a large piece of paper.

None of those devices existed in this place.

My East African friend had an idea. He constructed my drawing physically by using what was available—two benches, some sticks from a tree, some fist-sized rocks, a Bible, and a pair of glasses. The presentation that day was *so good*, so much *clearer* and more *concrete*, that we never went back to the whiteboard or the chalkboard or even paper. *Everywhere* we went after that, even in urban settings, I was asking for sticks, rocks, benches, a Bible and someone else's glasses (because I need mine). The physical representation was so helpful that we kept it in place for two more days, referring to it often.

Figure 1. Physical Representation of Chalkboard Drawing

---

[1] Jean-Marc Éla, *My Faith as an African* (Eugene: Wipf and Stock, 1988), 45.

Hiebert explains why this worked so well:

We who are literate tend to think only in terms of storing and communicating the gospel in spoken and written forms. We fail to realize that oral societies are not "illiterate." They have, in fact, a rich supply of cultural knowledge and many different ways of storing it. In such societies, we must present the gospel in concrete ways that the people will recall.[2]

I learned that concrete, physical illustrations are powerful with Oral Learners.

Brush Stroke: Women and Men

Oil and water...sometimes you need oil and water together, when baking, for example; yet sometimes, oil and water should separate. I got the sense during the training that the women were holding back. Whether they were deferring to the male leaders, most of whom were pastors, or whether it was just a nudge from the Holy Spirit, I felt led to separate the women from the men. The mission team with me had men and women, so I "wisely" separated the group by gender, asking the "pastors" and any other men to go outside under the tree with me. In my "wisdom," I had not considered that some of the women present were also pastors. Not smart...

However, the results quickly demonstrated that the Spirit had nudged me, and the impact was palpable. Within a short time, we heard murmuring coming from inside the church. The murmuring grew more urgent, then it turned to crying and loud praying. Like children not wanting to miss out, we quietly stole over to peek inside the windows. We were greeted with a wonderful scene. In the same amount of time that the pastors had moved outside and gotten settled under the tree, made introductions and just began to get organized, the women had launched into caring for each other's hurts, needs and desires. Their cries and prayers shot straight up to heaven.

Paul Koehler described what we witnessed that day: "The theologies of oral people will often reflect their experiences of God revealing himself by meeting their needs."[3] *I learned to follow the Spirit and observe the culture.*

Brush Stroke: Contextual Creators

Meanwhile, in the "pastors" group outside, we covered the next session of the oral teaching and made assignments for the next day. They were to go home and think about a problem in their community. Then, think about a Bible story that they could use to address that problem and tell us the next day, how they would put these together. On the next day, we were receiving the imaginary results of the "thinking" assignment. Several pastors had given

---

[2] Paul G. Hiebert, *Transforming Worldviews* (Grand Rapids: Baker, 2008), 162.
[3] Paul Koehler, *Telling God's Stories With Power* (William Carey Library, 2010), 78.

their ideas when a non-pastor male spoke up: "Some of the rest of us would like to give our reports also." I yielded to Francis.

Francis explained that since he cannot read or write, he could only go home and think about the assignment. He knew some problems in the community, but he could not look up any Bible stories to potentially match. He developed his own solution. He knew that idol worship was a problem. He knew that these manmade idols did not actually have any real power, but they held powerful influence over many people. Not being able to read or reference a story, he created his own story.

In his story, a father was on his way to the fields to work for the day. As he looked at the sky, he thought that it might rain later, so he instructed his son to bring the idols inside if it rained so they would not be damaged. He was very unhappy when he returned home at the end of the day to find that the idols were still outside and had indeed been damaged by the rain.

He angrily asked his son why he did not obey his instructions to bring the idols inside? His son thoughtfully replied, "Father, you always say that the idols have power and that we pray to them to get help. I thought that if they have so much power, then they could help themselves."

Francis did not merely think about this problem in his community; he made up this wonderful story. He did not merely work on an assignment for this oral storytelling workshop; he went next door to his neighbor and told him this same story. His neighbor is an idol worshipper, by the way.

When his neighbor heard the story and had a brief discussion with Francis, he announced two decisions:

1. I will stop worshipping these idols,
2. I will follow you to your church.

I learned that oral learners do not rely on the same resources as literate learners and that they learn well through immediate application. From Francis, an illiterate non-pastor, *I learned the true power of locally contextualized, worldview-specific stories.* (By the way, Francis' son has since gone on to become a pastor!)

Brush Stroke: Sing It!

Northern Ghana at that time of year was over one hundred degrees Fahrenheit. All of our team was struggling in the heat, with no electricity for air conditioning, or even ceiling fans, and the walls of the large church effectively blocking any available breeze. I had an idea that I thought would buy us about a twenty-minute break. Earlier, in Madagascar, we had observed groups of people working to create songs after discussing Bible stories. I had heard that the people in Northern Ghana also loved to sing. Once confirmed, I challenged each of the six small groups to create a song based on the Bible story they had been assigned. They were to stand up to indicate when they were finished creating their song. I then told the team to get some water and take a break. Before we were even able to relax, the first small groups began to stand. It had only been two minutes. I immediately apologized for my instructions not being clear enough. I re-explained that they were to create a unique song based upon the Bible story their group had discussed earlier in the day. They assured me that they understood—they were simply finished. As the first two groups explained this to me, the remaining groups also stood. I looked at the team, shrugged my shoulders and asked for the first group to share their song, still not convinced that they understood me.

I was *so* wrong. Each group took time to share their unique song, each with its own cadence, movement and...joy. Wow. Before the workshop ended, each group had also taught their story and their story song to all of the other groups such that by the end of the three days, everyone left knowing ten Bible stories and ten brand new Bible story songs.

In *Hymns of the Everlasting Hills*, Arrington refers to this song-based memory enhancement as "liturgical literacy."[4] As I come from a different ecclesiastical bent, I'd like to refer to this as "Lyrical Literacy." *I learned the power of communicating in song.*

Brush Stroke: Evangelism and Planting Churches

Remember that guy that was so "laid back"? Turns out I was wrong about him also. Edward was not just there for the free lunch. He must have been doing some sort of Memory Masters Jedi mind trick because he was actually absorbing *all* that was shared such that he became an indispensable orality leader in northern Ghana. During the workshop, he realized there was going to be a need. Immediately after the workshop, he called together many of the women who had attended. Each Saturday, he would teach them a new Bible story. They would discuss it, practice repeating it, and create a song or two.

Then the women would scatter like chickens blown about by a sudden wind and go village to village sharing their song and Bible story. The results? Well, the District Superintendent for that area had told me at the end of the workshop that this training was actually an answer to ten years of praying. In that area, 95 percent of the people do not know how to read or write, and while they had once been active in church planting, they had *run out* of literate pastors to lead the churches, so they had stopped planting churches.

Now, armed with a way to easily remember the Bible stories, create new songs, and the empowerment they felt, they were able to start planting churches again. In fact, in just two months' time, eight new fellowships had been started and two of them were already officially organized new churches.

---

[4] Aminta Arrington, "Hymns of the Everlasting Hills: The Written Word in an Oral Culture in Southwest China" (Ph.D. product, Biola University, 2014), 245.

In addition, one Muslim father, after observing the direct and wonderful impact of the Bible stories on the behavior of his two teenage daughters, gave them each permission to start their own churches in two different nearby villages. Margaret Mead's words do justice in describing what transpired: "A small group of thoughtful people could change the world. Indeed, it's the only thing that ever has."[5] *I learned that empowerment is limitless.*

Brush Stroke: Hold it in Your Head

Edward demonstrated such successful leadership that he accompanied me to Sierra Leone to help lead a rather large orality training. At one point during an afternoon break, I asked him how he is able to remember all the stories involved in these three-day workshops. His long, blank stare told me he did not understand my question, which intrigued me. We moved on to other topics.

That evening, I asked the same question in a different way. He recognized my half-hearted attempt at being clever and rewarded my effort with that same long blank stare. In desperation, I asked him how he could so easily remember all the content for a full three-day workshop. I explained that though we do not allow use of printed materials during trainings, we can always go back to our notes at night and review for the next day. In *Voices of Mong Elders*, Thao said it this way: "They said that a primary oral person could take their knowledge with them everywhere they go, whereas a literate person has to depend on books. A literate person does not function well without books."[6] Similarly, Edward saw my literate limitations and guided me to a new realization. *I learned that listening well is a first step to remembering well.*

Brush Stroke: Intentional Movements, Local Illustrations

At one point, a western-based illustration had failed to communicate properly, so we looked for a local way to explain a part of the process of creating orality-based content. We decided to use the everyday example of gathering food, preparing food, and sharing the food. We adapted this to gathering information from a Bible story, then preparing that story by careful study and thought, and finally thinking about how we would go about sharing those insights with others in such a way that they would take it home inside themselves. After trying this out in the next Bible story session, we saw the eagerness with which it was received and the ease with which it was

---

[5] Margaret Mead, *The World Ahead: An Anthropologist Anticipates the Future* (New York: Berghahn, 2005), 12.

[6] Yer Thao, "The Voices of Mong Elders: Living, Knowing, Teaching, and Learning within an Oral Tradition" (Ph.D. product, Claremont Graduate University, 2002), 242.

repeated, complete with hand motions. Edward explained that such things made it so easy to remember all the words that went with such tools.

Figure 2. Intentional Hand Motions

This surfaced again when I had presented a paper to a group of Ph.D. candidates at a large African University. Unbeknownst to me, one of the highly literate students there was also taking our orality-based courses due to the pressing need in her birth country. During the Q&A, she asked me why we did not include hand motions in every course, as those had proven to be excellent mnemonic tools for recalling the content, including for the current "Christian Theology 1" course.

Her insightful inquiry pierced me such that I spent the hour after the presentation ended creating a series of hand signs for that theology course. Now *all* of the pastor's training courses are accompanied with intentional hand signs. Thigpen says, "It would seem that we need to take informal means into formal places so more people can learn in the manner most suited to their ways of learning."[7] Jean-Marc Éla states, "God communicates with humanity under the veil of symbols; words, gestures, and signs must all work together to manifest God."[8] *I learned that successful mnemonics can include contextually derived intentional hand motions.*

Brush Stroke: Repetition

You are likely familiar with the old adage, "Use it or lose it." It is true of skills as well as knowledge. This applies to our memory as well. I once knew Latin, Spanish and Greek. Lack of using those languages caused them to cease

---

[7] L. Lynn Thigpen, *Connected Learning* (Eugene: Pickwick, 2020), 126.
[8] Jean-Marc Éla, *My Faith as an Africa* (Eugene: Wipf and Stock, 1988), 43.

to occupy a useful space in my memory. Now, I mostly remember that *gato* is not something I want to order from a restaurant. (*Gato* is Spanish for "cat.")

Was there a time when you remembered people's phone numbers, rather than which single digit to press on your phone to speed dial them? In some ways, technology and internet search engines have made us lazy. I suggest that most of us today, especially in Western society, listen out of a sense of politeness.

Oral learners, however—those without the reliance or ability go back and read important details—listen differently. They listen for survival. When someone without the ability to rely on written literature hears about a man who will be hiring day laborers starting on Monday at 7:30AM at a new jobsite, which is three blocks past the bank with the two massive trees in front of it, there's no need to repeat the information. The potential worker, who happens to be in need of a job, captures all the details at the first hearing.

It is true that longer narratives or detailed instructions about how to properly administer a certain medicine to a sick child may take repetition to ensure that the details are all correct. However, as I have observed among oral learners, many will learn long narratives in just two to three repetitions. Literate learners struggle to understand this because we cannot perform at the same level. The difference is motivation. We listen for politeness; they listen for survival. *I learned that repetition is not boring but vital to oral learners.*

Brush Stroke: Local Art, Local Stories

Most of the year in West Africa it is *hot*! Both as a way to combat the heat and as a cultural practice, most of the women wear headscarves. An idea surfaced as our team was thinking about how to help people remember a set of Bible stories about the life of Jesus. Why not create headscarves with pictures of the Bible stories? As no good reason not to do this surfaced, they contracted with a West African artist, designed and printed thousands of headscarves. They neither sold them nor gave them away.

In a brilliant move, people could "earn" a headscarf by telling from memory the twelve stories shown on the scarf. Many women demonstrated their ability to accurately tell all twelve stories, and quite a few men did as well. The men typically carried theirs in a backpack or turned the scarf into a shirt. We heard multiple stories of women in the market being questioned about their unique headscarves, which lead to lots of Bible stories being told! *I learned that leaving space for local ownership is mandatory.*

Figure 3. The Story Headscarf

Brush Stroke: Long-term Memory

A few years before having an impromptu reunion, we had visited one church on a Wednesday night and orally presented a Bible story. To say the response was positive would have been an understatement. The response was electric. People eagerly shared insights they were seeing and sensing from what was thought to have been a well-known and well covered Bible story. This evening however, the story took on a life of its own in the hearts of those gathered. It stood on its own feet. Healey and Sybertz explain, "Telling stories frees, reveals, opens up, and empowers—both in relation to the narrator and the hearers. There is a grace of naming, a journey of self-understanding and self-discovery and a healing of memories."[9]

The pastor went on to tell us person-by-person who shared what discovery. The impact on him was contagiously exciting as his broad smile kept flashing while he recalled that experience. Watching him relive that night with such clarity, my wife pressed in for a question that would bring its own insight. She inquired, "Pastor, do you remember how long ago it was that we visited your church?"

He thought for a moment as his eyes grew nearly as wide as his smile and replied while laughing, "*That was 4 years ago!*"

Then with the timing of a sensei, my wife asked, "Do you remember what you preached last Sunday?" It took the pastor a few beats before he recalled the last sermon he had preached, but then, sensing the intent of the question, he added that he could not remember his own sermon from two weeks ago! *I*

---

[9] Joseph Healey and Donald Sybertz, *Towards an African Narrative Theology* (Maryknoll: Orbis, 1996), 325.

13

learned that shared embedded experiences are powerful tools for long-term memory.

Conclusion

Why have I told you all of these stories? Because each of these stories represents an inflection point of connected learning leading to where we are today in a continuing iterative innovation process of providing appropriate resources for oral learning communities around the globe. Thigpen's research in *Connected Learning* led her to conclude what DeCapua and Marshall stated well: "The cornerstone of learning is the unity of people and knowledge."[10]

Some of the ways we are working to create more unity of this nature include:

- Literate teachers becoming much more oral themselves in order to teach and model proper principles and practices that are easily reproducible.
- Avoiding printed materials during training workshops.
- Unlearning what we've always known so that we can learn to teach in ways that are not comfortable or natural to us, preferring others ahead of us.
- Trusting that the Spirit of God still moves over His spoken Word in ways that breathe life into those who have ears to hear and makes the Word of God "stand on its feet."
- Being willing to have as small a footprint as possible so that we empower global partners to do what they can do, far beyond our initial efforts.
- Riding the waves of global change to find, adapt, encourage, and equip our oral learning partners within their means and abilities.
- Generational grading, driving teaching of generations through multiple languages.
- Zoom classes, catylized by COVID—for good and for aggravations—and those aggravations then driving us to find other new models, including custom Android apps designed for oral learners, with visual navigations, supported by local-dialect audio content.

One case study to highlight was an Old Testament Survey class taught over Zoom to sixteen people across West and North Africa. We used everything we were learning from our friends in the field to stumble our way forward in this new iteration of online oral teaching. I built in a graduated grading system which awarded up to 75% of their grade during the first-generation class. The additional 25% could be earned by teaching another generation. It

---

[10] Thigpen, *Connected Learning*, 164.

worked. It was less likely that people wanted to earn the remaining portion of their grade, and more likely that they were encouraged and empowered by the format we used to convey a simple yet powerful way of knowing, remembering, and applying what we learned together from the stories of the Old Testament.

Key elements being used at that time included a family-based outline, hand motions, local proverbs, stories connected to major topics, pictures, repetition, spaced learning, audios and videos for review.

Those few students faithfully taught a second generation, who taught a third generation, who taught a fourth generation, who taught a fifth, sixth, seventh, and into an eighth generation of students, eventually growing to over twenty-six thousand students!

Pre-COVID, costly international flights month after month after month over a decade did not reach the same number of people. Yet in four months, this was accomplished in an adaptation from the initial delivery over Zoom, migrating to face-to-face, all the while transferring from one local language to another! *I have learned that God does indeed, still do amazing things beyond what we could ask or imagine.*

"Now all glory to God, who is able, through his mighty power at work within us, to accomplish infinitely more than we might ask or think" (Ephesians 3:20, NLT).

Bibliography

Arrington, Aminta. *Hymns of the Everlasting hills: The Written Word in an Oral Culture in Southwest China.* Ph.D. product, Biola University, 2014.

Éla, Jean-Marc. *My Faith as an African.* Eugene: Wipf and Stock, 1988.

Healey, Joseph and Donald Sybertz. *Towards an African Narrative Theology.* Maryknoll: Orbis, 1996.

Hiebert, Paul G. *Transforming Worldviews.* Grand Rapids: Baker, 2008.

Koehler, Paul. *Telling God's Stories with Power.* Pasadena: William Carey, 2010.

Mead, Margaret. *The World Ahead: An Anthropologist Anticipates the Future.* New York: Berghahn, 2005.

Thigpen, L. Lynn. *Connected Learning.* Eugene: Pickwick, 2020.

Thao, Yer. *The Voices of Mong Elders: Living, Knowing, Teaching, and Learning within an Oral Tradition.* PhD product, Claremont Graduate University, 2002.

Chapter 3:
Jumping Away from Syncretism: The Use of Orality to Close the Gap Between Formal and Folk Religion

Danyal Qalb & Jay Angeles

Abstract[1]

Evangelical missions largely used text-based approaches for worldwide evangelism. An oral world was reached by low orality reliant (LOR) methods with the result of many folk beliefs that are high orality reliant (HOR) in nature to continue in the background. Syncretism and folk religion result from inadequate contextualization. Formal/high/orthodox religion often fails to address local everyday concerns because, due to its primarily literacy/text-based nature, it is less accessible for HOR people. Most people that call themselves Christians today in HOR cultures are part of a religion that was/is propagated and grounded with LOR methods. We call this the Folk Religion Orality Gap (FROG). It means that formal religion often fails to connect with HOR people, creating a gap that folk beliefs and practices can fill using orality. The lack of orality in formal religion often creates a vacuum where folk beliefs and practices flourish and open the doors for syncretism. We conclude that orality alone will not suffice to solve the problem of syncretism, but it is a vital part for Kingdom transformation among HOR peoples. Our recommendations include making orality principles and methods central in missions and missionary training, continued research and provision of resources, and oral development of leadership and theology.

Maguindanao Spirit World (Danyal Qalb)

A few years ago, a team of missionaries hosted an event for Maguindanao[2] youth. I had the privilege to witness it. About one hundred young people enjoyed the program that ended with a message and a time for fellowship. It was already dark by the time they departed for home. Some of the youth had come from a neighboring village and their overloaded vehicle did not make it up the hill, causing some of the youth to walk for a few hundred meters to the crest. While walking, one of the girls heard the voice of her mother calling from the direction of a coconut plantation. She turned around and followed

---

[1] This chapter is adapted from an article in the Journal of Asian Mission: Jay Angeles & Danyal Qalb, "Deterring Syncretism: The Use of Orality to Close the Gap between Formal and Folk Religion," *Journal of Asian Mission* 23, no. 2 (2022): 39–63.

[2] Muslim people group from the Philippines.

the voice that only she could hear. Her friends did not realize what was happening and when they looked back, they observed how an evil spirit (*saitan*) with the appearance of a white dog entered her mouth. This is just one of many cases of a Maguindanao being possessed by a spirit.

The Philippines is a storytelling country[3] and its mythology is filled with stories about spirit beings and ancient deities.[4] Maguindanao mythology tells of many spirits with much of their folklore surrounding the theme of water. The *Bwaya*[5] spirit is the dominating figure with many ceremonial traditions having the crocodile being in the center of the ritual.[6]

These myths are not officially taught, but when people are facing an existential crisis, they seek help from the spirits of their ancestors through soliciting the assistance of the sorcerer (*tabib*). This person uses orality methods in his rituals like interpretating the position of a baby in the placenta by "reading" an egg, reciting a formula for defense against evil spirits, or wearing of amulets for protection.[7] Formal Islam often does not have answers for these needs, leaving the door wide open for folk beliefs to fill the gap.[8] These spirits and ancestors are more accessible than Allah, who is unapproachable for these worldly problems.[9] Malinowski argues that religion is in the making when people are confronted with an existential crisis that cannot be explained.[10] They do so because their limited "toolbox" helps

---

[3] Dianne De Las Casas and Zarah C. Gagatiga, *Tales from the 7,000 Isles: Filipino Folk Stories*, World Folklore Series (Santa Barbara: Libraries Unlimited, 2011), xxvi.

[4] Lusito Batongbakal, "The Ancient Mindanao Deities of Philippine Mythology," FilipiKnow, accessed January 14, 2021, https://filipiknow.net/the-ancient-mindanao-deities-of-philippine-mythology/.

[5] Maguindanao term for crocodile.

[6] Mark Williams, "Bwaya as Spirit-Being: Filipino Islam and the Supernatural," *JAM* 7, no. 1 (2005): 119–21.

[7] Rod Cardoza, *Sourcery Among Maguindanaon of Barrio Bunao* (unpublished manuscript, San Jose State University, 1986), 14–17.

[8] Mark Williams, "A Short Examination on Beliefs in Popular Islam.," *Musafir: A Bulletin of Intercultural Studies* 2, no. 2 (2008): 3–4; Mark Williams, "Causality, Power, and Cultural Traits of the Maguindanao," *Philippine Sociological Review* 45, no. 1–4 (1997): 35–36.

[9] Williams, "Causality, Power, and Cultural Traits of the Maguindanao," 39; Craig Gustafson, "Qualities of an Adored Maguindanaon Leader" (DIS product, Fuller Theological Seminary, 2014), 73; Paul G. Hiebert, "The Flaw of the Excluded Middle," *Missiology: An International Review* 10, no. 1 (1982): 40, https://doi.org/10.1177/009182968201000103; Michael A. Rynkiewich, *Soul, Self, and Society: A Postmodern Anthropology for Mission in a Postcolonial World* (Eugene: Cascade, 2011), 144–45.

[10] Rynkiewich, *Soul, Self, and Society*, 142; Bronislaw Malinowski and Robert Redfield, *Magic, Science and Religion and Other Essays*, Text Edition (Glencoe, IL: The Free Press, 1948), 67.

to explain the situation.[11] The explanation often involves spiritual beings.[12] This also makes sense in a Biblical worldview since God created all dominions, yet we can only see one—our physical earth domain.

For Malinowski, "traditional magic is nothing else but an institution which fixes, organizes and imposes upon the members of a society the positive solution in those inevitable conflicts which arise out of human impotence in dealing with all hazardous Issues by mere knowledge and technical ability."[13] For the Maguindanao, magic also functions as a means to give a sense of control over the domain of the spirit world.[14]

When our team received the message of this girl being possessed, four of my teammates went to the girl's village home while the rest prayed on our site. Upon arrival, the sorcerer was doing his rituals like massaging the girl to feel where the spirit was located within the body and reciting Arabic formulas, but the spirit did not leave her. After the ritual was completed, our teammates prayed over the girl in the name of Jesus and the evil spirit left her and she regained control over her body again. As explanation of why the Spirit left after our team prayed over the girl, the local imams later told their people that it was a Christian spirit that possessed the girl.

As we have seen, the spirit world is a part of the everyday life of Maguindanao. They fear the spirits, and storytelling is a natural way of passing on the knowledge of who they are and how to contend with these spirits. "Very few of these myths are written; the great majority of them are preserved by oral tradition only."[15] Storytelling is an important part of shaping and sharing culture.[16] Maguindanao love songs and ballads sung by older men serve as an example.

Folk beliefs are intertwined into the lyrics, keeping their traditions alive.[17] Still, missionaries rarely have the chance to openly talk about the spiritual world with Maguindanao. On one side, they are often not equipped to do so,

---

[11] Paul G. Hiebert, R. Daniel Shaw, and Tite Tiénou, *Understanding Folk Religion: A Christian Response to Popular Beliefs and Practices* (Grand Rapids: Baker Academic, 1999), chap. Explanation Systems.

[12] Paul G. Hiebert, *Transforming Worldviews: An Anthropological Understanding of How People Change* (Grand Rapids,: Baker Academic, 2008), 57.

[13] Bronislaw Malinowski, "The Role of Magic and Religion," in *Reader in Comparative Religion: An Anthropological Approach*, ed. William Armad Lessa and Evon Z. Vogt, 4th ed. (New York: Harper & Row, 1979), 43.

[14] Cardoza, *Sourcery Among Maguindanaon of Barrio Bunao*, 16–26; Williams, "A Short Examination on Beliefs in Popular Islam.," 3.

[15] Henry Otley Beyer, *Origin Myths among the Mountain Peoples of the Philippines* (Project Gutenberg, 2014), 4, http://www.gutenberg.org/ebooks/46024.

[16] Hiebert, *Transforming Worldviews*, 85; Michael Wesch, *The Art of Being Human: A Textbook for Cultural Anthropology* (Manhattan, KS: New Prairie Press, 2018), 332, https://newprairiepress.org/ebooks/20.

[17] Dennis Merritt, *Warp and Woof: The Persvasive Influence of Folk Beliefs and Practices upon Philippine Islam* (unpublished manuscript , Fuller Seminary, 1986), 298.

and on the other side, Maguindanao do not easily open up about their beliefs about the spirit world.[18] This example shows us how missionaries often struggle to meaningfully engage with the spiritual world of cultures that are highly reliant on oral communication.

Folk Religion Orality Gap

Today, most missionaries emphasize contextualization of the gospel, but their communication forms and modes often fall short. Written materials and propositional and exegetical sermons still prevail as the preferred ways of communicating the gospel. From our own experience, we know that it is frustrating when people read discipleship materials or hear a text-based sermon listening to us but syncretize them by holding on to their old beliefs and practices in need of Kingdom transformation.

Unlike in formal[19] religion, for people who adhere to folk beliefs[20] and practices, no faith acknowledging spirits and the invisible world is required. For them, the existence of spirits and the unseen world is a mutually shared reality and unquestioned. Spirits simply live among us as a part of nature.[21] The knowledge of this spiritual reality is encapsulated and passed on in a people's mythology, rituals, stories, and daily activities, all in high orality reliance (HOR) forms and functions in nature and a key component in shaping their worldview.[22] We define orality as "a complex of how oral cultures best receive, process, remember, and replicate (pass on) news, important information, and truths."[23] Orality is therefore a means of how people interpret and propagate their worldview.

Contrasting the HOR of folk beliefs and practices is the low orality reliance (LOR) of formal religion. Both must be seen as two poles of a continuum.[24] In *The Flaw of the Excluded Middle* (FEM), Hiebert made the point that folk religion gives answers to people that formal religion does not address. Formal religion is concerned with the physical and spiritual world that is beyond our reach, but only folk religion gives answer to people's everyday life that relates to the invisible but real world between those two realities.[25]

---

[18] Compare Hiebert, "The Flaw of the Excluded Middle."

[19] With formal religion we describe the high- or orthodox religion with its written dogmas.

[20] Folk beliefs are animistic beliefs and practices that are not part of formal religion but are nevertheless practiced by people adhering to that religion.

[21] Wesch, *The Art of Being Human*, 253–56.

[22] Hiebert, *Transforming Worldviews*, 85–89.

[23] Charles Madinger, "A Literate's Guide to the Oral Galaxy," *Orality Journal* 2, no. 2 (2013): 15 (cf. Tom Steffen and William Bjoraker, *The Return of Oral Hermeneutics: As Good Today as It Was for the Hebrew Bible and First-Century Christianity* [Eugene: Wipf & Stock, 2020], 72).

[24] Steffen and Bjoraker, *The Return of Oral Hermeneutics*, 67.

[25] Hiebert, "The Flaw of the Excluded Middle."

This paper attempts to add a different dimension to FEM. In addition to its concept that formal religion often assumes or overlooks addressing people's everyday concerns, "the middle" is also less accessible because formal religion (especially Christianity and Islam) is primarily literacy based. The result is that HOR people, more than eighty percent of the world's population,[26] have a communication preference that led them to stay within the realm of folk religion even after formerly converting. Most Muslims or Christians belong to HOR cultures but are part of a religion promoted though LOR methods.

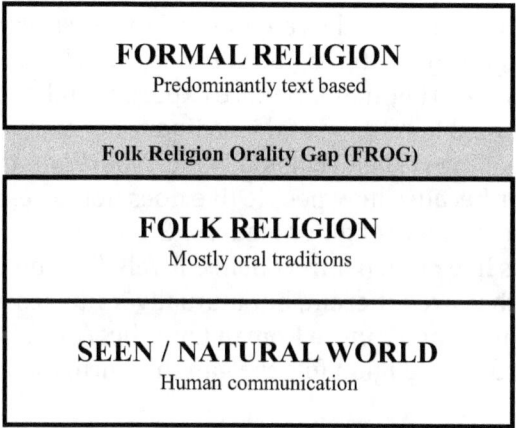

FORMAL RELIGION
Predominantly text based

Folk Religion Orality Gap (FROG)

FOLK RELIGION
Mostly oral traditions

SEEN / NATURAL WORLD
Human communication

Figure 4. Folk Religion Orality Gap. Adapted from FEM.[27]

We call this expanded FEM the Folk Religion Orality Gap (FROG). It means that formal religion fails to connect intellectually with HOR people, creating a gap that folk beliefs and practices can fill using principles and methods of orality (dance, myths, folklore, songs, art, poetry, etc.). Basically, the lack of orality in formal religion creates a vacuum where folk beliefs and practices can flourish. The lack of orality is not the only reason for folk religion to remain, but as we like to show, it's a major contributing factor.

During the early twentieth century, some deemed the missionary priority of translating the Bible and developing literacy in foreign cultures that became known "as a translation movement."[28] By relying on written text and teaching people how to read and write, western missions reasonably yet naively tried to educate people away from higher orality reliance. Among

---

[26] Grant Lovejoy, "The Extent of Orality: The Word Become Flesh," *Orality Journal* 4, no. 2 (2015): 29.

[27] Hiebert, "The Flaw of the Excluded Middle," 40.

[28] Scott Sunquist, *The Unexpected Christian Century: The Reversal and Transformation of Global Christianity, 1900-2000* (Grand Rapids, MI: Baker Academic, 2015), 22.

other factors, this led to the *Orality Gap* as described by Charles Madinger.[29] This is the distance between where people function in HOR and where LOR trained pastors and missionaries use their acquired preferences and skills to teach and preach.

Unlike Ferdinand de Saussure, who suggested that written language is just a representation of oral speech,[30] Walter Ong recognizes that visualizing oral speech does have a profound impact on communication.[31] Therefore, a case can be made that using LOR methods for teaching and discipleship rather than using HOR can lead to syncretism among HOR people.[32]

Furthermore, Robert Redfield calls formal religion "Great Tradition," based on the official teachings of the religion and mostly reliant on intellectual knowledge and written materials. It is the religion of the clergy. "Little Tradition," on the other hand, is more experimental and based on oral traditions. It is the tangible religion of the ordinary believer and referred to as folk religion.[33] Looking at the Great and Little Traditions, they seem to contradict each other because how people live does not necessarily reflect what they are taught by their religious leaders. Sidney Williamson writes that "Most Christians live on two unreconciled levels."[34] However, Chiu Eng Tan points out that they are different, but mutually influence each other. In his writing about Philippine-Chinese Roman Catholics/Buddhists, he explains how the orality-based folk religion fills the gap that formal religion does not address.[35]

We make the argument here that Kraft's concept of *dynamic equivalence*[36] and Hiebert's *critical contextualization*[37] extend beyond translation of language and incorporate all the disciplines of orality in order to close the

---

[29] Charles Madinger, "Applications of the Orality Discussion," *Evangelical Missions Quarterly* 53, no. 1 (2017).

[30] Ferdinand de Saussure, *Course in General Linguistics*, ed. Charles Bally, Albert Sechehaye, and Albert Riedlinger, trans. Wade Baskin (New York: Philosophical Library, 1959), 23–24.

[31] Walter J Ong, *Orality and Literacy: The Technologizing of the Word* (London: Routledge, 2002), 11–12.

[32] "Making Disciples of Oral Learners (LOP 54)," Lausanne Movement, 2004, https://www.lausanne.org/content/lop/making-disciples-oral-learners-lop-54.

[33] Robert Redfield, *Peasant Society and Culture: An Anthropological Approach to Civilization* (Chicago: University of Chicago, 1956), 70.

[34] *Akan Religion and the Christian Faith: A Comparative Study of the Impact of Two Religions*, ed. Kwesi Dickson (Accra: Ghana Universities, 1965), 158.

[35] Pascal D Bazzell and Aldrin Peñamora, eds., *Christologies, Cultures, and Religions: Portraits of Christ in the Philippines* (Mandaluyong City: OMF Literature, 2016), chap. 6.

[36] "Dynamic Equivalence Churches," *Missiology: An International Review* 1, no. 1 (January 1973): 39–57, https://doi.org/10.1177/009182967300100108.

[37] Paul G. Hiebert, *Anthropological Insights for Missionaries* (Grand Rapids: Baker, 1985), 188.

FROG. As Rodney Henry points out, people "will not reject old beliefs and rituals unless they are replaced with suitable alternatives."[38]

Javanese Rituals and Tumpeng (Jay Angeles)

We can observe another example of the FROG in Central Java, Indonesia, where every life transition is celebrated with a ritual. Even among university students immersed in their academic and social engagements, rituals play a significant role in daily life. It is a part of culture seated deeply in their worldview. According to Lloyd Warner, rituals are practiced in every transition as *"rites de passage"* in life, from conception to death. He highlighted their role in society to stress their significance for every person and the whole community.[39] Tom Steffen describes rituals as the expression of traditional stories and symbols which define one's worldview.[40] These rituals are being passed from one generation to another through the principles and methods of orality.

In general, Javanese have a lot of things to tell us about transition rituals from pregnancy—such as *mitoni,* or the salvation ritual of the seventh month pregnancy of a Javanese. This tradition originally used some symbols like water in a jar (*kendi*) or rice and chicken in a casserole while chanting.[41] This carried over into Islam and was culturally syncretized into the recitation of Al-Barzanji and some chapters from the Qur'anic chapters of Yusuf and Maryam.[42]

Some young people in East Java are obliged to join community rituals like *Labuhan Pantai Ngliyep* (Ngliyep Beach Tradition)[43] where community fishermen and their families offer food to *Kanjeng Ratu Kidul* (Queen of the Sea), and decorate their village with coconut tree leaves and other plants, to protect them from any danger. It is also a celebration of thanksgiving for

---

[38] Rodney L. Henry, *Filipino Spirit World: A Challenge to the Church* (Mandaluyong City: OMF Literature, 2001), 157.

[39] Lloyd W. Warner, *The Living and the Dead: A Study of the Symbolic Life of Americans*, Yankee City Series (New Haven: Yale University, 1959), 303 cited in Turner, n.d., 235.

[40] Tom Steffen, *Worldview-Based Storying: The Integration of Symbol, Story, and Ritual in the Orality Movement* (Richmond: Orality Resources International, Center for Oral Scriptures, 2018), 163.

[41] Wakit Abdullah, "Local Knowledge and Wisdom in the Javanese Salvation of Women Pregnancy 'Mitoni' (an Etholinguistic Perspective)," *Jurnal Unissula*, n.d., 178.

[42] Abdullah, 173.

[43] Adib Gatama, "Makna Tradisi Labuhan Gunung Kombang Bagi Masyarakat" (Malang, Universitas Muhammadiyah, 2019), http://eprints.umm.ac.id/56026/2/BAB_I_PDF%5B1%5D.pdf; Faylescha Virgitta Liyanara, "Perubahan Budaya Larung Sesaji Dalam Perspektif Kearifan Lokal Di Pantai Ngliyep Desa Kedungsalam" (Malang, Universitas Brawijaya, 2018), http://repository.ub.ac.id/id/eprint/11293.

saving the community, and happens during a day in the Muslim calendar.[44] The Ngliyep Beach Tradition takes place as part of the East Java culture that was passed down to them, orally, from different generations even before the formal religion came to the area.

These examples introduce the wide varieties of rituals in Java common to everyone regardless of their formal religion. Some rituals vary by region and city. Both Muslims and Christians still engage with these kinds of rituals in their community even though they are obvious animistic practices outside the orthodoxy of both. Some people join in to maintain peace with their fellow citizens and not to create an ostracizing conflict if they do not attend those events. Additionally, some young people only join to celebrate without knowing the deeper meaning behind the celebrations. The reason could be that Islam and Christianity do not address these traditions, nor do either have any knowledge of means to deal with them.

According to Wu, those celebrations may not be consciously perceived as rituals, but rather viewed as transitional celebrations. They are significant events as they celebrate and express cultural meanings.[45] I agree with Sherwood Lingenfelter, that some people do not know the meaning of those rituals because they became routine.[46]

Some rituals may just be social transitions from old to new positions and power status, but they can also incorporate spiritual matters. Moreover, people use these rituals to reinforce their relationships with one another, with God, and with their ancestors.[47] With the symbols that they use during the celebration, it can be related to the ritual that Turner[48] defined as a "prescribed formal behavior for occasions not given over to technological routine, having reference to beliefs in mystical beings or powers."[49] Many of those events in Java (and most of Indonesia) are celebrated with and symbolized by *tumpeng*, a set of cone shaped rice in the middle of a serving plate, usually surrounded by seven kinds of side dishes. According to

---

[44] Liyanara, "Perubahan Budaya Larung Sesaji Dalam Perspektif Kearifan Lokal Di Pantai Ngliyep Desa Kedungsalam," chaps. 2, 4.

[45] Qiao Wu, "The Structure of Ritual and the Epistemological Approach to Ritual Study, " *The Journal of Chinese Sociology* 5, no. 1 (August 23, 2018): 1, https://doi.org/10.1186/s40711-018-0081-x.

[46] Sherwood Lingenfelter, *Agents of Transformation: A Guide for Effective Cross-Cultural Ministry* (Grand Rapids: Baker, 1996), 166.

[47] Lingenfelter, 166.

[48] Victor Turner, *The Forest of Symbols: Aspects of Ndembu Ritual* (Ithaca: Cornell University, 1967), 19.

[49] Turner, 2.

Wulandari[50] and Jati,[51] the rice symbolizes that their lives are meant to worship God. Wulandari believed that it originated from a Javanese (and most like Hindu) belief of a god, named *hyang* in the mountain of Mahameru.[52] The side dishes are believed to be the *pertolongan,* or help from the seven hands of God.[53] Other authors like Aw point out that some of the ingredients like *urap urap* (mixed grated coconut) promote interaction and friendship whereas *rempeyek teri* (small fried chips) communicate harmony (e.g., boiled eggs as gentleness, catfish as humility, etc).[54]

Some Javanese do transition rites privately only with their friends or close relatives. Others do it in the traditional way of *Slametan,* amidst the waves of Western influences in post-modern societies. In this case, it is a gathering of the families, friends and neighbors for a communal feast and is one of the most widely practiced rituals in Java.[55] According to Nurdien Kristanto, it "symbolizes the mystic and social unity of those participating in it."[56] It is a mystic unity because of the Javanese's belief that participants are being united with a spirit and with the dead ancestors; and it brings social unity because they gather to eat the same food in the same location for all classes of society.

The purpose of this is for everyone to prevent facing untoward events or even facing sicknesses.[57] When the food is ready, including the main dish *tumpeng* and all kinds of food that the host can prepare, the official speaker starts with *Salawat,* or short praise to the Prophet Muhammad, followed by the recitation of *sura Alfatiha* and additional prayer for welfare in Arabic.[58] This is basically outside the Islamic belief and why it is considered a syncretistic ritual of Islamic and Javanese tradition by Hakam.[59] The *tumpeng*

---

[50] Retno Wulandari, "The Hidden Meaning Of Nasi Tumpeng," brilio.net, August 24, 2016, https://en.brilio.net/food/hidden-meanings-in-indonesian-traditional-dish-nasi-tumpeng-160823z.html.

[51] Ignasius Radix A.P. Jati, "Local Wisdom behind Tumpeng as an Icon of Indonesian Traditional Cuisine," ed. Mr Bernie Quinn Dr Claire Seaman, *Nutrition & Food Science* 44, no. 4 (January 1, 2014): 324–34, https://doi.org/10.1108/NFS-11-2013-0141.

[52] Wulandari, "The Hidden Meaning Of Nasi Tumpeng."

[53] Wulandari.

[54] Nedi Putra Aw, "The Philosophical Significance of Indonesia's 'Tumpeng,'" *The Jakarta Post*, March 30, 2020, https://www.thejakartapost.com/life/2020/03/30/the-philosophical-significance-of-indonesias-tumpeng.html.

[55] Ahmad Hakam, "Communal Feast Slametan: Belief System, Ritual, and the Ideal of Javanese Society," *Indonesian Journal of Multidisciplinary Islamic Studies* 1, no. 1 (January 2017): 98, https://doi.org/10.21009/hayula.001.1/06.

[56] Nurdien H. Kristanto, "The Javanese Slametan as Practiced as Tradition and Identity," *International Journal of Humanities and Social Science* 6, no. 11 (November 2016): 92.

[57] Hakam, "Communal Feast Slametan: Belief System, Ritual, and the Ideal of Javanese Society," 98.

[58] Hakam, 99.

[59] Hakam, 97.

was originally meant for idol worship and acknowledging Hindu gods was then intertwined with Islamic beliefs.

I agree with Turner that the concept beneath those rituals is structurally "invincible" and the students or other witnesses themselves do not see it, especially when their minds are conditioned to see a tradition as historically and communally expected.[60] Furthermore, the Javanese mind unconsciously does that as witnessed in their foundational belief that understands "the spiritual unseen as a source of hope and help from which the human beings are dependent on."[61]

Possible Responses to the FROGs

In the above example from Central Java, Christians can use these remarkably colorful traditional rituals by redeeming the culture and directing this belief to the One true God. I (Jay) think that we can utilize the same food symbols in a purposeful gathering to unite family and friends, and at the same time use the opportunity to acknowledge God and incorporate the biblical truths and values symbolized by the side dishes of the *tumpeng* and the *Slametan*. Significantly, these rituals are full of meaning that can easily complement biblical truth and Christians should take advantage them. Christians can and must always connect at the deepest levels fulfilling the Great Commission. That means connecting to and with peoples in their community to redeem their rituals and the use of *tumpeng* as the highlight of their rituals or celebrations.

It is no different than the Western church taking the rituals celebrated in Roman pagan religions that we now call Christmas. As we do so, we can even incorporate the Psalms with their prayers that give thanks to God and acknowledge His wonderful works for us. This can mirror the early church's method of bringing people to Christ, as Bosch says, "[t]he community around Jesus was to function as a kind of *pars pro toto*, a community for the sake of all others, a model for others to emulate and be challenged by."[62] Local Christians and missionaries can purposely involve themselves in those celebrations to incorporate the realities of our God and his fallen family in our presentation of the gospel. In doing so, we bridge the FROG.

There are also good ways for engaging the Maguindanao and the Filipino in conversations about their beliefs. In 2019, I (Danyal) met a Muslim Background Believer (MBB) at a conference for cross-cultural workers among

---

[60] Victor Turner, *Betwixt and Between: The Liminal Period in Rites de Passage.* (Symposium on New Approaches to the Study of Religion, 1999), 235.

[61] Rosyada 1995, 12 quoted in Abdullah, "Local Knowledge and Wisdom in the Javanese Salvation of Women Pregnancy 'Mitoni' (an Etholinguistic Perspective)," 174.

[62] David Jacobus Bosch, *Transforming Mission: Paradigm Shifts in Theology of Mission*, Twentieth anniversary ed, American Society of Missiology Series, no. 16 (Maryknoll: Orbis, 2011), 51. Italics by the author.

Muslims in the Philippines. He is Maguindanao and intimately familiar with their spirit world. He uses this talent in music, arts, and media to share the gospel with his own people. He just produced a movie called *Pangitain Ni Noraisa*.[63] This forty-five-minute film centered around a girl experiencing visions at night that accurately predicted future events. She fears the spirits and goes to a sorcerer to free her from these visions. This film goes deep under the skin and raises pertinent questions.

The MBB shows this movie via laptop or projector to initiate transformational dialogues with his fellow Maguindanao. Movies like this can also be broadcast through social media to provoke questions, discussion, and to answer viewer questions. This is a prime example of how someone used orality to directly bridge the gap by tackling folk beliefs among Maguindanao. Just like most Filipinos, Maguindanao are drawn to mystical movies and television series like *Indarapatra and Sulayman*, *Diwata*, and *Aswang*. According to Muriel Orevillo-Montenegro, these mystical television series are one way for Filipinos to express their beliefs and folklore.[64]

Wrapping It Up

During the sixteenth to eighteenth centuries Western missionaries normally held little regard for the value of other cultures, calling them primitive,[65] barbaric and savage.[66] Many held convictions that animistic beliefs and practices "had to be destroyed before Christianity could be built up."[67] Just like other aspects of culture, orality was also a devalued and limiting aspect of primitive cultures, neither for contextualization nor in proclamation. Even today, most missionaries struggle to contextualize and resist presenting the gospel by embracing the principles of orality.

As we tried to show in the arguments and evidence above, the historic neglect of understanding our God-given orality resulted in an inevitable syncretism. Animistic beliefs and practices among HOR peoples were unilaterally condemned and cross-cultural workers called for converts to abandon them and divorce themselves from all the cultural trappings of their own people. There was no transforming a culture. People had to be converted to a new Christian culture,[68] adopting new Christian names, and never participating in traditional family gatherings. All this simply reflected a

---

[63] *Pangitain Ni Noraisa* (The Storyteller Films, 2019).

[64] Bazzell and Peñamora, *Christologies, Cultures, and Religions*, chaps. 5, Introduction.

[65] Hiebert, Shaw, and Tiénou, *Understanding Folk Religion*, chap. Missionary Worldview.

[66] William Carey, *An Enquiry into the Obligations of Christians to Use Means for the Conversion of the Heathens* (Leicester: Ann Ireland, 1792), 67, https://www.wmcarey.edu/carey/enquiry/anenquiry.pdf.

[67] John Pobee cited in Hiebert, Shaw, and Tiénou, *Understanding Folk Religion*, chap. Missionary Worldview.

[68] This also applies to the expansion of Islam.

syncretism of Western Christian preferences. The lack of using orality in contextualizing and in proclaiming the gospel left a gap that could not be filled with a religion that is mostly LOR. We believe that what Hiebert calls *Critical Contextualization*[69] cannot occur without taking a people's orality into account. All this is seen in the two examples above. The FROG is real.

Formal religion, as preached by many missionaries, portrays God as a sovereign cosmic being who will decide over our afterlife. By doing so, folk religion continues to thrive as people struggle to find answers to their everyday problems. Especially in the Western world, savings accounts, modern medicine, insurance, technology, and science became the solutions for these everyday challenges.[70] These solutions, however, are often unattainable for HOR cultures. To bridge the FROG, we must return to a holistic theology where God is at the center of finances, medicine, technology, and science. Only by doing so, can God become the solution for people's everyday struggles again.[71] In the Philippines many Christians still go to the *albularyo*[72] when sick despite knowing that formal Christianity prohibits it. Instead of a systematic lesson about healing and prayer, they must hear stories about healing. They also must have practical solutions. The church can have an herb garden and emergency pharmacy while teaching members how to use the plants and medicines. For emergencies, the churches can have funds set aside and a list of members who are willing to assist with transportation to the doctor and elders who will pray for the sick. These simple steps would drastically reduce the albularyo visits because people connect better with stories, and one main hindrance (access to resources) for people to visit the doctors is eliminated.

Admittedly, some oral traditions lost their original meaning over time. Many practitioners of oral traditions neither know their origins nor their original intent. For example, much of the rice cone dish became just a tradition. Even so, we argue that these rituals still exist because missionaries failed to redeem and reinterpret them with new meaning using orality. Surely the rice dish can be used to point people to Jesus by repurposing its meaning just as Jesus did with the Passover meal that became the ritual, which we call today, Communion or the Lord's Supper. Many HOR people fear the uncontrollable powers of the unseen world. As seen with the Maguindanao example, orality can be used to pinpoint the issue, but it must also be used to point people to a God who is in control and near to those who call upon His name (Psa 145:18).

---

[69] Hiebert, *Anthropological Insights for Missionaries*, 188.
[70] Compare Hiebert, Shaw, and Tiénou, *Understanding Folk Religion*, chap. Roots of the Problem.
[71] Hiebert, Shaw, and Tiénou, chap. A Holistic Theology.
[72] Medicine man or faith healer.

Interestingly, many western practices originated from orality expressions and lost their original meaning. One example is that many Christians in the world fold their hands while praying. In the New Testament, believers would lift their hands to pray (1 Tim 2:8), but missionaries to the Germanic tribes around the twelfth century found that people would fold their hands as sign of surrender and trust during their rituals. The folding of hands was nicely incorporated into the Christian faith as a sign of surrendering to and trusting in God. Germans today do not have any animistic association with folding hands and usually do not even know its origins. In fact, many are taught that the purpose of folding hands is to ensure that one is not distracted during prayer. This is a good example of how orality was used to redeem an animistic practice. However, instead of contextualizing forms from other cultures, Western forms have been introduced to the oral world. Today, many Christians around the world fold their hands for prayer just like Germans do, and even Christmas is uncontextualized as a celebration wholly and unconsciously observed through Western conception, practiced with no associations or understanding of its origins.

Instead of utilizing a people's orality reliance, schools and hospitals are built ensuring people study the way it is done in the West. Because of this, medicine is used to treat people's physical problems with little regard for their question about the origin of the sickness. In HOR cultures, sickness is often believed to be caused by broken relationships.[73] While the Bible supports that broken relationships can be a cause for sickness (1 Cor 11:30),[74] missionaries seldom, if ever, make this connection.

After reading the arguments and envisioning the examples above, can the case be made that orality will solve the FROG? Not entirely. Still, we can see that the lack of orality is a major contributing factor that led to FROGs. As such, orality must be part of the solution for syncretism that is practiced in folk religion as anthropological literature and missiological praxis shows. This was also the realization of missionaries working with New Tribes Missions back in the late seventies and early eighties that led to the chronological storytelling approach and started the orality movement.[75]

"Finally, it is important to study worldviews to transform them. Too often conversion takes place at the surface levels of behavior and beliefs; but if worldviews are not transformed, the gospel is interpreted in terms of pagan worldviews, and the result is Christo-paganism."[76] Since much of the worldview of HOR cultures is based on and uses orality, it is also paramount

---

[73] Wesch, *The Art of Being Human*, 49.

[74] While the verses 17-34 are instructions for the Communion, reading the verses makes it clear that relationships in the church are the major issue that Paul is addressing.

[75] Tom Steffen, "Orality Comes of Age: The Maturation of a Movement.," *International Journal of Frontier Missiology* 3, no. 31 (2014): 139.

[76] Hiebert, Transforming Worldviews, 89.

that missionaries understand the orality characteristics and expressions of a culture so they can use orality to bring about worldview-level transformation. Only then can we bridge the FROG.

Implications and Recommendations

This paper advocates from first-hand experience that the understanding and practice of orality is effective for discipling, and yet it is underused by most missionaries. Our research shows that there is significant overlap of HOR cultures and the syncretism of these cultures because many of their animistic beliefs and practices morph into local religion. The oral nature of folk religion is fertile soil and appealing for HOR cultures and peoples. The LOR nature of formal religion unintentionally creates an additional hurdle for Kingdom contextualization for people who prefer oral communication. Now we conclude by elaborating some implications and recommendations for effectively bridging the FROG among HOR people.

Oral Learners

Orality leadership – Most training methods and materials are created by and made for LOR leaders. This puts HOR learners at an extreme disadvantage which in turn is reflected in the leadership positions of churches, seminaries, and mission organizations. The system caters exclusively to the learned skills of LOR learners which makes it hard for HOR leaders to succeed in these systems or be promoted to positions of responsibility. One need not look far to find that the overwhelming majority of mission leaders, influential pastors, and excelling seminary students are almost exclusively LOR. To overcome this, we must not look at formal resumes but consider qualified leaders who are close to the learning preference of the target people. In fact, they are the ones who should be given those options over well-versed LOR leaders.

Edward Neil Benavidez launched a Bible School in Mindoro, the Saleng Leadership Institute, to equip churches with oral learners from the Mangyan people group. Very few of them have formal education and most have not even obtained a high school degree. This is a good example of a school that uses HOR methods and does not rely much on written materials to train future leaders. They train to proficiency in knowing the Word, sharing the Word, and helping their churches build transformational communities.

Oral theologies – Most people of HOR cultures must be able to defend and comprehend their faith without the need to rely on written text. Only then, Daniel Shear implies, can these people move away from syncretism.[77] Daniel Shaw reports that the Samo people successfully replaced their animistic

---

[77] Daniel Sheard, *An Orality Primer for Missionaries*, 2007, chap. Orthodoxy on the Oral Frontier.

beliefs with the Biblical message of incarnation by incorporating the Biblical message into their own stories and songs.[78] As a result, oral theologies based on stories, memory verses, songs, rituals, etc. are necessary for HOR people. "Self-Theologizing" must become more of an insider, locally-driven process rather than an outsider prompted product.[79] Their stories, songs, music, dance, and dramas are most often redeemable and remarkably transforming when seen as a bridge to living in the Kingdom. They need narrative and character theology, oral hermeneutics (without full reading/literacy skills) and teaching patterns that begin with the concrete before moving to abstract principles. Teaching through their rituals, practices, proverbs, folktales, and myths unlock powerful links to the Word of God.

Missionaries

Focus on orality – In most cases, orality as a method is seen by missionaries as just an afterthought or something for children in Sunday school. At best, they see it as a stand-alone methodology of "Bible Story-Telling." We suggest that orality be taught in churches and seminaries as a crucial toolbox to shape and share the gospel for oral learners. Before going to the field, missionaries must be familiar with making use of music, drama, food, dance, mythology, etc., as vehicles to convey the gospel. We must recognize orality as people's 'heart language' and put more effort into presenting the gospel message in a way that can be easily understood, remembered, and passed on. Missionaries and pastors must take time and effort to learn the orality heart language of the people they are ministering to. This should also include new media formats that already are HOR by design. The widespread use of smartphones worldwide makes this form of orality accessible to most people regardless of cultural and social background.

Training – Missionaries, both Western and non-Western, should be trained and aware of orality not just as a tool for evangelism but also for discipleship, community development, and even for academic teaching in Bible schools and seminaries. They must also be trained in methods of participant observation to learn how orality speaks into their target group and what it means to them. Teaching Western LOR patterns of church planting is not necessarily to be avoided but HOR methods must be a dominant and significant part of all training as well.

The last point has special relevance for emerging sending churches and mission organizations from nations in Africa, Asia and Latin America that tend to copy the Western model instead of using their innate orality. Bible

---

[78] Steffen and Bjoraker, *The Return of Oral Hermeneutics*, chap. Foreword.
[79] Compare Jay Matenga, "Centring the Local: The Indigenous Future of Missions" (Together in Christ, Virtual: Wycliffe Global Alliance/SIL, 2021). https://jaymatenga.com/pdfs/MatengaJ_CentringLocal.pdf.

schools and seminaries must consider oral learners, and incorporating orality in their curriculum and instructional methods in their courses can be a good response. The Asian Graduate School of Theology (AGST) just introduced a new program offering ThM, Graduate Certificate, and PhD in Orality Studies (https://www.agstphil.org). This will pave the way for more academic leaders to develop more HOR curricula for HOR leaders both for the church and mission fields. The Institutes for Orality Strategies (https://i-ostrat.com), a partner with AGST, also offers a professional certification in orality with 4 course modules and an integrative project (https://i-ostrat.com).

Academics

Orality resources – In recent years, the Lausanne Movement, with the International Orality Network or ION (https://orality.net) and others have advocated for and written about orality. These are good starting points to gather information. Other resources include various seminars on storytelling, ethnomusicology, ethnohermeneutics, ethnoarts, etc., that can be attended by missionaries. ION's *Orality Journal*, books on orality, and other sources about the specific orality of host cultures should be studied. Internet searches, especially images and videos, are another useful resource, and provide a starting point to discover the orality of specific cultures.

Further research – This paper with its initial findings reveals the need to engage HOR peoples with aspects of orality. It uncovers some shortcomings of LOR methods among oral preference learners. Furthermore, it suggests that there is a connection between HOR cultures and folk-religion. However, this is not meant to be an extensive analysis, and needs further research to validate orality as a constructive vital tool and show its effectiveness in the difficult task of contextualizing communication, curricula, and strategies in the face of folk beliefs and their tendencies toward syncretism. A group of orality experts is working on the Global Orality Mapping Project, (https://gomap.pro), a resource and a tool to research and understand unreached oral cultures around the world. This is expected to assist missionaries to improve their strategies in dealing with their respective people groups.

Final Note

We believe FROGs can be bridged! As missionaries, we must rediscover the power of orality as part of God's design for humanity. Like Jesus and his approach to communication (John 12:48-49), we too can share the gospel with the oral majority in a way that does not lead to syncretism, but to Kingdom transformation of cultures. People can once and for all leave their folk beliefs and practices behind and find Jesus in their midst, loving them as a unique people and using their cultural expressions to display His truth and glory.

Bibliography

Abdullah, Wakit. "Local Knowledge and Wisdom in the Javanese Salvation of Women Pregnancy 'Mitoni' (an Etholinguistic Perspective)." *Jurnal Unissula*, n.d., 172–78.

Aw, Nedi Putra. "The Philosophical Significance of Indonesia's 'Tumpeng.'" The Jakarta Post, March 30, 2020. https://www.thejakartapost.com/life/2020/03/30/the-philosophical-significance-of-indonesias-tumpeng.html.

Bazzell, Pascal D, and Aldrin Peñamora, eds. *Christologies, Cultures, and Religions: Portraits of Christ in the Philippines.* Mandaluyong City: OMF Literature, 2016.

Beyer, Henry Otley. *Origin Myths among the Mountain Peoples of the Philippines.* Project Gutenberg, 2014. http://www.gutenberg.org/ebooks/46024.

Bosch, David Jacobus. *Transforming Mission: Paradigm Shifts in Theology of Mission.* Twentieth anniversary ed. American Society of Missiology Series, no. 16. Maryknoll: Orbis, 2011.

Cardoza, Rod. *Sorcery Among Maguindanaon of Barrio Bunao.* Unpublished manuscript, San Jose State University, 1986.

Carey, William. *An Enquiry into the Obligations of Christians to Use Means for the Conversion of the Heathens.* Leicester: Ann Ireland, 1792. https://www.wmcarey.edu/carey/enquiry/anenquiry.pdf.

De Las Casas, Dianne, and Zarah C. Gagatiga. *Tales from the 7,000 Isles: Filipino Folk Stories.* World Folklore Series. Santa Barbara: Libraries Unlimited, 2011.

Gatama, Adib. "Makna Tradisi Labuhan Gunung Kombang Bagi Masyarakat." Universitas Muhammadiyah, 2019. http://eprints.umm.ac.id/56026/2/BAB_I_PDF%5B1%5D.pdf.

Gustafson, Craig. "Qualities of an Adored Maguindanaon Leader." DIS product, Fuller Theological Seminary, 2014.

Hakam, Ahmad. "Communal Feast Slametan: Belief System, Ritual, and the Ideal of Javanese Society." *Indonesian Journal of Multidisciplinary Islamic Studies* 1, no. 1 (January 2017): 97–110. https://doi.org/10.21009/hayula.001.1/06.

Henry, Rodney L. *Filipino Spirit World: A Challenge to the Church*. Mandaluyong City: OMF Literature, 2001.

Hiebert, Paul G. *Anthropological Insights for Missionaries*. Grand Rapids: Baker, 1985.

———. "The Flaw of the Excluded Middle." *Missiology: An International Review* 10, no. 1 (1982): 35–47. https://doi.org/10.1177/009182968201000103.

———. *Transforming Worldviews: An Anthropological Understanding of How People Change*. Grand Rapids: Baker Academic, 2008.

Hiebert, Paul G., R. Daniel Shaw, and Tite Tiénou. *Understanding Folk Religion: A Christian Response to Popular Beliefs and Practices*. Grand Rapids: Baker Academic, 1999.

Kraft, Charles H. "Dynamic Equivalence Churches." *Missiology: An International Review* 1, no. 1 (January 1973): 39–57. https://doi.org/10.1177/009182967300100108.

Kristanto, Nurdien H. "The Javanese Slametan as Practiced as Tradition and Identity." *International Journal of Humanities and Social Science* 6, no. 11 (November 2016): 290–95.

Lingenfelter, Sherwood. *Agents of Transformation: A Guide for Effective Cross-Cultural Ministry*. Grand Rapid: Baker, 1996.

Liyanara, Faylescha Virgitta. "Perubahan Budaya Larung Sesaji Dalam Perspektif Kearifan Lokal Di Pantai Ngliyep Desa Kedungsalam." Universitas Brawijaya, 2018. http://repository.ub.ac.id/id/eprint/11293.

Lovejoy, Grant. "The Extent of Orality: The Word Become Flesh." *Orality Journal* 4, no. 2 (2015): 11–40.

Madinger, Charles. "A Literate's Guide to the Oral Galaxy." *Orality Journal* 2, no. 2 (2013): 13–40.

———. "Applications of the Orality Discussion." *Evangelical Missions Quarterly* 53, no. 1 (2017).

Lausanne Movement. "Making Disciples of Oral Learners (LOP 54)," 2004. https://www.lausanne.org/content/lop/making-disciples-oral-learners-lop-54.

Malinowski, Bronislaw. "The Role of Magic and Religion." In *Reader in Comparative Religion: An Anthropological Approach*, edited by William Armad Lessa and Evon Z. Vogt, 4th ed., 37–46. New York: Harper & Row, 1979.

Malinowski, Bronislaw, and Robert Redfield. *Magic, Science and Religion and Other Essays*. Text Edition. Glencoe, Illinois: The Free Press, 1948.

Matenga, Jay. "Centering the Local: The Indigenous Future of Missions." Virtual: Wycliffe Global Alliance/SIL, 2021. https://jaymatenga.com/pdfs/MatengaJ_CentringLocal.pdf.

Merritt, Dennis. *Warp and Woof: The Pervasive Influence of Folk Beliefs and Practices upon Philippine Islam*. Unpublished manuscript, Fuller Seminary, 1986.

Ong, Walter J. *Orality and literacy: the technologizing of the word*. London: Routledge, 2002.

Pangitain Ni Noraisa. The Storyteller Films, 2019.

Radix A.P. Jati, Ignasius. "Local Wisdom behind Tumpeng as an Icon of Indonesian Traditional Cuisine." Edited by Mr Bernie Quinn Dr Claire Seaman. *Nutrition & Food Science* 44, no. 4 (January 1, 2014): 324–34. https://doi.org/10.1108/NFS-11-2013-0141.

Redfield, Robert. *Peasant Society and Culture: An Anthropological Approach to Civilization*. Chicago,: University of Chicago, 1956.

Rynkiewich, Michael, A. *Soul, Self, and Society: A Postmodern Anthropology for Mission in a Postcolonial World*. Eugene: Cascade, 2011.

Saussure, Ferdinand de. *Course in General Linguistics*. Edited by Charles Bally, Albert Sechehaye, and Albert Riedlinger. Translated by Wade Baskin. New York: Philosophical Library, 1959.

Sheard, Daniel. *An Orality Primer for Missionaries*, 2007.

Steffen, Tom. "Orality Comes of Age: The Maturation of a Movement." *International Journal of Frontier Missiology* 3, no. 31 (2014): 139–47.

———. *Worldview-Based Storying: The Integration of Symbol, Story, and Ritual in the Orality Movement*. Richmond: Orality Resources International, Center for Oral Scriptures, 2018.

Steffen, Tom, and William Bjoraker. *The Return of Oral Hermeneutics: As Good Today as It Was for the Hebrew Bible and First-Century Christianity*. Eugene: Wipf & Stock, 2020.

Sunquist, Scott. *The Unexpected Christian Century: The Reversal and Transformation of Global Christianity, 1900-2000*. Grand Rapids: Baker Academic, 2015.

Batongbakal, Lusito. "The Ancient Mindanao Deities of Philippine Mythology." FilipiKnow. Accessed January 14, 2021.

https://filipiknow.net/the-ancient-mindanao-deities-of-philippine-mythology/.

Turner, Victor. *Betwixt and Between: The Liminal Period in Rites de Passage.* Symposium on New Approaches to the Study of Religion, 1999.

———. *The Forest of Symbols: Aspects of Ndembu Ritual.* Ithaca: Cornell University, 1967.

Warner, Lloyd W. *The Living and the Dead: A Study of the Symbolic Life of Americans.* Yankee City Series. New Haven: Yale University, 1959.

Wesch, Michael. *The Art of Being Human: A Textbook for Cultural Anthropology.* Manhattan, KS: New Prairie, 2018. https://newprairiepress.org/ebooks/20.

Williams, Mark. "A Short Examination on Beliefs in Popular Islam." *Musafir A Bulletin of Intercultural Studies* 2, no. 2 (2008): 3–4.

———. "Bwaya as Spirit-Being: Filipino Islam and the Supernatural." *JAM* 7, no. 1 (2005): 119–31.

———. "Causality, Power, and Cultural Traits of the Maguindanao." *Philippine Sociological Review* 45, no. 1–4 (1997): 34–63.

Williamson, Sidney. *Akan Religion and the Christian Faith: A Comparative Study of the Impact of Two Religions.* Edited by Kwesi Dickson. Accra: Ghana Universities, 1965.

Wu, Qiao. "The Structure of Ritual and the Epistemological Approach to Ritual Study." *The Journal of Chinese Sociology* 5, no. 1 (August 23, 2018): 1–19. https://doi.org/10.1186/s40711-018-0081-x.

Wulandari, Retno. "The Hidden Meaning Of Nasi Tumpeng." brilio.net, August 24, 2016. https://en.brilio.net/food/hidden-meanings-in-indonesian-traditional-dish-nasi-tumpeng-160823z.html.

Chapter 4:
Native Knowing, Western Knowing, and Scripture's Knowing

James Miller

Abstract

Native American, First Nations, and Alaska Native knowledge systems have struggled for survival in the presence of Western knowledge systems, often brought by Christian missionaries. In recent years, missiologists have recognized the damaging effect of an Enlightenment epistemology on the Western missionary enterprise. This paper examines recent developments in both Native epistemology and biblical epistemology and offers a culturally appropriate, biblically faithful model of knowing that goes beyond the rationalism and individualism of Western epistemology. This model is founded upon the nature of humans as relational beings and extends to actions, values, and beliefs to create a holistic approach to knowing.

Introduction

Since first contact with Western culture, Native[1] knowledge systems have struggled for survival in the presence of Western knowledge systems and the dominance of its bearers. One of those bearers of Western knowledge was the Christian missionary. Though Christian missionaries may have played a role in the destruction of Native knowledge systems, recent Christian scholarship challenges the notion that the knowledge system they brought was consistent with Scripture's knowing. Recognizing that Western Christianity has been heavily influenced by Greek rationalism since before the Enlightenment compels us to reexamine the missionary enterprise and re-envision the relationship of Christianity with Native knowing. This chapter will attempt to highlight the similarities between the process of Native knowing and the process of Scripture's knowing, to demonstrate the differences between Western knowing and Scripture's knowing, and to envision for the future a new relationship between Native knowing and Scripture's knowing.

---

[1] The terms "Native" and "Indigenous" are used interchangeably to identify Native American, Alaska Native, and First Nations people. "Indigenous" is generally the term used by First Nations scholars, and "Native" is generally used by Alaska Native and Native American scholars.

Methodology

This chapter will lay a foundational framework to understand and compare Native knowledge systems with Scripture's knowledge system ultimately, but with a Western Christian knowledge system intermediately. This framework will be built on a literature review of Native scholarship to identify key features of Native knowing. Likewise, works from Western philosophers, scientists, theologians, and missionaries will be used to analyze Western knowing and Scripture's knowing and the application of that analysis to evaluate the characteristics of Western Christianity which has been brought to the Native people. Especially important will be observations of the epistemological processes in each system rather than the specific content of the belief systems, though it will be impossible to completely distinguish the process from the content.

Though comparing the content of Native knowledge and Scripture's knowledge is not the focus of this paper, it is helpful to understand that many Alaska Native elders do not see great discontinuity between the content of Christianity and Native beliefs. Several Iñupiat women from the Seward Peninsula who were interviewed by Kristin Helweg Hanson concurred that "continuity was evidenced in: 1) understanding of the Creator, 2) similar spiritual practices and values, and/or 3) Iñupiaq prophecy prior to the arrival of whites."[2] Chief Peter John explains that many of the Athabascan beliefs can harmonize with Christian beliefs.[3] Perhaps more continuity can be discovered as more similarities in epistemological foundations are established.

Limitations

As a Western researcher, I acknowledge my own limitations when discussing Native knowledge. I am an outsider, looking into Native knowledge. Native knowledge is a lifelong process, yet this research has been conducted over a short period of time. Native knowledge is based on orality; this research has been exclusively based on written documentation. Native knowledge is experiential while this research documents and analyzes others' experiences or their own analyses of their experiences. Western knowledge is an end product, a stand-alone fact or set of facts that make up a body of knowledge when combined with other facts. Native knowledge, however, is not the end product isolated from the process. There is no end to Native knowing. There is no point at which someone stands outside the process of

---

[2] Kristin Helweg Hanson, *Alaska Native (Iñupiaq) Translations and Transformation of Protestant Beliefs and Practices: A Case Study of How Religions Interact* (Lewiston, NY: Edwin Mellen, 2015), 33.

[3] Peter John, *The Gospel According to Peter John* (Fairbanks: Alaska Native Knowledge Network, 1996), 8–13.

obtaining knowledge, having already obtained. Coming to know and knowing are part of a cycle that continues throughout life and into the next.

Further Research

This paper is only an initial foray into the interplay of three large bodies of literature concerning the related topics of Native knowing, Western knowing, and Scripture's knowing. The limitation of space given to each topic in this paper is clear. Much more needs to be written about the impact of Western epistemology on missions and how understanding both biblical epistemology and Native epistemology can reduce and even reverse that impact.

A major research project on the impact of Western epistemology was conducted in the final years of the twentieth century and was published as *To Stake a Claim.* This five-year study concluded that "the area of epistemology is not marginal to mission reflection and action, but raises acute, central concerns that missiology cannot afford to ignore if it wishes to engage realistically and self-consciously with the relevance of Christian faith in societies shaped by the history, culture, and ideals of the West."[4] One of the conclusions by the editor, J. Andrew Kirk, was that they had not fully examined the relationship of doing, being, and knowing. He stated that "the unfinished work can be distributed under four main headings: the justification of beliefs, the question of truth, the relation of knowing and doing (belief and action), and intercultural communication."[5] The importance of a relational epistemology for missions has been addressed by Enoch Wan and Mark Hedinger in *Relational Missionary Training* (2017), and it merits a more thorough treatment than offered in this paper. This paper focuses on modernism as characteristic of Western knowing. Consideration could also be given to postmodernism and whatever lies beyond postmodernism and the impact on Western missiology.

Since the initial writing of this chapter, more research has been done on biblical knowing, particularly on the activities of knowing. Johnson's 2019 book, *Human Rites,* would be a worthwhile contribution to this study. His book also intersects in many areas with James K.A. Smith's works on Radical Orthodoxy. Johnson's works largely deal with the Old Testament; more work needs to be done on the epistemological content of the New Testament. This research could focus on the interplay of Hebraic knowing, Greek knowing, and Christian knowing as a result of both. Hermeneutical considerations have arisen during this research, particularly the impact of the modern subject-object approach to interpreting Scripture.

---

[4] J. Andrew. Kirk and Kevin J. Vanhoozer, *To Stake a Claim: Mission and the Western Crisis of Knowledge* (Maryknoll,: Orbis, 1999), ix.

[5] Kirk and Vanhoozer, 235.

This study has uncovered several needed areas of research in Native epistemology. Lansdowne states that there are no truly "indigenous epistemologies" because there are not enough Indigenous scholars in Western philosophical studies.[6] Though it may not end in a Westernized epistemological format, Native epistemology could benefit from more interaction with Western epistemology. Despite a lack of formal Native epistemology, much of the epistemological content produced by Native scholars is in the area of indigenous educational reform. Shawn Wilson developed a Native research paradigm based around familiar philosophical categories—epistemology, ontology, methodology, and axiology (see Figure 5).

Ontology   Axiology   Epistemology   Methodology

Figure 5. Indigenous Research Paradigm[7]

The role of axiology in Native knowing was largely absent from the original draft of this chapter, though it is an essential part of Native epistemology. Some axiological content has been added to each section, but values or ethics play a larger role in Native epistemology than is represented in this chapter. Also, the role of relationships within each of these categories and knowing in general needs more research. History as a source of Native knowing needs more attention. Understanding colonialism's impact on Native sources of knowledge, research conducted on Native people, and Native scholarship's struggle to conduct research in culturally significant yet academically approved ways are all areas that could yield significant epistemological information.

Native Knowing

Indigenous scholars have identified being (ontology), doing (methodology), and knowing (epistemology) as elements of Native

[6] Carmen Rae Lansdowne, "Bearing Witness: Wearing a Broken Indigene Heart on the Sleeve of the Missio Dei" (PhD diss., Graduate Theological Union, 2016), 71.

[7] Shawn Wilson, *Research Is Ceremony* (Black Point, NS: Fernwood Publishing, 2008), 70.

knowledge.[8] Other Native scholars have added the importance of values (axiology) and the centrality of relationship to all elements of knowledge. In this study, I propose that these elements create a cycle or process of knowing.[9] This process of being, doing, valuing, and knowing will provide the outline for my examination of Native knowledge.

Where does a circle begin? As humans enter the world, they come into being. As beings they act, and those actions shape values, are shaped by values, and ultimately create knowledge. As experiences of action and knowledge occur, the person's being experiences change and growth. These changes in being bring new experiences which bring new knowledge, and the cycle continues.

Native Ontology

Humans always find themselves situated in a particular context. The Western, individualistic mind tries to separate one's being from the rest of its context, but in Native knowing, the context is an integral part of being. This context includes physical location, family, community, natural world, spirit world, and themselves in relationship within the context. Oscar Angayuqaq Kawagley, a Yup'ik scholar, illustrates this through a tetrahedral diagram in which the self interacts with the human realm, the natural realm, and the spirit realm (see Figure 6). A person's existence, or being, in relationship to these three realms forms the basis for his worldview. Each of these realms becomes part of the process of knowing.

---

[8] Kathleen E. Absolon, *Kaandosswin: How We Come to Know* (Winnipeg: Fernwood, 2011), 55; Vine Deloria Jr., *The Metaphysics of Modern Existence* (Golden: Fulcrum, 2012), 263;

A. Oscar Kawagley, *A Yupiaq Worldview: A Pathway to Ecology and Spirit* (Long Grove, IL: Waveland, 2006), 7; Blair Stonechild, *The Knowledge Seeker: Embracing Indigenous Spirituality* (Regina: University of Regina, 2016), ch 8.

[9] Wilson, *Research is Ceremony*, 62–96; Sharon Henderson Singer, "Diné Research Practices and Protocols: An Intersectional Paradigm Incorporating Indigenous Feminism, Critical Indigenous Research Methodologies and Diné Knowledge Systems" (PhD diss., Arizona State University, 2020), 32.

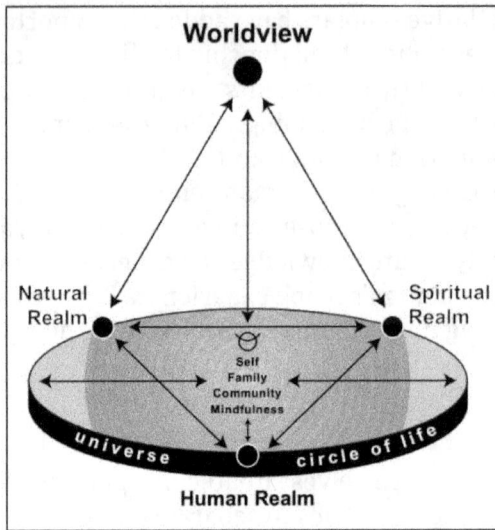

Figure 6. The Yupiaq Worldview[10]

Human Realm

Native existence is conspicuously tied to human relationships. Native kinship relationships, community relationships, and ancestral relationships differ greatly from Western relationships.

A traditional Native person finds his existence in many ways determined by kinship. Though customs vary from people group to people group, many Native kinship systems can determine or at least restrict marital and occupational expectations. Position and role in a community, such as chief, shaman, or servant, can follow matrilineal patterns. Marriage is often restricted by clan. Even certain economic or social conditions in a child's life can be dramatically altered through formal or informal adoptions. Though many of these customs are fading with modern times, a Native person finds his or her existence greatly affected by kinship.

Native community goes beyond extended family and can also be defined in relationship to location. Whether living in the village or not, most Native people view themselves as from a particular location and belonging to the people who are connected to that location. Connection to the land goes beyond human relationships and serves as the link to the natural and spiritual realms associated with that location.[11]

While all realms are interrelated, ancestors provide the clearest link between the human realm and the spirit realm. Elders are held with deep

---

[10] Kawagley, *A Yupiaq Worldview*, 15.
[11] Absolon, *Kaandosswin*, 72; Kawagley, *A Yupiaq Worldview*, 11, 99.

respect, not only as the holders of key elements of knowledge but also as those who will soon join the ranks of ancestors.

Natural Realm

Animals, plants, mountains, valleys, rivers, streams, and bodies of water all make up the natural realm, and each Native person finds self uniquely situated in the natural realm. With the growth of urbanization among Natives comes a disconnection from the land. As connection to the land is lost, the effect extends into the Native being and even robs the Native person of his humanity. To be human is to be connected to the natural realm.[12]

Just as knowledge begins by finding oneself in a particular context in the human realm, so knowledge also begins in one's relationship to the natural realm. Knowledge is attained by observation of animals, plants, weather patterns, water, wind, and stars. Observation of animal behavior teaches moral and spiritual lessons and lessons about the divine nature and human nature.[13] Knowledge, however, is not simply transmitted from the natural realm to the individual, rather knowledge is shared with all of Creation, across all realms.[14]

Spirit Realm

One's existence in relationship to the spirit realm is also crucial to the Native process of knowing. "Spirituality is inherent in Indigenous epistemology, which sees everything in relation to Creation and recognizes that all life has Spirit and is sacred."[15] Awareness of spirit in everything is part of consciousness and existence as a human being.[16] Starting from one's existence with the spirit realm, the search for knowledge extends beyond the natural and human realms into the spirit realm. Recognizing knowledge from the spirit realm affects methodology as well as epistemology.[17]

Native Methodology

As the Native person finds himself situated among the human, natural, and spirit realms, he must know how to act. Doing, or methodology, becomes integral to the process of coming to know. Methodology flows from relationship with the world around him.

---

[12] Harold Napoleon, *Yuuyaraq: The Way of the Human Being*, ed. Eric Christopher Madsen (Fairbanks: Alaska Native Knowledge Network, 1996), 5.
[13] Kawagley, *A Yupiaq Worldview*, 11.
[14] Absolon, *Kaandossiwin*, 76.
[15] Absolon, *Kaandossiwin*, 61.
[16] Kawagley, *A Yupiaq Worldview*, 14; Napoleon, *Yuuyaraq*, 5
[17] Absolon, *Kaandossiwin*, 118–20.

During her doctoral studies, Kathleen Absolon, an Anishinaabe/Ojibwe researcher, found great contrast between Indigenous methodologies and those of the Western academic environment. Indigenous methodologies flow from being: "They include the Spirit, heart, mind and body because Indigenous methodologies are wholistic [sic] in nature and encompass the whole being."[18] She discovered for each area of being a diversity of methodologies. Methodologies related to the spirit, included "use of sacred protocols, medicines, ceremony, ritual, and prayer. Use of intuition, reflection and inner knowings." Methodologies which flowed from the heart included "circle work, dialogue, Elders, family, community, learning, friendships, gatherings, feasts, visiting, searching with heart, nurturing good feelings and relationship connections." Methodologies of the mind were listed as "enact respectful research, reclaim memory, anti-colonial attitude, privilege, Indigenous scholars, genealogy of knowledge." The body evoked "physical action: walk, run, dance, sing, participate, listen, observe, wait, create space, paint, photograph, bead, sew, poetry, tell stories, experience and 'do.'"[19]

Even though Absolon's methodologies center on self, they relate self to the human, natural, and spirit realms. Storytelling is a methodology that works in community. Many stories repeated over a lifetime combine to create a body of knowledge for the entire community. Indigenous languages require an effort from communities and the elders who will teach the language and the unique knowledge that comes with it. Rituals and ceremonies such as prayers, dances, and offerings that revolve around interactions with the natural realm like hunting and fishing are often a community event and recognize the spirit realm which is at work alongside the physical realm.[20] These methodologies not only flow from the three realms, but they also maintain balance with them.[21]

Orality as a Native methodology is distinct from Western written forms of conveyance. Kawagley observes,

Hearing stories being told in the *qasegiq* (community house) allowed the children and other hearers to savor the words and visualize the events. For the duration of the story, they became a part of the imagery. The modern written word is useful for many things, but it removes the reader from the human interaction element. In the *qasegiq*, the hearer becomes a part of the story, an essential participant-observer in the events.[22]

---

18 Absolon, *Kaandosswin*, 118.
19 Absolon, *Kaandosswin*, 119.
20 Kawagley, *A Yupiaq Worldview*, 21.
21 Absolon, *Kaandosswin*, 120; Napoleon, *Yuuyaraq*, 6.
22 Kawagley, *A Yupiaq Worldview*, 16.

Absolon adds that orality is not separated from community. Sharing the air, water, land, joy, and grief are all part of the common experience of those who participate in the oral history.[23]

Native methodologies reflect ontological realities in family and gender. Boys and young men learned their roles and prescribed methods of hunting, fishing, and trapping. They were taught how to perform their duties in balance with both the natural and spirit realm. Girls and young women learned prescribed methods of cooking, preparing and sewing skins, raising children, keeping the home, and avoiding taboos involving gender interactions and times of menses. Kawagley concludes, "They made up a team, complemented one another, and were very much equal in standing."[24]

Native Axiology

Native axiology (values or ethics) is inseparable from Native knowing. Shawn Wilson, an Opaskwayak Cree from Manitoba, defines axiology as "the ethics or morals that guide the search for knowledge and judge which information is worthy of searching for."[25] Jim Cheney, a professor of American Indian Philosophy at the University of Wisconsin, argued that Western philosophy not only tries to separate ethics and knowledge but also orders them incorrectly. Cheney and Anthony Weston have "argued that the standard understanding of the relationship between ethics and epistemology is mistaken. The standard view, in part, is that ethical action is a response to our knowledge of the world. Knowledge comes first; then, and only then, practice."[26] He argued that ethical action, especially in relation to the natural world, opens up the possibility of more knowledge of the world than if it is reversed. Burkhart argued for the inseparability of knowledge from ethics. He wrote, "The idea is simply that the universe is moral. Facts, truth, meaning, even our existence are normative. In this way, there is no difference between what is true and what is right...The guiding question for the entire philosophical enterprise is, then: what is the right road for humans to walk?"[27]

The ethical dimension includes what is right for everyone and everything. Rather than the Western practice of isolating and analyzing individual facts

---

[23] Absolon, *Kaandosswin*, 24.

[24] Kawagley, *A Yupiaq Worldview*, 18.

[25] Wilson, *Research Is Ceremony*, 34.

[26] Jim Cheney, "The Moral Epistemology of First Nations Stories," *Canadian Journal of Environmental Education* 7, no. 2 (Spring 2002): 90.

[27] Brian Yazzie Burkhart, "What Coyote and Thales Can Teach Us: An Outline of American Indian Epistemology," in *American Indian Thought: Philosophical Essays* (Malden, MA: Blackwell, 2004), 17.

and their individual correspondence with reality, Native knowing is viewed holistically, involving "all my relations."[28]

Native Epistemology

Ethics-based methodologies shape and distinguish Native epistemology from Western epistemology. Just as Native methodologies are shaped by interaction with the three realms, so Native epistemology is derived from human, natural, and spirit relationships. Western knowledge attempts to be objective and detached from personal influence. Shawn Wilson explains a distinctive feature of Native knowledge:

> An Indigenous paradigm comes from the fundamental belief that knowledge is relational. Knowledge is shared with all of Creation. It is not just interpersonal relationships, just with the research subjects I may be working with, but it is in relationship with all of Creation. It is with the cosmos, it is with the animals, with the plants, with the earth that we share this knowledge. It goes beyond the idea of individual knowledge to the concept of relational knowledge.[29]

While Western knowledge demands detachment, Native knowledge requires relationship.

Native knowledge from the natural realm is very similar to the modern, scientific method. Outdoor activities require extensive observations of weather, hydrology, zoology, botany, and biology. Much of this rational knowledge can be passed along by elders, but it can also be added to and improved upon by observation and experimentation. Though observations of the physical world produce factual knowledge, moral and spiritual lessons can also be learned. Kawagley distinguishes between mystical and rational knowledge: "Our mystical knowledge cannot have been gained merely by observation, which is the main basis for rational knowledge. To obtain mystical knowledge, observation must be coupled with the participation of our whole being—mind, body, and soul—with the universe."[30]

The spirit realm is also a source of Native knowledge. An individual may gain knowledge by intuition, dreams, and premonitions. These sources of knowledge are not to be ignored, and even enigmatic knowledge is to be considered and contemplated in search of meaning.[31] An individual can add to his knowledge through others' interactions with the spirit realm. Though

---

[28] Barbara Deloria, Kristen Foehner, and Sam Scinta, eds., *Spirit and Reason: The Vine Deloria, Jr. Reader* (Golden: Fulcrum, 1999), 52; Cheney, "The Moral Epistemology of First Nations Stories," 95.

[29] Shawn Wilson, "What Is an Indigenous Research Methodology?" *Canadian Journal of Native Education* 25, no. 2 (January 1, 2001): 176–77.

[30] Kawagley, *A Yupiaq Worldview*, 29.

[31] Deloria, *The Metaphysics of Modern Existence*, 131.

some dreams and premonitions are not to be shared, lest they cause havoc in someone's life, some of this knowledge can be shared. Artists, story tellers, dancers, and song writers also share knowledge from the spirit realm through their crafts. Shamans have a special connection between the human, natural, and spirit realms and provide specialized knowledge when other forms of knowledge do not provide an answer. For example, they may possess cures for diseases for which a natural cure is not known.[32]

Western Knowing

What is "Western knowing"? The history of Western science and philosophy can be traced back to the sixth century B.C. to the Ionians in the city of Miletus. Later came Pythagoras with his mathematical discoveries. From these scientific discoveries came the great philosophers Socrates, Plato, and Aristotle who sought to define the nature of existence, the basis of knowledge, and the resultant ethics. Science, math, art, philosophy, and religion all developed together in Western culture through the rise of Christianity, the medieval period, the middle ages, and into the modern era.[33] Modernity had the greatest influence on Christianity during the period of first contact with Native Americans and Alaska Natives and will be the bulk of our consideration of Western knowing.

History of Western Knowing

Though the beginning of movements of thought and eras in science and philosophy can be difficult to define, a few major persons and developments can be identified which brought rationalism to Western knowing. Thomas Aquinas is attributed with providing the theological and philosophical grounds for separating knowledge into two categories: natural and supernatural, or reason and revelation. By developing his five rational arguments for the existence of God, he opened the door to knowledge about God apart from revelation.[34] Since revelation and its interpretation belonged to the church, the foundation was laid for reason to become separated from religion.[35]

Three hundred years after Aquinas, a renewal, or *Renaissance,* of Greek art, science, and philosophy began. A renewed interest in Greek art inspired

---

[32] Absolon, *Kaandosswin: How We Come to Know*, 93; Kawagley, *A Yupiaq Worldview*, 110; Napoleon, *Yuuyaraq*, 8.

[33] C. Stephen Evans, *A History of Western Philosophy: From the Pre-Socratics to Postmodernism* (Downers Grove: IVP Academic, 2018), 11.

[34] James F. Engel and William A. Dyrness, *Changing the Mind of Missions: Where Have We Gone Wrong?* (Downers Grove: InterVarsity, 2000), 59; Evans, *A History of Western Philosophy*, 184.

[35] Ian G. Barbour, *Issues in Science and Religion* (Englewood Cliffs, NJ: Prentice-Hall, 1966), 19–20.

works by Leonardo de Vinci (1452-1519) and Michelangelo. Nicholas Copernicus' (1473-1543) renewal of interest in Pythagorean mathematics began the era of modern science as he proposed the new theory that the earth moved around the sun.[36] Scientists like Galileo Galilei (1564-1642) adopted materialism and atomism from fifth century B.C. Greek philosopher Democritus.[37] These movements toward Greek philosophy culminated in a new era of modern philosophy begun by Renè Descartes (1596-1650) whose rationalism dominated European philosophy until the late 1700s and continues to dominate modern scientific method.[38]

Modern Ontology, Methodology, and Epistemology

Descartes' rationalism began with doubting what can be known and led to a search for an epistemology rooted in science rather than relationship or revelation. This crisis of knowledge and epistemological uncertainty has characterized the modern age. Cartesian dualism suggested an ontology that separates mind and body and further reduces those parts to explain mankind's existence as a mechanical construction of so many parts. The scientific method of the modern era attempts to explain those parts from a position of disconnectedness governed by rules rather than connected in relationship to the surrounding universe.

In the twentieth century, philosophers, scientists, and theologians began to question rationalism and began looking toward a more holistic and relational epistemology. In his book, *Personal Knowledge,* Michael Polanyi challenges the scientific method that seeks to detach itself from human influence and truth that stands by itself. Ian Barbour, in *Issues in Science and Religion,* challenges the notion that science and religion are separate enterprises. Bible scholars and missiologists are noting the impact that modernity has had on Christianity and its presentation of truth to the non-Western world.[39]

---

[36] Evans, *A History of Western Philosophy*, 239; Michael Polanyi, *Personal Knowledge: Towards a Post-Critical Philosophy* (Chicago: University of Chicago, 1958), 5.

[37] Evans, *A History of Western Philosophy*, 239; Polanyi, *Personal Knowledge*, 8.

[38] Evans, *A History of Western Philosophy*, 578.

[39] Engel and Dyrness, *Changing the Mind of Missions*, 57–62; Os Guinness, "Mission Modernity: Seven Checkpoints on Mission in the Modern World," *Transformation: An International Journal of Holistic Mission Studies* 10, no. 4 (1993): 3–13, https://doi.org/10.1177/026537889301000402; Lesslie Newbigin, "Truth and Authority in Modernity," in *Faith and Modernity*, ed. Philip Sampson, Vinay Samuel, and Chris Sugden (Oxford: Regnum Books International, 1994), 60–88; E. Randolph Richards and Brandon J. O'Brien, *Misreading Scripture with Western Eyes: Removing Cultural Blinders to Better Understand the Bible* (Downers Grove: InterVarsity, 2012), 157.

Modernity and Christianity

Indigenous scholars have noted the dualistic character of modernity that has influenced Christianity. Vine Deloria, Jr. observed, "Knowledge seems to be divorced from experience. Even religion is a process of memorizing creeds, catechisms, doctrines, and dogmas—general principles that never seem to catch the essence of human existence."[40] Kathleen Absolon records a similar observation in an interview with an Indigenous scholar: "But my experience of growing up with western religion was it was very compartmentalized, that it was relegated to Sunday between 11:00 and about 2:00 and after coffee hour and then the rest of the time was, you know, kind of the rest of your life."[41] This compartmentalization of knowledge has created a Christianity that is disconnected from relationship.

Missiologists have also noted dualism's impact on Christianity which segregates spiritual matters from the rest of life in the world. Richards and O'Brien note that with the increase of scientific knowledge about the natural laws that govern the universe, many Christians began to look at natural processes apart from God.[42] God became less a part of the natural world and was relegated to spiritual matters. Thus, Christianity became a means of eternal salvation which had little to do with everyday life except to provide a list of rules by which to live morally. With the bifurcation of knowledge, only that which was considered objectively true was fit for public consumption. Subjective matters, such as religion, were deemed a private matter.[43] Faith became a personal choice rather than knowledge that was shared within the community. Lesslie Newbigin connected the public-private distinction to a separation of knowledge from values. He argued, "This is what underlies the decisive feature of our culture that can be described both as the division of human life into public and private, and as the separation of fact and value."[44] As a result, modernism forced Christians into either knowledge-free values or value-free knowledge.

Scripture's Knowing

Scripturally based epistemology is a relatively new field of study according to Dru Johnson. In his books, *Scripture's Knowing* and *Biblical Knowing,* he explores the topic in the Old Testament (Hebrew) Scriptures and the Gospels. He states that there is little work on biblical epistemology being done in the

---

[40] Deloria, *The Metaphysics of Modern Existence*, 1.
[41] Absolon, *Kaandosswin: How We Come to Know*, 61.
[42] Richards and O'Brien, *Misreading Scripture with Western Eyes*, 170.
[43] Engel and Dyrness, *Changing the Mind of Missions*, 60.
[44] Lesslie Newbigin, *Foolishness to the Greeks: The Gospel and Western Culture* (Grand Rapids: William B. Eerdmans, 1986), 34.

New Testament epistles.[45] In this study, we will limit our examination to Johnson's work in the book of Exodus, written by Moses.

Johnson demonstrates from these Scriptures that "knowing well entails listening to trusted authorities and doing what they prescribe in order to see what they are showing you."[46] Here we see a pattern similar to Native knowing. The individual exists in a community (ontology) in which resides authoritative truth. Within that community, the individual follows prescribed methodologies. Those methodologies lead to knowing or seeing what the authorities of the community see (epistemology).

Scripture's Ontology

In Exodus, both Israel and the Pharaoh are called to know through the plagues and eventually Israel's exodus from Egypt. Epistemology is at the heart of this narrative. However, a clear difference is seen between the knowledge of Pharaoh and the people of Israel. This difference begins with ontology. Pharaoh demonstrates that he has no relationship with YHWH (the Hebrew name for God) in his question, "Who is YHWH that I should listen to Him and let Israel go?" (Exodus 5:2). Pharaoh is called to know things about God—"That I AM YHWH, that there is none like me, etc.," but Israel is called to "know YHWH."[47] How were they to know Him? Johnson emphasizes YHWH's instruction to hear Moses (whose authority was established by miracles) and eventually by doing what Moses prescribed (methodology), but the narrative also lays an ontological foundation. Before giving the Ten Commandments (YHWH's list of prescribed actions), He reaffirms His relationship (ontology) with Israel, "I am YHWH your God" (Exodus 20:2).

Scripture's Methodology

The truth-action-knowing pattern brings into focus the rituals of scripture. Westerners, who dichotomize between thinking and acting, tend to view rituals as merely symbolic or instructive of an underlying truth. Johnson and Smith argue that knowing comes from the act of the ritual as much as from understanding the meaning behind it.[48] For example, the Abrahamic covenant is a ritual that answers Abram's question, "How will I know that I shall possess it?" (Genesis 15:8). The answer comes in the form of a ritual animal sacrifice, or "cutting" of the covenant.[49]

---

[45] Dru Johnson, *Scripture's Knowing: A Companion to Biblical Epistemology*, Kindle, Cascade Companions Book 24 (Eugene: Cascade, 2015), 122.

[46] Johnson, 16.

[47] Johnson, 36, 43-44.

[48] James K. A. Smith, *Imagining the Kingdom: How Worship Works* (Grand Rapids: Baker Academic, 2013), 30.

[49] Johnson, *Scripture's Knowing: A Companion to Biblical Epistemology*, 73.

Scripture's Axiology

Though Johnson does not address axiology, Smith emphasizes that Scripture's methodologies are designed to engage the heart to effect a different kind of knowledge. "Liturgies are the most loaded forms of ritual practice because they are after nothing less than our hearts. They want to determine what we love ultimately."[50] A methodology that aims at the heart creates a deep-seated knowledge that affects the whole being.

Scripture's Epistemology

Western knowing is very different from that found in the Hebrew Scriptures. Westerners believe knowledge or truth is something that can be obtained in a moment, apart from a relationship with the knower. In the Old Testament, however, truth is a "quality that is borne out over 'time and circumstance.'"[51] To be true is to be consistently proven to be what one ought to be. Scripture's knowing is intimately tied to the being of the knowledge giver and the knowledge receiver. Johnson teaches that the Hebrew word *yadah* (know) is related to the word for faith or belief. He suggests that faith is not blind belief but trust in what has been demonstrated over time to be true. The proven action that flows from being creates a knowledge that reaches beyond the mind and into the heart.

Conclusion

Native knowing is a process which begins with one's being, situated in the Creator's universe. Native methodologies (ways of acting), axiology (ways of valuing), and epistemology (ways of knowing) flow out of a relationship with human, natural, and spirit realms. Native methodologies transcend the mind, heart, spirit, and body and produce knowledge that is relational and experiential. In contrast, Western knowing in the modern era has attempted to be detached from human ontology, seeking to keep knowledge as objective as possible. The scientific method strives for total objectivity, uninfluenced by personal biases, intuition, or personal belief. Consequently, knowledge must be derived through rational thought or empirically, and only that which can be observed, tested, and repeated is considered to be true.

Scripture's knowing shares ontological, methodological, axiological, and epistemological characteristics with Native knowing. Scripture's ontology begins with the being of God and His people's relationship to Him. Scripture's methodologies incorporate mind, body, heart, and spirit and are conducted in ethical ways that value all relationships. These actions create a knowledge

---

[50] James K. A. Smith, *Desiring the Kingdom: Worship, Worldview, and Cultural Formation* (Grand Rapids: Baker Academic, 2009), 86.

[51] Johnson, *Scripture's Knowing: A Companion to Biblical Epistemology*, 9.

which brings the knower into a deeper relationship with the Creator as his being is transformed into His image (Rom 8:29; Phil 3:10). When integrated together, Native knowing and Scripture's knowing produce an epistemological model that includes being, doing, valuing, and knowing as a holistic process with relationships at the center affecting the entire process (see Figure 7).

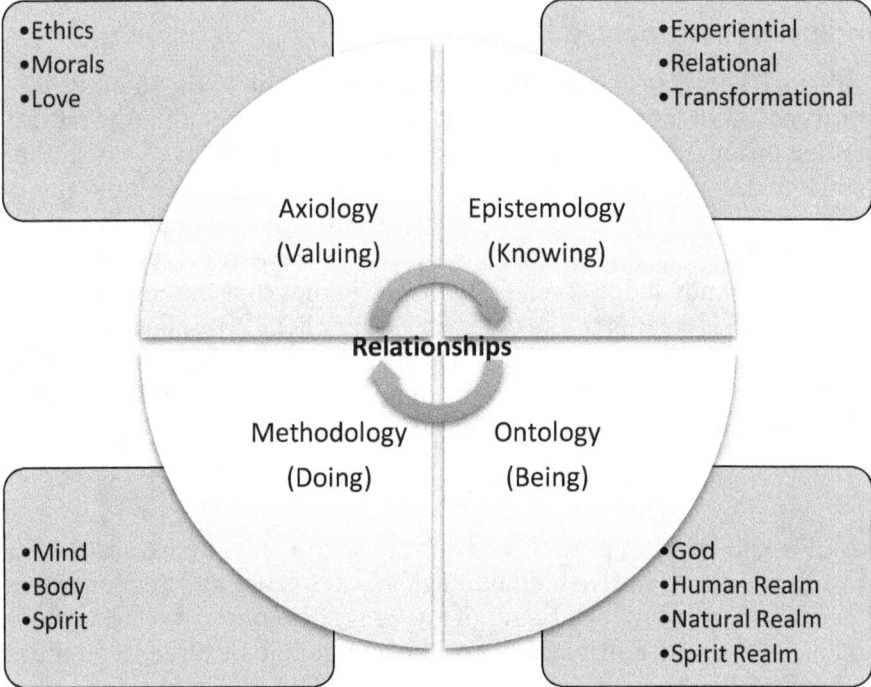

- Ethics
- Morals
- Love

- Experiential
- Relational
- Transformational

Axiology (Valuing)   Epistemology (Knowing)

Relationships

Methodology (Doing)   Ontology (Being)

- Mind
- Body
- Spirit

- God
- Human Realm
- Natural Realm
- Spirit Realm

Figure 7. An Integrated Epistemology for Missions

Modern Christianity has adopted characteristics of Western knowing and often holds knowledge as abstract truth apart from being. The negative consequences on Western Christianity can be seen in the results of modern missionary work among Native people. Neither Native knowing nor Scripture's knowing, however, is designed to be a cerebral process of obtaining abstract truth. Scripture's knowing is meant to bring a person into a relational knowledge of the Creator, His world, and His people. There is much to sort through when comparing the content of Scripture's knowing and Native knowing, but by seeing the similarities in the process we might glimpse a future where true humanity is restored in the knowledge of the Creator.

Bibliography

Absolon, Kathleen E. *Kaandosswin: How We Come to Know*. Winnipeg: Fernwood, 2011.

Barbour, Ian G. *Issues in Science and Religion*. Englewood Cliffs, NJ: Prentice-Hall, 1966.

Bastien, Betty, and Jürgen W. Kremer. *Blackfoot Ways of Knowing: The Worldview of the Siksikaitsitapi*. Calgary: University of Calgary, 2004.

Biderman, Shlomo. *Scripture and Knowledge: An Essay on Religious Epistemology*. Leiden: E.J. Brill, 1995.

Brokensha, David, Dennis M. Warren, and Oswald Werner. *Indigenous Knowledge Systems and Development*. Washington: University Press of America, 1980.

Buckingham, Will. *The Philosophy Book*. London: DK, 2011.

Burkhart, Brian Yazzie. "What Coyote and Thales Can Teach Us: An Outline of American Indian Epistemology." In *American Indian Thought: Philosophical Essays*, 15–26. Malden, MA: Blackwell, 2004.

Charles, Mark, and Soong-Chan Rah. *Unsettling Truths: The Ongoing, Dehumanizing Legacy of the Doctrine of Discovery*. Downers Grove: IVP, 2019.

Cheney, Jim. "The Moral Epistemology of First Nations Stories." *Canadian Journal of Environmental Education* 7, no. 2 (Spring 2002): 88–100.

———. "Truth, Knowledge, and the Wild World." *Ethic and the Environment*, Special Issue on Epistemology and Environmental Philosophy, 10, no. 2 (Autumn 2005): 101–35.

Dellinger, Lisa A. "Reclaiming Indigenous and Christian Narrative Epistemologies: Refusing U.S. Settler Colonialism's Theological Anthropology of Sin." PhD diss., Garrett-Evangelical Theological Seminary, n.d.

Deloria, Barbara, Kristen Foehner, and Sam Scinta, eds. *Spirit and Reason: The Vine Deloria, Jr. Reader*. Golden: Fulcrum, 1999.

Deloria, Vine, Jr. *The Metaphysics of Modern Existence*. Kindle. Golden: Fulcrum, 2012.

Engel, James F., and William A. Dyrness. *Changing the Mind of Missions: Where Have We Gone Wrong?* Downers Grove: InterVarsity, 2000.

Ermine, Willie. "Aboriginal Epistemology." In *First Nation Education in Canada: The Circle Unfolds*, edited by Marie Battiste and Jean Barman, 101–12. Vancouver: UBC, 1995.

Evans, C. Stephen. *A History of Western Philosophy: From the Pre-Socratics to Postmodernism*. Downers Grove: IVP Academic, 2018.

Gegeo, David Welchman, and Karen Ann Watson-Gegeo. "'How We Know': Kwara'ae Rural Villagers Doing Indigenous Epistemology." *The Contemporary Pacific* 13, no. 1 (Spring 2001): 55–88.

Grenier, Louise. *Working with Indigenous Knowledge: A Guide for Researchers*. Ottawa: International Development Research Centre, 1998.

Guinness, Os. "Mission Modernity: Seven Checkpoints on Mission in the Modern World." *Transformation: An International Journal of Holistic Mission Studies* 10, no. 4 (1993): 3–13. https://doi.org/10.1177/026537889301000402.

Hanson, Kristin Helweg. *Alaska Native (Iñupiaq) Translations and Transformation of Protestant Beliefs and Practices: A Case Study of How Religions Interact*. Lewiston, NY: Edwin Mellen, 2015.

Henderson Singer, Sharon. "Diné Research Practices and Protocols: An Intersectional Paradigm Incorporating Indigenous Feminism, Critical Indigenous Research Methodologies and Diné Knowledge Systems." PhD diss., Arizona State University, 2020.

Hester, Lee, and Jim Cheney. "Truth and Native American Epistemology." *Social Epistemology* 15, no. 4 (2001): 319–34. https://doi.org/10.1080/02691720110093333.

John, Peter. *The Gospel According to Peter John*. Fairbanks: Alaska Native Knowledge Network, 1996.

Johnson, Dru. *Biblical Knowing: A Scriptural Epistemology of Error*. Havertown, PA: James Clarke & Co, 2014.

———. *Scripture's Knowing: A Companion to Biblical Epistemology*. Cascade Companions Book 24. Eugene: Cascade, 2015.

Kawagley, A. Oscar. *A Yupiaq Worldview: A Pathway to Ecology and Spirit*. Long Grove, IL: Waveland, 2006.

Kirk, J. Andrew., and Kevin J. Vanhoozer. *To Stake a Claim: Mission and the Western Crisis of Knowledge*. Maryknoll: Orbis, 1999.

Lansdowne, Carmen Rae. "Bearing Witness: Wearing a Broken Indigene Heart on the Sleeve of the Missio Dei." PhD diss., Graduate Theological Union, 2016.

McCarty, Teresa L., Tamara Borgoiakova, Perry Gilmore, K. Tsianina Lomawaima, and Mary Eunice Romero. "Editor's Introduction: Indigenous Epistemologies and Education: Self-Determination, Anthropology, and Human Rights." *Anthropology & Education Quarterly*, Indigenous Epistemologies and Education: Self-Determination, Anthropology, and Human Rights, 36, no. 1 (March 2005): 1–7.

McIsaac, Elizabeth A. "Indigenous Knowledge and Colonial Power : The Oral Narrative as a Site of Resistance." MA Thesis, University of Toronto, 1995.

Napoleon, Harold. *Yuuyaraq: The Way of the Human Being.* Fairbanks: Alaska Native Knowledge Network, 1996.

Newbigin, Lesslie. *Foolishness to the Greeks: The Gospel and Western Culture.* Grand Rapids: William B. Eerdmans, 1986.

Newbigin, Lesslie. "Truth and Authority in Modernity." In *Faith and Modernity*, edited by Philip Sampson, Vinay Samuel, and Chris Sugden, 60–88. Oxford: Regnum, 1994.

Papineau, David. *Western Philosophy: An Illustrated Guide.* Oxford: Oxford University, 2004.

Polanyi, Michael. *Personal Knowledge: Towards a Post-Critical Philosophy.* Chicago: University of Chicago, 1958.

Richards, E. Randolph, and Brandon J. O'Brien. *Misreading Scripture with Western Eyes: Removing Cultural Blinders to Better Understand the Bible.* Downers Grove: InterVarsity, 2012.

Sampson, Philip, Vinay Samuel, and Chris Sugden. *Faith and Modernity.* Oxford: Regnum, 1994.

Smith, James K. A. *Desiring the Kingdom: Worship, Worldview, and Cultural Formation.* Cultural Liturgies, vol. 1. Grand Rapids: Baker Academic, 2009.

———. *Imagining the Kingdom: How Worship Works.* Cultural Liturgies, vol. 2. Grand Rapids: Baker Academic, 2013.

Stonechild, Blair. *The Knowledge Seeker: Embracing Indigenous Spirituality.* Regina: University of Regina, 2016.

Tanaka, Michele T. D. *Learning and Teaching Together: Weaving Indigenous Ways of Knowing into Education.* Vancouver: University of British Columbia, 2016.

Wan, Enoch, and Mark Hedinger. *Relational Missionary Training: Theology, Theory, and Practice.* Skyforest, CA: Urban Loft, 2017.

Wilson, Shawn. *Research Is Ceremony.* Black Point, Nova Scotia: Fernwood, 2008.

———. "What Is an Indigenous Research Methodology?" *Canadian Journal of Native Education* 25, no. 2 (January 1, 2001): 175–79.

Chapter 5:
Orality and Accuracy: The Danger of Uncritical Conflation

Phil Henderson

Abstract

The idea that oral peoples have great ability to accurately recall information is a hallmark of the Orality Movement. Much of oral methodology is premised on this point. However, there are other features of oral communication that need to be considered in order to provide balance to the idea of accurate recall. One of those important features is that the ability *to recall information accurately is not the same as* valuing *accuracy in retelling. Oral cultures are uniquely susceptible to inaccurate retellings. This paper will explore some of the reasons for that susceptibility and what can be done to evaluate and reduce content drift. Finally, the missiological implications of this susceptibility will be explored, especially as they relate to those missiological approaches characterized by what the author terms "movementism," that is, Church Planting Movements (CPM) and Disciple Making Movements (DMM) where the emphasis is more on facilitating movement (--M) than on the church planting (CP-) or the disciple-making (DM-).*

Introduction

One important foundation of oral ministry is that oral people have better recall ability than others. My intention is not to contest that particular point, per se, but to contest the assumption that usually follows, namely, that because they can *recall* accurately, therefore they will *retell* accurately. My contention is that when we conflate the *ability* to recall accurately with the *desire* to recall accurately, we are in danger.

The concept of accuracy presupposes a standard and a means of evaluating conformity to that standard. A text can serve as the standard and provides the means for evaluating conformity. When I speak of a "text" I am not necessarily thinking of something written. I am following Konrad Ehlich's definition of a text as "retrieved communication," that is, a message that has become fixed in some medium (either recorded or written) and is independently accessible.[1] In oral communication, on the other hand, there is no means for evaluating conformity. A message spoken is disappearing as it is being spoken. There is no objective way to go back and verify if there is correspondence between the memory of the spoken message and what was actually spoken. While an oral person might be able to remember more of the

---

[1] Jan Assmann, *Religion and Cultural Memory* (Stanford: Stanford University, 2006), 103.

spoken message than someone else, in general the practical outcome of that lack of objectivity is a diminishment of accuracy in a society.

Ordinarily, that diminishment of accuracy might not be worth worrying about. But in ministry contexts, where we are communicating the very Word of God, with all its eternal consequences, accuracy is critical. In ministry contexts we cannot afford to take accuracy lightly, especially when we have in mind more than learning a set of one to one hundred simple, straightforward Bible stories. No doubt the typical set of simple, straightforward narratives used in many oral ministries is a good start, but our ministry goals among unreached people groups should be much more profound than where those story sets leave off. To help the church handle and accurately reproduce, over the long haul, the complexity of Paul's propositional argumentation in 2 Corinthians is quite different. However, if a church is to be truly mature, they are going to have to handle that level of complex content accurately. For oral ministries to be more effective, they need to understand, first, the ways in which oral cultures are uniquely susceptible to inaccurate retellings and, second, what can be done to ensure accuracy.

Pressures Against Accuracy That Impact Oral Communicators

The pressures against accuracy that will be discussed here are felt by all communicators, not just oral communicators. Because of the unique nature of oral communication, oral communicators feel these pressures to a greater degree than others. I suggest a number of reasons for this increased pressure.

Oral Retellings Have No Objective Basis

The first pressure against accuracy has already been mentioned, namely, that an audible message is disappearing as it is being spoken. There is no objective way to go back and verify if there is correspondence between the memory of the spoken message and what was actually spoken. Disagreements between audience members about what was said quickly degenerate into a "he said, she said" scenario. We use that phrase in modern English as a label for situations where we despair of being able to figure out who is really telling the truth. Oral peoples live in that situation perpetually.

Audience Expectations Influence Retellings

As human beings, we all want to be liked, and good storytellers shape their stories to what their audiences want to hear. Good storytellers are known for entertaining, and they take that seriously, sometimes to the point of changing the facts of a story. This is true of all communicators, oral or not.

Oral communicators would sympathize with the Roman historian Livy who said he would gladly change the winner of the battle of Pharsalia to

Pompey if the rhyming of his poem about the battle required it.[2] Cicero, another Roman historian, said "the privilege is conceded to rhetoricians to distort history in order to give more point to their narrative."[3] All communicators make adjustments to the audience, but oral communicators are likely to make more radical adjustments. Ernst Breisach points out that "In the absence of an 'authoritative' written text, the bards could adjust their messages to the changing preferences and realities of collective life."[4]

The *Physical* Proximity of the Audience Influences Retellings

Another of the reasons for increased audience pressure on oral communication is that speaker and audience must be physically co-present. "The writer is normally absent when the reader reads, whereas in oral communication speaker and hearer are present with one another."[5] That face-to-face proximity inherent in oral communication causes the speaker, on the one hand, to take greater care in saying anything contrary to the expectations of the audience, and on the other, to take greater liberty in saying what pleases. Difficult messages are mitigated, while pleasing messages are enhanced. Physical distance has always bred boldness.

The *Relational* Proximity of the Audience Influences Retellings

Not only is physical proximity a factor, but relational proximity is also a factor. In most oral communication situations, the audience is known to, or even related to, the speaker. If a respected family elder or a hostile neighbor is present, and the message the speaker wishes to communicate might be offensive, the speaker is likely to make significant adjustments. If accuracy, in itself, is not a strong value, while pleasing the audience is a strong value, the amount of change the message could undergo can be significant.

The pressure of relational proximity also works in the opposite direction, from audience to speaker. If the respected family elder says something publicly that a member of the audience knows isn't true, the likelihood that that member of the audience would publicly shame the elder by trying to correct him is diminished. In oral societies it is even more difficult to separate the messenger from the message, and, because oral cultures tend to be honor/shame oriented, the higher the authority of the messenger making the "mistake," the less likely it is to be corrected.

---

[2] David Hackett Fischer, *Historians' Fallacies: Toward a Logic of Historical Thought* (New York: Harper Torchbooks, 1970), 87.

[3] Jonathan A. C. Brown, *Misquoting Muhammad: The Challenge and Choices of Interpreting the Prophet's Legacy* (London: Oneworld, 2014), 235.

[4] Ernst Breisach, *Historiography: Ancient, Medieval, and Modern* (Chicago: University of Chicago, 1983), 6.

[5] Walter J. Ong, *Orality and Literacy: The Technologizing of the Word* (New York: Routledge, 1982), 171.

In a communication situation dominated by literacy, however, there is greater physical, relational, and temporal distance between message sender and message receiver. Kenneth Boulding points out,

> The invention of writing marks the separation of the communication from the communicator and enables individuals to receive messages from people that they have never met, will never meet, and could never meet. With the invention of writing, messages from individuals may penetrate the time space of the society far beyond the life span of the individuals concerned. In some degree, of course, this is possible in a nonliterate society through the transmission of an oral heritage. Writing, however, enormously magnifies this effect.[6]

The increased physical and relational distance between communicator and audience facilitates a sense of anonymity which allows the speaker to craft the message, or the audience to respond to the message, differently than they would if face to face. I mentioned that physical distance breeds boldness, and relational distance (anonymity) does too. The separation of communicator and audience allows for the message to be evaluated more critically than otherwise. Because of the anonymity inherent in written communication, the audience can develop what Bourgault terms "critical distanced postures."[7] This posture of evaluating the message for the message's sake, unfettered by relational pressures, has the potential to increase accuracy.

The Cultural Proximity of the Audience Influences Retellings

The final pressure that affects communicators is worldview pressure. Worldviews are the assumptions (about the way the world is) that we use to think with. Our worldviews are like gravity, a force exerting consistent pressure on everything we do and say and hear, pulling it inexorably towards a given conclusion.

Kathleen Callow reminds us,

> As rational beings, we have the fundamental capacity to relate things to each other coherently; indeed, we have the incapacity not to. We are under a strong inner compulsion to hold our world in our minds in a way that makes sense...We expect coherence enough to search for it actively.[8]

And if we don't find coherence, we will adjust the material until it makes sense to our worldview. Jan Vansina adds: "Finally, there is the known

---

[6] Kenneth E. Boulding, *The Image: Knowledge in Life and Society* (Ann Arbor: University of Michigan, 1956), 55.

[7] Louise M. Bourgault, "Press Freedom, the Oral Tradition, and the Press in Sub-Saharan Africa," *Journal of Third World Studies* XIII, no. 1 (Spring 1996), 64.

[8] Kathleen Callow, *Man and Message: A Guide to Meaning-Based Text Analysis* (Lanham: University Press of America, 1998), 28–29.

tendency of the mind to construct a coherent discourse. This leads to structuring of the same topics over and over again so that they become more meaningful in terms of the worldview of the culture in question."[9] Hippolyte Delehaye gives us an example of what this worldview pressure looks like practically:

> Through not listening properly or through forgetfulness, someone fails to mention an important circumstance and the coherence of the story is thereby impaired. Somebody else, more careful, notices something is missing, and uses his imagination to try and repair the omission; he invents a new detail here, and suppresses another there, till the requirements of likelihood and logic appear to him to be satisfied. This is generally achieved at the expense of truth, the speaker or writer not realizing that he has substituted a quite different story for the primitive version. Sometimes again a story is transmitted through someone who finds it embarrassing, and contributes seriously to its falsification by some twist of thought or expression.[10]

Because both the speaker and the audience in most oral situations share the same worldview, the effects of the pressure are likely to remain unnoticed. The worldview pressure to match "the requirements of likelihood and logic" that is put on the speaker matches the expectations of the audience, so any adjustment made by the speaker is readily accepted by the audience.[11] This is especially critical when the material being conveyed comes from a far-away land and a far-away culture and a far-away time and told in a far-away language, like any Bible story would be. The potential for worldview mismatch is great, and the speaker and audience will both facilitate and appreciate the drift towards their own perspective.[12]

These reasons (lack of objectivity, audience expectations, the physical, relational and cultural proximity of the audience) combine to contribute significant pressure on communication accuracy in an oral situation.

Characteristics of Oral Messages

Apart from the community pressures that work against accuracy in an oral situation, there is the general characteristic of oral communication in itself that also makes recall difficult. In this section I will discuss the

---

[9] Jan Vansina, *Oral Tradition as History* (Madison: University of Wisconsin, 1985), 171-72.

[10] Hippolyte Delehaye, *The Legends of the Saints*, Donald Attwater (Dublin: Four Courts Press, 1955), 14.

[11] Breisach, 19; Robin Horton, "African Traditional Thought and Western Science," in *Africa and Change*, ed. Colin M. Turnbull (New York: Alfred A. Knopf, 1973), 510.

[12] For more on how to address this issue, see: Tom Steffen and William Bjoraker, *The Return of Oral Hermeneutics: As Good Today as It Was for the Hebrew Bible and First-Century Christianity* (Eugene: Wipf and Stock, 2020).

characteristic nature of oral communication and several techniques that oral cultures employ to compensate for it.

The characteristic nature of oral communication is that it typically proceeds without a clear plan, resulting in what Catherine Reissman describes as "stop-and-start" and "typically long, full of asides, comments, flashbacks, flashforwards, orientation and evaluation."[13] In short, a typical oral communication is often a jumble of chaotic elements because the telling of the message unfolds without much forethought. Some communicators are better than others at producing a coherent message, like a chess master thinking many moves ahead, but the average oral person doesn't.[14] Each language develops discourse features to help the audience track the many changes and shifts, but the chaotic nature of oral communication remains.

When an oral communicator does want to have the message or story remembered, one of the techniques they can employ is repetition. This can be both in terms of number of times a message is repeated as well as the number of listeners who hear the message (collective memory). With repetition and the triangulation of collective memory, getting an audience to consistently remember a straightforward Bible story, like Daniel being thrown into the lion's den, is not especially difficult.

For longer stories (like epics) and more complicated topics the speaker will put in more effort and fashion the story using meter and formulas. Recall is enhanced when the form of the message is presented mnemonically. But while meter can enhance recall, it is a double-edged sword, it also pressures the message away from accuracy. Remember the earlier mention of the historian Livy who said he would gladly change the winner of the battle of Pharsalia to Pompey if the rhyming of his poem about the battle required it. Jan Vansina mentions that one of the greatest pressures to alter the telling of a story is "the working of mnemonic dynamics."[15] David Fischer describes the impact of poetic pressure on the work of the Roman poet-historian Lucan:

> Lucan actually wrote a long epic poem, commonly called the *Pharsalia.* Though he did not reverse the outcome of the battle for poetic effect, he revised nearly everything else, in the interest of aesthetic perfection. For the sake of his meter he rearranged the geography of the Mediterranean, substituting *Emathios* for *Thessalios* in the first line, because *Thessalios* would not scan after the opening *Bella per.* He removed the capital of Parthia from crude, clumsy-sounding Ctesiphon, to beautiful, euphonious Babylon. Like many another Roman poet after Virgil, he made the battles of Pharsalia and Philippi take place on the same spot, though more than

---

[13] Catherine Kohler Riessman, *Narrative Analysis*, Qualitative Research Methods Series (Newbury Park: Sage, 1993), 13-14, 43.

[14] Ong, 141-142, 147, 164-65.

[15] Vansina, *Oral Tradition*, 144.

150 miles lay in between. He changed the sequence of consuls when it suited his poetic purpose, promiscuously mixed real and fictitious persons, improved the inconvenient topography of Greece, reversed the Persian Gulf and the Red Sea, revised the career of Pompey, and brought Cicero to the battlefield for dramatic effect.[16]

In summary, while meter enhances recall of the message, it also supplies pressure that will intentionally or unintentionally shape the message. In a society where strict accuracy isn't valued highly, that can have devastating effects on a message. Paul Connerton points out,

> These large scale performative utterances have to be cast in a standardised form if there is to be any chance of their being repeated by successive generations; and the rhythms of oral verse are the privileged mechanisms of recall...But rhythm sets drastic limits to the verbal arrangement of what might be said and thought...By substituting a visual record for a phonetic one, the alphabet frees a society from the constraints of rhythmic mnemonics.[17]

To this idea Reuven Firestone adds:

> Proper rendition of oral epic poetry is possible only when the bard or rhapsodist has mastered the various formulae of which it is comprised. He does not memorize and recite the oral poem verbatim, but rather relates its matter through the infinitely creative combination and adjustment of oral literary formulae and formulaic expressions. Each rendition of the "same" poem is different; the nature of oral literature therefore remains fluid...It is the nature of oral literature, whether poetic song or prose legend, to change and evolve in the course of repeated tellings. Each individual rendition is unique because it consists of interactive communication between the performer (the storyteller or singer of epic poetry) and the audience. The performer reacts to visual and auditory cues that are received from the audience, and will knowingly or unconsciously vary the rendition accordingly. The fluid nature of oral literature therefore lends itself to adaptation to its naturally changing cultural environment.[18]

Northrop Frye says, "symmetry, in any narrative, always means that historical content is being subordinated to mythical demands of design and form."[19] As mentioned earlier, oral communications, in their natural state, are difficult to remember, and some of the techniques (like meter and

---

[16] Fischer, *Fallacies*, 88.

[17] Paul Connerton, *How Societies Remember* (Cambridge: Cambridge University, 1989), 76.

[18] Reuven Firestone, *Journeys in Holy Lands: The Evolution of the Abraham-Ishmael Legends in Islamic Exegesis* (Albany: State University of New York, 1990), 16.

[19] Todd Lawson, *The Quran: Epic and Apocalypse* (London: Oneworld, 2017), 195.

formulas) that oral people employ to make the message easier to recall, can, ironically, also facilitate content drift.

Implications

When we discuss orality in *ministry* situations, that is, where God's revealed word is the basis of our appeal, we cannot be satisfied with inaccuracy in any form. If we believe we have been given a message by God Himself, a message to be shared with all people everywhere, a message with eternal consequences for those that hear, then accuracy has to be important. We are obligated to ensure accuracy is highly valued and modeled. I conclude my paper with implications in four ministry areas.

Theological Implications

My first point is that we need to be aware of an insufficient authority base for our ministries. Assuming an oral person with an ability to recall information becomes convinced of God's message and of the need to pass it on accurately—what will they be accurate to? As mentioned earlier, the concept of accuracy presupposes a standard and a means of evaluating conformity to that standard. What will serve as the authority for their accurate retelling? And how will they know they are attaining their goal?

Will we provide God's Word itself (a translation) or just a summary (a story)? In other words, is the Bible itself the authority, or do we insert an alternative level of authority between them and God's Word—a buffer, so to speak? Often this buffer that substitutes for God's revealed Word are a set of finely crafted stories. The rationalization for this buffer is that the stories are "biblically accurate." Indeed, they might be biblically accurate, but they aren't the Bible. Of course, in locations where the Bible is already translated and available in audio form, a set of carefully crafted stories is very helpful. But where the scriptures are not yet translated, such a "buffer" should not substitute for the actual Word. Such strategies are justified by invoking the word "oral." Because oral peoples have good recall ability, this ability is considered sufficient to ensure accuracy. That might be true if we employ techniques like repetition and collective memory, and the content is merely a set of carefully crafted stories. But my contention in this chapter is that the audience being "oral" is not a sufficient basis for ensuring God's revealed Word remains accurately reproduced. Once God's Word is made available in "text" form, it exists independently and objectively it is able to exert authoritative influence into a situation.

Practical Implications

We need to be aware of an insufficient understanding of the worldview of our audience. We need to understand what direction their worldview is going to bend what they hear and be able to mitigate the pressure it will place on the interpretation and retelling of the message. Without some sort of back pressure to slow the drift, the content of the message that God gave us will suffer.[20]

Motivational Implications

We need to be aware of "good" ministry objectives when "best" ministry objectives are available. Because of the popularity of CPMs and DMMs, I want to make specific mention of the danger of "movementism." This is my term for when, in the course of pursuing church planting movements (CPMs) and disciple making movements (DMMs), the values of speed and movement trump the values of developing solid disciples and churches—when breadth is more important than depth.

"Best" usually means hard work, and sometimes oral methodologies are chosen to justify avoiding hard work (like Bible translation and long-term discipleship) or to justify ministry short-cuts in order to facilitate movements. Another place where shortcuts are sometimes justified is when we come to ministry with time constraints. When time constraints enter in, we have to lessen what would be best for what would be manageable, and that kicks the door open to a host of short-cuts, and the subsequent need to rationalize those short-cuts.

These choices are sometimes given a noble coloring by invoking the role of the Holy Spirit in bringing people to maturity. The Holy Spirit certainly has an important role, but pushing off onto Him the discipleship responsibility that He has squarely placed on our shoulders is not noble, it is a dereliction of duty.

Notice the repeated use of the word "sometimes." I am not making a blanket statement about oral ministries. But I am saying that we need to be aware of our motivations when the choice between "good" and "best" is before us.

Prejudicial Implications

My final point is that we need to be aware of perpetuating the chronic under-development of our oral friends in a rapidly globalizing world. I realize that the use of the word "under" in this context is itself prejudicial, but my point is that sometimes our ministry choices and methodologies are not sufficiently holistic.

---

[20] I say "slow" the drift because, even if you translate God's word accurately, you can't really prevent the drift. Worldview pressure inevitably twists the interpretation of the accurate translation towards its own understanding. See E. Randolph Richards and Brandon J. O'Brien, *Misreading Scripture with Western Eyes: Removing Cultural Blinders to Better Understanding the Bible* (Downers Grove: IVP, 2012).

The fact is, globalization is influencing our oral friends more and more each day. We can't resist it any more than we could stand in the ocean and try to hold back the tide. It is coming whether we like it or not, or whether it is good or not. The world is changing out from under them, and either we are helping them be prepared for it or we are contributing to their being left even further behind. We should be asking ourselves what world our friends will be living in in 30 years' time and whether there is more we can do to help them be prepared for it.

Bibliography

Boulding, Kenneth E. *The Image: Knowledge in Life and Society*. Ann Arbor: University of Michigan, 1956.

Bourgault, Louise M. "Press Freedom, the Oral Tradition, and the Press in Sub-Saharan Africa." *Journal of Third World Studies* XIII, no. 1 (Spring 1996): 57–96.

Breisach, Ernst. *Historiography: Ancient, Medieval, and Modern*. Chicago: University of Chicago, 1983.

Brown, Jonathan A. C. *Misquoting Muhammad: The Challenge and Choices of Interpreting the Prophet's Legacy*. London: Oneworld, 2014.

Callow, Kathleen. *Man and Message: A Guide to Meaning-Based Text Analysis*. Lanham: University Press of America, 1998.

Connerton, Paul. *How Societies Remember*. Cambridge: Cambridge University, 1989.

Delehaye, Hippolyte. *The Legends of the Saints*. Donald Attwater. Dublin: Four Courts, 1955.

Firestone, Reuven. *Journeys in Holy Lands: The Evolution of the Abraham-Ishmael Legends in Islamic Exegesis*. Albany: State University of New York, 1990.

Fischer, David Hackett. *Historians' Fallacies: Toward a Logic of Historical Thought*. New York: Harper Torchbooks, 1970.

Horton, Robin. "African Traditional Thought and Western Science." In *Africa and Change*, ed. Colin M. Turnbull, 454–520. New York: Alfred A. Knopf, 1973.

Lawson, Todd. *The Quran: Epic and Apocalypse*. London: Oneworld, 2017.

Ong, Walter J. *Orality and Literacy: The Technologizing of the Word*. New York: Routledge, 1982.

Richards, E. Randolph, and Brandon J. O'Brien. *Misreading Scripture with Western Eyes: Removing Cultural Blinders to Better Understanding the Bible*. Downers Grove: InterVarsity, 2012.

Riessman, Catherine Kohler. *Narrative Analysis*. Qualitative Research Methods Series. Newbury Park: Sage, 1993.

Steffen, Tom, and William Bjoraker. *The Return of Oral Hermeneutics: As Good Today as It Was for the Hebrew Bible and First-Century Christianity*. Eugene: Wipf and Stock, 2020.

Vansina, Jan. *Oral Tradition as History*. Madison: University of Wisconsin, 1985.

Part 2: Oral Discipleship Training

Chapter 6:
Integration of Chronology with Oral Bible Story Telling

Larry Dinkins

Abstract

I did my doctoral research on the Walk Thru the Bible Chronological teaching method in the context of the Thai. Through this qualitative research I was able to clearly see the benefits of presenting the meta-narrative of the Scriptures as a foundation for Thai believers who often had a very fragmented understanding of God's Word. Being able to reproduce the basic structure and storyline of the Bible including the key characters, events, time elements, and geography through WTB proved to very beneficial. However, a needed further step was a thorough familiarity with the individual stories that make up the redemptive storyline and an ability to reproduce those stories orally for the purposes of discipleship, leading small groups, evangelism, church planting and preaching. There have been many positive developments and materials produced for presenting the chronological metanarrative, but those advances need to be matched with practical training in oral Bible story telling. This chapter shows how these two aspects can be integrated and effectively taught so that the majority of our world which is made up of preferred primary and secondary oral learners can be reached with the gospel.

Bumpy Road to Orality

A monumental paradigm-shift in my missionary career in Thailand, which now spans four decades, occurred in 2006 when I was invited by Thai friends who had completed a five-day storytelling workshop in Hemet California called *Simply the Story* (STS). My initial shock was not being allowed to take any written notes for five days. Like other highly literate ministers in the training, I almost went into "diabetic shock" at this stipulation and actually found my hand tracing invisible notes as I listened. This first jarring jolt began to wear off, however, as I actually learned to enjoy orally told Bible stories and especially the participatory experience of unpacking them with others. Each story we heard was presented in its pure form so that anyone seeking to bring in a comment from their vast knowledge of theology or years of study of cognate passages was politely asked, "But where is that in this particular story." In this way everyone felt that they were on "a level playing field" with no one person able to dominate the discussion.

At the end of the training, each participant was instructed to present a story for evaluation so that a certificate of competency could be given. The director, Dorothy, singled me out for special scrutiny. I felt good about my presentation. I had flown through many academic workshops in my day and thought this one would be no different. At the end, a Thai participant asked Dorothy if I had passed. Dorothy responded, "I'm afraid Dr. Dinkins didn't pass. He violated too many of the basic principles of telling the story."

At that point I began to lose my sanctification and actually became angry. A number of lay people, including the Thai, had received their certificates. Yet Dorothy had the audacity to flunk the Reverend Larry M. Dinkins! By then I had been a cross-cultural missionary for 25 years with a PhD and was enough Thai that the thought of "losing face" was unacceptable. I returned home that day and informed my wife of this perceived injustice. She replied, "That is the first academic assignment you have failed to pass since I have known you. Actually, it's good that you flunked. You needed to be humbled. I sense that you have run into a topic that you truly don't understand and so you probably need to investigate it more."

The truth hurt. The Reverend Dr. Dinkins didn't know how to follow seemingly simple directions for telling a Bible story. You teach as you have been taught and the cumulative effect of 25 years of western education based mainly on lecture became all too apparent. Usually, I could rectify any perceived lack of competency in a given field of learning by simply doing more study or working through key books in that area. Many academic subjects can be mastered in this way, but not oral Bible story telling. Failing STS set me on a quest to expose myself as much as possible to the whole field of orality and especially how oral-aural communication relates to teaching the meta-narrative of scripture and the intersection of that grand narrative with the individual stories of which it is composed.

Exposure to Walk Thru the Bible

My appreciation for a big picture view of the Sacred Storybook came during my first year at Dallas Theological Seminary in 1975. It was then that Bruce Wilkinson visited Dallas Theological Seminary (DTS) and put on a seminar which treated the Bible chronologically. The roots of the method he brought to DTS can be traced back to 1963 when Ralph Braun began a participatory home Bible study following a chronological approach using hand signs and geographic locations laid out as a map in a living room. He called this unique method, "An Old and New Testament Walk-Through."[1] Braun's method was a fast-paced group Bible study of biblical covenants taught in a memorable way. It was used with Christians or evangelistically in small groups of 5 to 20 people over a 13-week period.

The following techniques were employed by Braun: group participation, hand signs, OT clothesline (events hung in sequence), and spatial maps.

---

[1] Ralph Braun, *Old and New Testament Walk–through* (Grand Rapids: Zondervan, 1975).

These proved to be precursors of the one-day seminar that Wilkinson presented to myself and ten other DTS students in 1975. Wilkinson spent five hours taking us through 77 key points of the Old Testament stressing the key characters, events, geography, and time components. He called the seminar *Walk Thru the Bible* (WTB).

Lessons Learned as TEE Mentor

I kept my exposure to WTB on the back burner as I applied to OMF and began my ministry in Central Thailand in 1981 with leprosy patients. The core group of believers usually had a fourth-grade education and were at best semi-literate. They were not at all impressed with my degrees, nor were they overly enthusiastic when I preached my expository sermons taken from outlines I had used in the States. I had been trained for four years as a critical thinker who could analyze the minutiae of a text in both Hebrew and Greek. My exposition of a biblical text was logical, purposeful, abstract, and weighted heavily in the doctrinal sections of the Epistles. You can imagine my enthusiasm when I discovered that the main teaching tool in my mission was called *Home Bible **Seminary*** (HBS).

A senior coworker instructed me to act as a mentor for my leprosy mentee and to teach him how to mark his Bible to a grammatical level of subject, verb and object and then transfer his analysis to what ended up being 66 workbooks (one for every book in the Bible). However, my fourth-grade level disciple struggled greatly with such a literate analysis.

When I asked the leader of HBS about this he replied, "Larry, we are using the cutting edge of a new trend in distance learning called TEE - Theological Education by Extension." Like the HBS leader, I too desired that all of our TEE students could develop in literate processing of the scriptures, but the reality was that most would remain at their core oral learners. At that time, I was a junior worker and had no answer for my very senior co-worker. However, four decades further on in Thai ministry I can now give a much more informed answer, having seen clearly how hard-wired for oral stories the Thai actually are.

I saw the Thai inclination towards narrative presentations each time I held up a preaching poster or showed the Jesus Film. At such junctures I could see a visible change in their demeanor as they inched closer to the speaker or screen and seemed to hang on every word. This tendency was especially pronounced when a Christian *likae* troupe visited our area. *Likae* is a Thai dramatic and musical theatre production that is performed on a stage in an open square or temple site.

Thai and the Dramatic Arts

The first *likae* I observed was performed by lay members of a rural church before four hundred captivated Thai. The actors, bedecked in colorful costumes, told the chronological story of the Bible from Genesis to the resurrection using traditional musical instruments, chants, songs, and dialogue. John Davis affirms the impact of this approach:

> To effectively communicate the message it needs to be packaged in a medium that will be culturally acceptable. For Thai this medium is drama. There seems to be no other means of communication which makes such a powerful impact on Thai audiences as the dramatic arts.[2]

Bible Fragmentation

This propensity for story and drama was even affirmed when I entered an academic environment as faculty at the Bangkok Bible Seminary (BBS). The students enjoyed hearing individual Bible stories, but I found that they seemed unable to piece together even a rudimentary picture of the plan of God as found in the Old and New Testaments. Tom Steffen finds this to be a universal problem: "Bible training institutes often promote fragmentation...A fragmented grasp of the Bible often results in some people missing the big picture. Caught up in the details of minutia, Bible students often fail to see God's overall plan."[3] In another article Steffen adds, "Too many of us are specialist in fragmentation when it comes to Scripture. We therefore continue to perpetuate a fragmented understanding of Scripture, and her Author. To grasp a more comprehensive picture of the face of God we must be able to move beyond the individual pieces of clothing placed on the clothesline, whether linear or circular, and learn to value how they all tie together to form a comprehensive wardrobe that brings honor to the Wearer."[4]

Hesslegrave observes the following in church contexts: "The church suffers from an approach that majors on the 'little stories' of Scripture without putting them in the 'larger story' of God's dealings with, and revelations to, humanity over the centuries."[5] Laity within the church are in turn directly impacted by this disjointed view of scripture. A Thai leader commented, "Thai Christians are unable to put events in the Bible into any

---

[2] John Davis, *Poles Apart?: Contextualizing the Gospel*, (Bangkok, Thailand: Kanok Bannasan, OMF Publishers, 1993), 14.

[3] Tom Steffen, *Reconnecting God's Story to Ministry: Cross-Cultural Storytelling at Home and Abroad*, (La Habra, CA: Center for Organizational & Ministry Development, 1996), 45, 46.

[4] Tom Steffen, *A Clothesline Theology for the World: How a Value-Driven Grand Narrative of Scripture Can Frame the Gospel*. Great Commission Research Journal, 1996, 235.

[5] David Hesslegrave, *Communicating Christ Cross-Culturally*, (Grand Rapids: Zondervan Publishers, 1978), 206.

sort of a timeline. This affects negatively their ability to understand both sermons and in their own personal study."[6]

Recognizing this deficiency and overall biblical illiteracy among believers, I harkened back to my WTB exposure at DTS and translated the OT/NT seminar into the Thai language. To better explain the need of this chronological approach, I used a familiar train trip that most all of them had taken. There are two trains that make a daily trip from Bangkok to Chiang Mai, a distance of 450 miles. One is an express train that makes very few stops along the way and covers the distance in 12 hours. The other is a painfully slow train that stops at most every village and takes much longer to travel the same distance. I explained that in this WTB seminar we would be riding on a "bullet train" that stops at only the most important depots. As life-long students of scripture they would have plenty of time to board the slower train in order to fill in what they missed in their Walk (actually run) Thru the Bible.

During my time at BBS I was able to teach WTB as a semester course but was also invited to Thai camps and local churches on a regular basis. Teaching the OT seminar to tribal groups in Thailand as well as an opportunity to teach in Mongolia and Russia served to further prove the cross-cultural effectiveness of the WTB approach.

Qualitative Research on WTB

I became so embroiled in WTB that I decided to make it the topic of my PhD at Biola University. The chance to do qualitative research on WTB was my goal, but possibly a greater goal was to find an answer for the slow growth of the church in Thailand. At that point, the nation was only about .3% Christian, a percentage that has only increased to .65% in 2022[7] despite almost 200 years of missionary presence in this country. I felt that the traditional Western and literate approach to communication in Thailand was a factor in these statistics, but I needed to do research to confirm it.

What followed were two years of classwork at Biola followed by five years of field testing, in which I taught the OT WTB seminar in Thai over 40 times in many parts of Thailand. A major help in my research was the groundwork laid by Trevor McIlwain of New Tribes Missions (now Ethnos360) in his tribal work in the Philippines. As with my struggles in Central Thailand, McIlwain's approach developed from a need to reach biblically illiterate oral learners with foundational chronological teaching. Hesslegrave highlights McIlwain's early trials: "McIlwain's approach arose out of difficulties he experienced in

---

[6] Manot Jaengmuk, *Walk Thru the Bible Bible Study Program and the Local Thai Church* (bachelor's thesis, Bangkok Bible College, 1992), 23.

[7] "Thailand People Groups, Languages, and Religions," Joshua Project, accessed September 15, 2022, https://joshuaproject.net/countries/TH.

working with the Palawano tribe on Palawan Island. He first tried to teach the Bible topically and later the Gospel of John expositionally, verse by verse. Both methods failed because the Palawanos 'had never been taught the basic Old Testament historical sequence of events as one complete story.'"[8] This teaching of "one complete story" is affirmed by Merrill Tenney: "If a student expects to comprehend any part of doctrine of the Scriptures, he must know what they teach as a whole. Each book is a part of that whole, and can be fully understood only when it is seen in relation to the entire stream of divine revelation that begins with Genesis and that ends with the apocalypse."[9]

McIlwain's approach became known as *Firm Foundations*, and started out as *Chronological Bible Teaching* (CBT) or *Foundational Bible Teaching* (FBT).[10] As seen by these titles, the stress was on the Bible itself as one story which is best understood by following the progressive historic development of God's revelation starting in Genesis and ending in Revelation. By following God's model of presenting the Old Testament first, one is able to show the need for salvation and resulting solution in the New Testament, and to correct various doctrinal errors related to salvation. CBT experienced wide acceptance on the field but still remained an overall literate approach covering many pages of print, and did not address how best to tailor the teaching for specific cross-cultural contexts. Possibly one of the best field examples of this approach presented more orally is seen in the Ee-Taow film, which traces the impact a panoramic story approach had on a tribe in Papua New Guinea.[11] I always tell my students, if they don't cry by the end of these videos, their grade will be reduced.

Building off the lead of McIlwain, I was able to complete my research on WTB, which only reinforced the strategic nature of a chronological approach as a first step in discipleship. The reasons for the warm reception that WTB received in Thailand is best described by Bruce Wilkinson himself in an interview with Hunt and McCauley:

---

[8] David Hesslegrave, *Communicating Christ Cross-Culturally* (Grand Rapids: Zondervan, 1978), 208.

[9] Merrill C. Tenny, *New Testament Survey* (Leicester: Inter Varsity, 2003), xii.

[10] Trevor McIlwain, *Building on Firm Foundations*, 9 volumes (Sanford, FL: New Tribes Mission, 1999).

[11] *Ee-Taow: The Mouk Story* (1989; Sanford: New Tribes Mission, 2002), DVD.

a) Synthetic - gives an overview of the "forest" (broad sweep of Bible) with little stress on the "trees" (details).
b) Teacher accepts responsibility for the student's learning.
c) It is memorable - contains a variety of mnemonic aids.
d) It's fun. [12]

These factors, coupled with a much shorter forty-point OTLive seminar stressing just the events and characters of the Old Testament, have confirmed this approach as an effective cross-cultural tool which is approaching fifty years of use in over one hundred countries.

WTB provides a basic story set covering the entire Bible by incorporating eighty key people and events. As a generic panorama of essential narrative elements, these eighty points are mainly presented in more literate contexts. However, when working in a non-literate or semi-literate culture it is possible to contextualize and adjust the story set to that specific people group. A suggested process is as follows:

1. Study the language and culture and gain a grasp of their world view.
2. Develop a more exhaustive story list that addresses those key world view issues.
3. Narrow the full list down to around thirty key stories that touch on essential doctrines and truths.
4. Field-test the story set for suitability.
5. Evaluate and debrief the results of field testing.
6. Finalize the story list and set up a training program.

A Missing Component

My research demonstrated the need for a chronological method and guidelines for developing a suitable cross-cultural approach for the Thai. I was then ready for the missing component: just how to fit the individual stories of the Bible into this chronological framework. Part of the answer came in the form of the Simply the Story Training in 2006 which so shook my Western mindset.

Simply the Story was actually the outgrowth of an eighty-minute video called "God's Story," which included a long introduction as a backdrop to Genesis 1 and then continued on from that point to Revelation using animation to cover fourteen key stories. The popularity of this media tool is seen by the fact that it has been translated into 426 languages. Those using God's Story began to ask for training in how best to tell the individual stories

---

[12] Angela E Hunt & Laurie McCauley, "Bruce Wilkinson Makes the Bible Come Alive," *Fundamentalist Journal* 7, no. 10 (1988): 17-18.

in an oral fashion, yet accurately and with understanding. Out of this felt need came the birth of *Simply the Story* (STS).[13]

The STS structure of training and the template for actually absorbing a story (as opposed to memorizing by rote) and telling it is quite straightforward. By listening repeatedly to an orally told Bible story and verbalizing it as best one can, the listener retains a high percentage of the story content itself. When each group member is exposed enough, then the process of unpacking the story by open-ended observational questions begins with applications based on those observations treated at the end. A storyteller then volunteers to tell the story to another group, and that person is then prepared through a six-step process to share the story:

1. Give the context of the story.
2. Tell the story accurately, but in your own words.
3. Ask for a volunteer to retell the story, or (in a less intimidating way) tell the story as best they can remember to a neighbor.
4. Lead through the story by retelling it in full together with your audience by inviting them to join with you in the retelling (i.e.. you start a sentence and the group chimes in to fill in the gaps you leave).
5. Ask spiritual observation questions of each part of the story.
6. Based on the lessons and principles revealed during the observation phase, make personal applications to life.

The whole purpose of STS is to train people to dig deeply into a Bible story and discover spiritual truths for themselves in a highly participatory group setting. The power of the story, however, is not just the oral absorption and analysis of the story, but in the actual retelling of the story to others.

In STS I saw the potential to actually follow 2 Timothy 2:2 with a training approach that can be passed down easily from generation to generation. In the West there is virtually no stress given to replicating what we hear. The typical sermon is not designed to be remembered long term nor packaged in such a way to be immediately transferable. Yet as cross-cultural workers who strive to make multiplying disciples, the need to design training that is readily conveyable to others is vital.

Jesus as the consummate oral communicator made his teaching eminently portable for his disciples and in turn, they passed it on quickly so that it was said, "These who have turned the world upside down have come here too" (Acts 17:6, NKJV). The following maxim should guide any trainer working with preferred oral learners: "Don't teach anything that is not immediately transferable." If this is your priority, then it will shape in a significant way the instructional design of your teaching materials—whether oral or in print.

---

[13] A downloadable 160-page handbook in eight languages, plus audio files of model stories can be found at www.simplythestory.org.

"Optimum" Stories with Content Accuracy

Besides its replicability aspect, STS is known for telling each story with content accuracy, as opposed to "crafting" a story. There is, of course, a place for crafting a story as seen in the *God's Story* video. Decisions must be made on what to leave out of a story when needing to summarize a long story like Joseph's, which covers twenty-one chapters. However, the principle of STS is to start a new oral storyteller with optimal stories of less than fifteen verses. The optimal aspect relates to the need to find stories with less dialogue and more action, with a plot that rises to a crisis or high point and concludes with a satisfying resolution within a minimum of verses. The more dramatic and sensory the story, the more memorable it will be.

Mark 4:35-41 which describes Jesus and his disciples in a storm is such a passage, and I have seen many small groups absorb these six verses in only ten minutes, with each member being able to tell it accurately in their own words. STS training does not encourage rote word-for-word memory of stories, which invariably slows the memory process. By seeing the story develop as a kind of movie storyboard in their mind and saying the story out loud repeatedly using appropriate gestures, the story is sealed into their heart pocket for further telling.

The nature of an orally told story commends itself to an accurate telling. We want non-literates to understand that we are telling a sacred story straight from God's word, a story that they can easily review no matter what translation is being used. A crafted story, by its very nature, changes according to the subjective decisions of whoever crafts the story and also demands a high level of spiritual maturity to decide just what to leave out.

Not Just for Children

Over time I became known as a narrative storyteller, but with that moniker came a common question: "What is it like telling stories to children?" I found that many people equated "storytelling" to ministry with small children, and at worst to simply spreading moralistic heroic tales. Donald Miller shares his early perceptions: "I associated much of Christian doctrine with children's stories because I grew up in church. My Sunday school teachers had turned Bible narrative into children's fables."[14]

I have to remind my students that the stories of scripture are for the most part designed for adults and that there are a number of them that are not tales suitable for small children because of sexual or violent content. In seminary contexts I had to remind students that my classes were andragogy

---

[14] Donald Miller, *Blue Like Jazz, Nonreligious Thoughts on Christian Spirituality* (Nashville: Thomas Nelson, 2003), 30.

more than pedagogy and were designed to train them in deep inductive Bible study but in an oral style.

What About the Epistles?

Invariably, another question was asked: "What about the epistles?" The answer to this inquiry is related to treating and interpreting each passage according to its biblical genre. The majority of the Bible is narrative genre as shown by Steffen's breakdown: narrative (55–65 percent), poetry (25–35 percent), and propositions (10 percent).[15] There are parts of the didactic epistles that lend themselves to a storyline and can be treated as such, but I always encourage students to use proper hermeneutical principles for propositional genre and interpret story sections according its narrative genre.

Integrating the Three Levels

As a coordinator for both Walk Thru the Bible and Simply the Story, I have had the privilege of seeing first-hand in local trainings around Asia and especially in Thailand the power of first laying a chronological framework and then filling that framework with orally told Bible stories. Fee and Stewart recognize this dynamic by describing three levels:

Top Level – whole plan of God; 2) Middle Level – Israel; 3) Bottom Level – individual narratives. Every individual OT narrative (bottom level) is at least a part of the greater narrative of Israel's history in the world (the middle level), which in turn is a part of the ultimate narrative of God's creation and his redemption of it (the top level). This ultimate narrative goes beyond the OT through the NT. You will not fully do justice to any individual narrative without recognizing its part within the other two.[16]

C. Wright's description revolves around concentric circles rather than levels:

Before we preach any of the stories in the Bible, we need to aim to preach the story of the Bible...When we think about preaching the narrative sections of the Bible, it is helpful to imagine a series of concentric circles increasing in size. The preacher's task is to set the nugget of the story on which he is preaching within the larger stories, which ultimately of course include the story of Christ.[17]

---

[15] Tom Steffen, "Pedagogical Conversions: From Propositions to Story and Symbol" *Missiology: An International Review* 38 no. 2 (2010): 150.

[16] Gordon D Fee. and Douglas Stuart, How *to Read the Bible for All Its Worth* (Grand Rapids: Zondervan, 1993), 14.

[17] C. Wright, "Preaching From Narrative," in *Preach the Word*, ed G. Haslam (Lancaster: Sovereign World, 2006), 341.

The practical outworking of being careful to set the nugget of the story into the larger story can be seen in an example from the OT Walk Thru outline. In the book of Judges there are a total of thirteen judges, of which three get the most coverage: Deborah, Gideon and Samson. I often ask my students if they know the three key judges and whether they can list them in order. To this question, I often get a blank stare. Yet after an OT WTB seminar they can at least remember the key people in Judges and put them in their proper sequence. Then, when they hear a sermon about Gideon, they can immediately place this important Judge in context between Deborah and Samson. Having a basic template of key people and events allows believers to then place the individual stories and details of scripture into their proper context.

Can You Share Just One Story?

In seminary contexts where I have taught a course on orality, I find that students often have a good grasp of the panorama of scripture and spend three or four years concentrating on the nuggets of scripture, often in the original Greek and Hebrew. Yet I consistently see a missing link in their biblical education in regard to the actual internalizing and telling of the epic and key stories of God's Word. One of my DTS ThM students, Mick Zubel, gave these comments after taking my orality class:

> Your class was unlike any other class I've taken at DTS. I've never been told not to take notes in any class. Initially it freaked me out, but it was one of the most beneficial and eye-opening experiences I've ever had. At my program at DTS we are taught to read Koine Greek and Classical Hebrew. I know the Bible inside and out and I can tell you the story of scripture from Genesis to Revelation. But when you ask us to share just one story with 100% content accuracy I didn't think I could do it. I was convicted and sat there. I could have summarized a story but I wouldn't be able to tell it accurately and I am a fifth-year student![18]

I totally understand Mick's sentiments, because in 2006, before my exposure to STS, I could not have told you one of the 500+ stories recorded in the Bible in an accurate manner. I could have summarized a number of them, and if you had given me a chance to thoroughly review a story, then I could have told it adequately. It made me wonder why I had such a high value on memorizing individual Bible verses along with their verse references (I knew well over one hundred), yet no one ever encouraged me to collect a database of key stories which I could then use in a winsome and natural way with my host audience. The challenge of STS has resulted in a master list of one

---

[18] Heart Pocket Podcast HPP0202. "DTS Student Overcomes His Fear," accessed August 23, 2022, http://www.heartpocket.org.

hundred favorite stories which I am ready to tell without review, a list which consists of over one thousand total verses. I am able to use this mental "rolodex" of stories in my evangelism, leading small groups, WTB seminars, seminary classes and even when preaching.

The Challenge of Understanding Oral Societies

There are many popular channels on YouTube that cover "fails" of people in every imaginable context. I started this chapter with the massive "fail" I encountered trying to gain a low-level certificate from an organization called *Simply the Story*. Looking back, I realized that even as a cross-cultural missionary with 25 years of experience among the Thai, I still did not comprehend the oral nature of my target group. I was a highly literate missionary who was "educated past my intelligence" as a PhD and was so immersed in my western training that I was blinded to the majority world who communicated much differently than myself.

The father of orality, Walter Ong, famously confessed to the same malady: "We—readers of books such as this—are so literate that it is very difficult for us to conceive of an oral universe of communication or thought except as a variant of a literate universe."[19] The classic confession in this vein must be the statement by the former editor of the journal *Missiology*, J. Nelson Jennings, who had to collate articles on the topic of orality for one volume: "As a wirelessly connected and lettered human being living in 2010, I find it next to impossible even to conceive of—much less interact with—those people living in 2010 who are embedded in oral societies."[20] Jennings as the editor of the flagship publication for missions is quite honest in his lack of understanding of the 70% of people in the world who either don't, won't or prefer not to process using print communication.[21] Their preference is, in fact, orally told stories, and the book that holds the most authoritative and powerful stories is the only true Sacred Story Book—the Bible.

---

[19] Walter J. Ong, *Orality and Literacy: The Technologizing of the World* (London: Methuen, 1982), 13.

[20] J. Nelson Jennings, *Missiology: An International Review* 38, no. 2 (April 2010): iii.

[21] Jim Slack, "2005 Findings from Field Research into the Effectiveness of Oral Strategy" (workshop at the 4th Conference on Reaching Oral Communicators. Anaheim, California July 13, 2005).

Bibliography

Braun, Ralph. *Old and New Testament Walk-through*. Grand Rapids: Zondervan, 1975.

Davis, John. *Poles Apart? Contextualizing the Gospel*. Bangkok: KanokBannasan, OMF, 1993.

Fee, Gordon D. and Douglas Stuart. 1993. *How to Read the Bible for All Its Worth*. Grand Rapids: Zondervan.

Heart Pocket Podcast HPP0202. "DTS Student Overcomes His Fear." Accessed August 23, 2022. http://www.heartpocket.org.

Hesslegrave, David. *Communicating Christ Cross-Culturally*. Grand Rapids: Zondervan, 1978.

Hunt, Angela E., and Laurie McCauley. "Bruce Wilkinson Makes the Bible Come Alive." *Fundamentalist Journal* 7, no. 10 (1988).

Jaengmuk, Manot. "Walk Thru the Bible Bible Study Program and the Local Thai Church." Unpublished bachelor's thesis, Bangkok Bible College, 1992.

Jennings, J. Nelson. *Missiology: An International Review* 38, no. 2 (April 2010).

McIlwain, Trevor. 1999. *Building on Firm Foundations*, 9 volumes. Sanford, FL: New Tribes Mission.

Miller, Donald. 2003. *Blue Like Jazz, Nonreligious Thoughts on Christian Spirituality*. Nashville: Thomas Nelson.

Ee-Taow: The Mouk Story. 1989; Sanford: New Tribes Mission, 2002. DVD.

Tenny, Merrill C. 2003. *New Testament Survey*. Leicester: Inter Varsity Press.

Slack, Jim. "2005 Findings from Field Research into the Effectiveness of Oral Strategy." Workshop at the 4th Conference on Reaching Oral Communicators. Anaheim, CA, July 13, 2005.

Steffen, Tom. "A Clothesline Theology for the World: How a Value-Driven Grand Narrative of Scripture Can Frame the Gospel." *Great Commission Research Journal*, 1996.

Steffen, Tom. *Reconnecting God's Story to Ministry: Cross-Cultural Storytelling at Home and Abroad*. La Habra, CA: Center for Organizational & Ministry Development, 1996.

Steffen, Tom. "Pedagogical Conversions: From Propositions to Story and Symbol." *Missiology: An International Review* 38 no. 2, April 2010.

"Thailand People Groups, Languages, and Religions." Joshua Project. Accessed September 15, 2022. https://joshuaproject.net/countries/TH.

Wright, C. *"Preaching from Narrative"* in Haslam, G. (Ed), Preach the Word. Lancaster: Sovereign World, 2006.

Chapter 7:
Chronological Bible Storying for ESL Learners

Yiyoung Yuk

Abstract

Chronological Bible Storying was used originally as a mission strategy and the application of it in the English as a Second Language (ESL) setting is less fully studied. There is no comprehensive study of finding out the perceived strength of using Bible Storying in an ESL setting. Even though there have been some ideas presented for Chronological Bible storying in the ESL field, few have attempted to examine the actual results. The researcher wrote and illustrated the entire curriculum and tested it. This study examines the participants' change from a missional perspective, discovers growth in their linguistic strengths of the Bible storying, and measures strengths of impact of active learning skills used in Bible storying. The research aims to synthesize the insights of two different fields: Bible storying and TESOL, adding a new perspective. The research was conducted in three different countries: the U.S., France and China. The researcher is ready to share all the positive results and also engaging Bible storying strategies Christian ELT's can use to advance His kingdom!

Journey into Chronological Bible Storying & ESL Ministry

This is the story of my eleven-year journey leading the Chronological Bible Storying/ESL ministry class. Each season brought its own unique challenges, from navigating new students and a new job, to developing team leaders and adapting to new technology in the face of COVID. However, with God's grace, I was able to learn how to be creative and adaptable, which enabled me to continue my ministry despite the obstacles. Bible storying has opened so many doors for me that I never knew existed. It has brought people from all different parts of the world and invited them to sit at the feet of Christ with open hearts. Looking back, I realize that it was the first domino and the fire that started to burn brightly in my heart. In 2012, I attended a Bible storying class at Southeastern Baptist Theological Seminary, taught by Dr. Don Barger, an IMB missionary. During the course, Dr. Grant Lovejoy also came as a guest speaker. I instantly fell in love with Bible storying. I searched for groups to join but failed to find any. After praying about it, I felt the Lord urging me to start a group, but I had my reservations and excuses. "No, Lord. I am a woman, a Korean woman, a minority." The seminary was mostly dominated by white males at that time. In spite of my uncertainties, I took the initiative to start a group. Initially, only my Korean friends joined, but eventually, women from different parts of the world became a part of our group. We had a great time together, laughing, sipping coffee, taking care of the kids, and sharing Bible stories. The international women, who spoke English as a second language, enjoyed telling the stories and asked me to create homework for them. This marked the humble beginning of my journey.

Before God called me into ministry, I was an ESL teacher. I started developing a curriculum for my international friends, using my M.Div. knowledge, TESOL/ESL teaching pedagogy, and my passion for art. I wrote and illustrated the curriculum with my Christian friends. With the Bible/ESL storying curriculum, I pioneered the ESL ministry for Chinese at the church. I have trained missionaries and educators worldwide ever since.

Currently, I am an ESL education director/teacher education faculty at Emmaus Bible College and lead the Bridge ESL ministry with my students. In our ESL ministry, we have a diverse group of 43 participants representing Afghanistan, China, Cyprus, Guatemala, Indonesia, Iran, Mexico, South Korea, and Turkey. Some participants don't know the Lord yet, and others continue to grow in the knowledge of God through storying. I train my students to do Bible storying; they have been teaching and reaching nations. Over the last eleven years, I have been sharing my curriculum for free with those who wish to start an ESL ministry. My lunch box offered to the Lord has been blessed, multiplied, and fed many hungry souls. I give all the glory to the Lord! This chapter is based on my research, my Ed.D. dissertation.[1]

ESL Teachers and Mission

When it comes to missions, English teachers have made a powerful impact and they play a significant role not only in America but throughout the world.[2] Michael Lessard-Clouston commented in his essay after collecting ideas from Christian English educators at the Christians in English Language conference in Toronto. "Despite some recent and helpful writings on faith and religion in language teaching and research, there has unfortunately been less focus on the Bible as it relates to second and/or foreign language teaching" (p. 7).[3] The reality is the same here in the U.S.[4]

---

[1] Yiyoung Yuk, "Chronological Bible Storying for ESL Learners" (Ed.D. diss., Southeastern Baptist Theological Seminary, 2019).

[2] Michael Lessard-Clouston, "Biblical Themes for Christians in Language Teaching," in *Thinking Theologically about Language Teaching* (Cumbria: Langham Global Library, 2011), 7.

[3] Lessard-Clouston, "Biblical Themes," 7.

[4] Lessard-Clouston, "Biblical Themes,", 7-9.

Churches hope to reach the population of people from various nations in their neighborhoods. However, there are few Bible-based curricula that combine ESL teaching methodologies, the Bible storying method, and theological training for ESL teachers. I hoped to find perceived strengths of the material in improving English proficiency, to gain Bible knowledge that will result in spiritual growth, and to discover the benefits of using active learning skills in class. Additionally, the researcher hoped to understand more about the population who used the curriculum so that Christian leaders could meet their linguistic and spiritual needs more effectively.

Rationale

Much has been written on exploring the benefits of Bible storying. Even though there have been some ideas presented for Bible storying applied in the ESL field, few have attempted to examine the actual results of this method in the ESL field. This research attempts to fill some of those gaps in the literature and proposes answers to some of the research questions. This research attempts to fill a gap in the literature by combining two major fields. One field is ESL, the other is missiology.

Chronological Bible Storying is a method that uses sequential narrative stories to reshape a people's warped worldview with the truth of the biblical worldview.[5] The Chronological Bible Storying model is used to teach both English and the gospel. In ESL terminology, it is a type of CLIL (Content and Language Integrated Learning) lesson, and the content is the Bible. However, as a way to do CLIL, I use a method called storying since "people can more easily embrace God's ways when they can see, hear, smell, taste, and touch the gospel."[6]

This study surveys the perceived benefits of the *Chronological Bible Storying for ESL learner's curriculum* on the mission field or in ESL ministries in the U.S. from a missional perspective, to discover the linguistic strengths of the Bible storying and the strengths of active learning skills used in Bible storying. The aim of this research is to synthesize the insights of two different fields: Bible storying and ESL ministry, adding a new perspective. Thus, as a strategy to help ESL ministries, the Bible storying method for ESL learners was created and tested.

For teachers of refugees, the importance and relevance of orality cannot be overstated. To ignore orality is to privilege students from literate cultures.

---

[5] Anthony F. Casey, "How Shall They Hear? The Interface of Urbanization and Orality" in *North American Ethnic Church Planting* (Louisville: Southern Baptist Theological Seminary, 2013).

[6] Avery T. Willis and Mark Snowden, *Truth that Sticks* (Colorado: Navpress, 2010), 43.

More specifically, for teachers of English in the United States who instruct refugees coming from oral cultures, the challenge is to harness these types of learning methods to use the unique cognitive characteristics that accompany orality. In this way, teachers can build an effective pedagogy of language instruction.

I am convinced that Bible storying for ESL learners is an effective pedagogy due to its oral nature. This literature and practical experience definitely show the benefits of Bible storying for oral learners and storytelling for students who have some issues with literacy.

Research Questions

I was guided by the following research questions:

1. What factors, if any, make Chronological Bible Storying for ESL Learners beneficial as a mission strategy?
2. What factors, if any, make Chronological Bible Storying bring about increased biblical knowledge for the ESL participants?
3. What benefits, if any, does the ESL Bible Storying method have on improving students' language proficiency for those who speak English as a second language?
4. What active learning skills included in Bible storying instruction are beneficial to ESL learners?
5. What spiritual changes, if any, do the instructors identify in their participants during the class?
6. What spiritual changes, if any, do the students identify as they participate in Chronological Bible Storying class for ten weeks?

Demographics of the Teachers

Five questions were asked to teachers before and after the ten-week training period to understand their backgrounds and perceptions of using the Bible in ESL ministry. Six teachers in different locations participated in the training. This section provides a summary of the demographics of the teachers from the survey.

Half the trainings were done in the United States. There were three teams consisting of international students, wives of international students, and immigrants. There were two house church groups in China; the last group was led by a missionary in France.

Demographic of Students

About half (47.8%) of the students were from China, 30.4% from South Korea, one student from Libya, two students from Tibet, and one student from Colombia. The total number of students who started and completed the ten-week training was twenty-two. Thirty-seven people came to the first interest meeting. Twenty-five people signed up for the ten-week training. Of those twenty-five, twenty-two were able to take a pre-test and a post-test. Teachers were able to share their observations on students' overall progress and testimony for all of the twenty-five people.

When students were asked to share their religious background, two people did not respond, 60.9% of the students identified themselves as Christians, 13.0% of the students were atheists, 8.7% were Buddhists, and 4.3% of the students were Muslim. It was my goal and desire to use this training for missions, and to use ESL ministry as a platform for evangelism and discipleship. Both non-Christians and Christians were able to participate and complete a 10-week training.

Research Findings

This section provides a helpful summary of the teachers' testimonies and their insights on factors that make Chronological Bible Storying for ESL learners beneficial as a mission strategy. I discovered various factors that contribute to Bible storying for ESL learners as a mission strategy through open-ended teacher surveys.

Research Question 1: What factors, if any, make Chronological Bible Storying for ESL Learners beneficial as a mission strategy?

Chronological Bible Storying is a beneficial mission strategy because it helps people understand the big picture of the Bible that leads to positive spiritual growth.

First, when people understand the Bible as one grand story, it can lead them to have a deeper understanding of each scripture. Thus, the storying method is beneficial as a mission strategy because students have a chance to learn the metanarrative of the Bible. In the open-ended survey, six teachers shared their opinions on the training. The teachers were asked: "In what ways has Chronological Bible Storying benefited you and your students?" All six teachers stated that they enjoyed teaching and students enjoyed learning the "Big Picture" of the Bible story. One teacher said, "We had a chance to see the Bible as one big mega-narrative and see how each story fits into God's big story." Another missionary in China said, "It helps the students to understand the gospel and God's salvation plan." An ESL teacher in China mentioned that "the connection points of the New Testament and Old Testament became much clearer" through the training. Without the great theme of redemption, and without understanding how each story fits into the great narrative, it is hard to understand why Jesus had to come and die, what His suffering meant and what kind of love human beings received. This confirms Kevin Vanhoozer's words that "To become a Christian is to be taken up into the drama of God's plan for creation, in this sense, our understanding of God is not so much about theology, but about theo-drama."[7]

Second, through Chronological Bible Storying, students gained the Bible knowledge that leads to spiritual growth. More details will follow as I answer each research question. Spiritual Growth Question 4 checked students' perceptions and attitudes of using Bible storying as a way to gain knowledge about God. Before the ten-week training, 56.5% of the students reported that they strongly agree that Bible Storying for ESL learners would help them to know more about God. I found this to be encouraging because 40% of the students were not even Christians, but they were open to taking part in a Bible-based ESL class for ten weeks. Not only that, more than half of responded that they strongly believed that learning more about God was beneficial. Another encouraging point is that there were not any neutral or even negative perceptions about using Bible Storying for ESL learners before or after the training. Non-Christians participated in the training as well, and it is amazing to see that they came to class regularly and gained more understanding of the Bible through this program.

When students had their Bible knowledge tested through pre-tests and post-tests, progress was made in 23 out of 30 questions (76.7%). Through the training, students made an improvement on the story of God's Creation and many other subjects. The most improvement was made on students' awareness of sins described in the Bible, the meaning of redemption, understanding faith, God's forgiveness of a woman caught in adultery, Jesus' death, repentance, Jesus' resurrection, Jesus' ascension, and the Great Commission.

Third, *repetition* coupled with *active learning skills* enhanced the students' learning experience greatly. According to the storying tips on the curriculum, students were encouraged to listen and retell the story at least five times in each session. Students were taught to retell the Bible story through various active learning skills to make the lesson more memorable and engaging. One teacher in China stated that "because the storying method used 'repetition' as one of the key ways to teach the Bible, students were able to gain more

---

[7] Kevin J Vanhoozer, *The Drama of Doctrine: A Canonical-linguistic Approach to Christian Theology* (Westminster John Knox, 2005), 71.

understanding." That means even non-Christians not only heard God's words, but they actively repeated the same story over five times. I believe that God's words have power and they bear fruit. Additionally, active learning in Bible storying helped the story "come alive." "People can more easily embrace God's ways when they can see, hear, smell, taste, and touch the gospel."[8]

Fourth, the ten-week training helped missionaries to pioneer an ESL ministry in America and overseas. More than half of the teachers who participated in training decided to start an ESL ministry because of the curriculum and coaching videos. Many missionaries are looking for creative ways and Bible-based resources to reach the lost populations. Jan Dormer expressed that "The demand for English has far outpaced many countries' capabilities for producing good English teachers and good materials."[9] Also, she argued that "English teachers are often the least prepared theologically, and sometimes culturally, for oversea missions"[10] Most of the teachers had positive comments about the curriculum and how it included a theological lesson for each lesson to educate the teachers as well as students. According to the research, all the teachers appreciated the Bible-based ESL material, and despite some ESL scholars' cautions, students were open to learning English through the Bible when they knew that that is what they were signed up for. As mentioned above, 40.0 % of the students were non-believers. As long as teachers were truthful and transparent about using the Bible as a resource, I strongly believe that God prepared the hearts of the people who were eager to learn the Bible.

Lastly, students grew spiritually as seen in their pre-test and post-test scores on spiritual growth question. More detailed data analysis regarding spiritual growth will be included in the analysis of Research Questions 5 and 6. As a result, I strongly argue that Chronological Bible Storying is a strategic tool as a mission strategy.

Research Question 2: What factors, if any, make Chronological Bible Storying bring about increased biblical knowledge for the ESL participants?

Students were able to make progress in Bible Knowledge and they made positive perception/attitude change toward Christianity. When students were asked to answer some Bible knowledge questions, out of thirty questions, students made progress in twenty-three of them (76.7%).

---

[8] Willis & Snowden, *Truth that Sticks*, 43.
[9] Jan Edwards Dormer, *Teaching English in Missions* (Pasadena: William Carey, 2011), 252.
[10] Dormer, *Teaching English*, 17.

Teaching them the Bible story in chronological order through the method of storying brought about positive change in students' Bible knowledge. In the words of Steffen, "Chronological Bible Storying builds a strong Old Testament foundation before presenting the gospel."[11] That is one of the benefits of doing narrative theology. As mentioned before, without the great theme of redemption, and without understanding how each story fits into the great narrative, it is hard to understand why Jesus had to come and die and what suffering meant and what kind of love humans received.

Research Question 3: What benefits, if any, does the ESL Bible Storying method have on improving students' language proficiency for those who speak English as a second language?

First, as a result of the instruction, students made progress in many areas of the English test. Quantitative data analysis shows that students made progress in fourteen out of twenty questions (70%). Three questions brought about positive improvements that were statistically significant. The pre-test and post-test were designed to monitor students' language progress on vocabulary, grammar, reading skills, and sentence structure. The data clearly showed that students made progress in those skills. Chronological Bible Storying for ESL learners brought about increased literacy skills among people who speak English as a second language.

Second, since the Chronological Bible Storying method emphasized improving oral proficiency skills, quantitative data alone cannot answer the research questions. Teachers' feedback and their observations on students' language progress in language arts, especially listening and speaking, were examined. In open-ended questions, all six teachers agreed that Bible storying challenged and helped the students greatly in their oral proficiency. When students were asked what skills they wanted to work on most before the test, "speaking" was the number one skill. All six teachers stated that Bible Storying for ESL learners helped students improve their speaking skills most because students have to repeat the story many times using various active learning models. The data analysis conforms to Sarah Telfer's argument that "using a range of storytelling activities in ESOL classroom can enhance learner engagement and interaction and promote language communication skills."[12]

---

[11] Tom A. Steffen, "Storying the Storybook to Tribal: A Philippines Perspective of the Chronological Teaching Model," *International Journal of Frontier Missions* 12, no.2 (April-June 1995), 99.

[12] Sarah Telfer, "Anecdotal Storytelling in the Adult ESOL and Literacy Classroom," in *Educational Features*, volume 9, (Bolton: University of Bolton, 2017), 2.

Third, when teachers were asked their views on the perceived strengths of using the curriculum, most of the teachers mentioned that, besides speaking skills, the curriculum also helped students with reading and grammar. All the teachers reported that the lessons were transferrable to everyday conversation or life. When it comes to ESL ministry, some people argue against using the Bible as a textbook because the lesson is not transferrable to everyday conversations or life situations due to the Bible's heavy focus on religious vocabulary. That is why I intentionally included a grammar section and activities that encouraged authentic language use so that students could actually learn something they could use as soon as the next day. I tried to include activities that are truly communicative.

Fourth, as a result of the Chronological Bible Storying for ESL Learners class, students made positive progress in both English proficiency and Bible Knowledge. This is a type of CLIL (Content and Language Integrated Learning) method. In this case, the Bible was used to teach English. Students were evaluated on their knowledge of the Bible and English abilities before and after the training. All the data showed that students made positive progress in both areas. Thus, it seems reasonable to conclude that the Chronological Bible Storying for ESL Learners curriculum made a positive impact on students' language proficiency.

Research Question 4: What active learning skills included in Bible Storying instruction are beneficial to ESL learners?

Engagement strategies such as using visuals, drawing the story, retelling the Bible story, Think-Pair-Share, drama, and the Strip Sequence are beneficial for ESL learners to improve their knowledge of the Bible and their English skills.

Upon analyzing the instructional strategies used in Bible storying, I found that they mostly involve active learning models. Teachers were asked to answer post-survey questions related to active learning skills used in Bible storying after they taught ten weeks. Communicative Language Teaching was introduced as a method to teach in English in the 1970s. Active learning skills that were applied in Chronological Bible Storying were activities that were used in communicative language teaching. Active learning skills gave students a chance to use authentic English in a real context.

Using visuals were highly effective. I illustrated all the pictures for the curriculum and added a separate visual story set specifically to help ESL learners. A large percentage (83.3%) of the teachers strongly agreed with the benefits of using visuals. As students describe the story based on the pictures, they are given chances to use what they know in language they can use. Students work on fluency and they become more communicatively competent. The vast majority (83.3%) of the teachers strongly agreed that visualizing a story by drawing it helped students' learning. I incorporated various creative and active teaching models for engaging learners and fostering creativity while helping them truly internalize the Bible. It helps students with active listening skills, and when students engage more senses in learning, the lesson is more memorable. All of the teachers strongly agreed that when students retell the Bible story, it helps their speaking skills. When students were asked before the training which skill they wanted to improve the most, the majority wanted to improve their speaking skills.

Half of the teachers strongly agreed that Think-Pair-Share helped students understand the Bible story better. Two-thirds (66.7%) of the teachers agreed that Think-Pair-Share helped students to develop communication skills. Repetition is crucial in language learning. However, when it is just a drill, it can be boring, and students might not be motivated. Students had ample opportunity to retell the story and, by doing that, they were able to work on speaking and pronunciation skills. Students became active communicators in Bible storying, which led to an increase in their oral proficiency.

A large percentage (88.3%) of the teachers agreed that using drama helped with students' pronunciation, new vocabulary, and structure. Also, all the teachers agreed that drama developed creativity and imagination which extended communication skills and encouraged sustained talking and thinking. When students use drama, they are engaged in role play.

One of the teachers stated,

> As I got to know these women, I noticed many of them would relate with God through their senses, so many of the stories incorporated the five senses. We smelled the myrrh that Mary poured on Jesus; we listened to songs that had to do with the story that week; we acted out dramas, and so much more.

Active learning skills added color to the class, bringing the story to life and enabling students to enjoy learning and improve their English proficiency and Bible knowledge.

Research Question 5: What spiritual changes, if any, do the instructors identify in their participants during the class?

All the students (both non-Christians and Christians) made positive spiritual growth, and two people were saved. It shows that Chronological Bible Storying for ESL learners is a great tool for evangelism and discipleship.

All the teachers were asked to share their observations of spiritual change in their classroom's students using the Engle's scale. Teachers wrote detailed descriptions of the students' change. All the feedback from the teachers' perspective emphasized that all the students made positive progress in spiritual change. The survey recorded students' spiritual positions before and after the training. According to the teachers' reports, thirty-seven people came to the first interest meeting. Twenty-five people signed up for ten-week training. Of those twenty-five, only twenty-two people were able to take a pre-test and a post-test. Teachers were able to share their observations on students' spiritual growth.

Out of 25 people, two people were saved, and everybody made a positive spiritual change. Sixty percent of the students were Christians when they began the training. These Christians had a strong desire to grow in the knowledge of God and to learn English as well. A group in China consisted of new believers who needed theological training. Leaders stated that many were discipled through the training and their spiritual growth was evident as they improved their spiritual disciplines. Chronological Bible Storying is a beneficial model for discipleship.

The other 40% of the students were not Christians. Through the training, students began to grasp important Bible truths: sin, the meaning of redemption, understanding of faith, God's forgiveness of a woman caught in adultery, Jesus' death, repentance, Jesus' resurrection, Jesus' ascension, and the Great Commission. Even though only two people were saved, all six teachers observed that the positive spiritual change was observed in each student. A missionary's job is to plant the seeds faithfully and leave the results to God. True success should be measured by missionaries' faithfulness in preaching the gospel. By the grace of God, during ten weeks of training, these people were able to hear the gospel and gained an understanding of Christian worldview through Chronological Bible Storying.

Research Question 6: What spiritual changes, if any, do the students identify as they participate in Chronological Bible Storying class for ten weeks?

By the grace of God, two people came to know Jesus and accepted Jesus as Savior as a result of the class. Spiritual Growth Question 1 asked students' perception or belief in the existence of God. Before the training, 52.2% of the students strongly agreed that they believe that God exists. The percentage improved to 60.9% after the training. Another encouraging point is that there were not any negative perceptions about using Bible storying for ESL learners before or after the training. Non-Christians participated in the training as well, and it is amazing to see that they came to class regularly and gained more understanding of the Bible through this program.

Conclusion

Jesus instructed his disciples to spread His message to all nations (Matt 28:19). The purpose of this research is to expand His kingdom using Chronological Bible Storying for ESL Learners. ESL ministry provides a strategic platform for both evangelism and discipleship. The Great Commission involves sharing the Good News across diverse cultures, and this curriculum serves as a means of connecting people to God and one another through language learning.

Although Bible Storying was originally intended for oral learners, it can also be effective when applied creatively using ESL teaching strategies. It has been observed that ESL students have benefited from this approach and have shown a strong desire to learn English as a literacy skill. I suggest that combining the Bible storying method with literacy teaching pedagogy can be highly beneficial for both oral learners and literate students who wish to improve their English skills. This is because the Bible storying method already incorporates a variety of effective teaching strategies. Missionary teachers play an important role in providing their students with the knowledge of both the English language and the Word of God. This creative combination of oral methods and literacy methods enables English language learners to improve language proficiency, cultural awareness, Bible knowledge, and spiritual sensitivity as they navigate the challenges of living in a foreign land. They also gain practical knowledge of the language as well as a deeper understanding of the giver of the language. Besides that, they can use ESL to grow a community of people who love God, language, and the foreigners.

In the words of Zoltan Dornyei, "Global English is becoming the lingua franca of Christianity in the twenty-first century."[13] ESL ministry is an open door to reach the mind and hearts of people who desire to learn English as a second language. All the teachers were strongly advised to inform students that they would use Bible-based ESL material in the beginning, to be transparent about their intent. From the above, it is apparent that God already prepared the hearts and the minds of people to have the desire to learn English using the Bible. If the educators and missionaries clearly but humbly communicate about using the Bible in the beginning, some students are more than ready to hear the good news. I believe that the Holy Spirit will empower the teachers with boldness and sensitivity as they share the

---

[13] Zoltan Dorney, "The English Language and the Word of God," in *Christian and Critical English Language Educators in Dialogue*, eds. Mary S. Wong and A. Suresh Canagarajah (New York: Routledge, 2009), 154-157.

curriculum. Christian educators need creativity and honesty, but also boldness to effectively share the gospel.

Bibliography

Casey, Anthony F. "How Shall They Hear? The Interface of Urbanization and Orality." In *North American Ethnic Church Planting* (Louisville: Southern Baptist Theological Seminary, 2013).

Dormer, Jan Edwards. *Teaching English in Missions.* Pasadena: William Carey, 2011.

Lessard-Clouston, Michael. *Biblical Themes for Christians in Language Teaching." in Thinking Theologically about Language Teaching.* Cumbria: Langham Global Library, 2017.

Steffen, Tom A. "Storying the Storybook to Tribal: A Philippines Perspective of the Chronological Teaching Model." *International Journal of Frontier Missions* 12, no. 2 (April–June 1995): 99-104.

Telfer, Sarah. "Anecdotal Storytelling in the Adult ESOL and Literacy Classroom." In *Educational Features,* volume 9. Bolton: University of Bolton, 2017.

Vanhoozer, Kevin J. *The Drama of Doctrine: A Canonical-linguistic Approach to Christian Theology.* Westminster John Knox, 2005.

Yuk, Yiyoung. "Chronological Bible Storying for ESL Learners." Ph.D. diss., Southeastern Baptist Theological Seminary, 2019.

Willis, Avery T., and Mark Snowden. *Truth that Sticks.* Colorado Springs: Navpress, 2010

Zoltan, Dorney. "The English Language and the Word of God." In *Christian and Critical English Language Educators in Dialogue,* edited by Mary S. Wong and A. Suresh Canagarajah. New York: Routledge, 2009

Chapter 8:
Oral Bible Storytelling:
Discovery, Impact, and Group Learning

Janet and Jim Stahl

Abstract

Formal education often rewards linear and analytical reasoning by entering the learning cycle or process through a theoretical or conceptual entry point, which is followed by collecting data and facts, and drawing conclusions. However, people often acquire other ways of processing knowledge and learning, such as recognizing intuitive responses to a typically oral communication experience and then verifying or adjusting their intuition by closely examining their experience.

In the Seed Company's Oral Bible Storytelling (OBS) approach, when people learn a portion of the Bible and practice telling it, they, the storytellers, rely on a group experience of hearing the Bible story being performed and then discuss their intuitive responses to the impact of the story. They are asked questions such as:

- *What images stood out from the story?*
- *What physical and other senses were provoked?*
- *What other stories came to mind that relate to this Bible portion?*

The process follows an experiential learning cycle that is carried out in groups and involves much repetition, discovery, and practice. In the verification stage of the approach, a framework or structure is used to guide the group through a thorough examination of the Scripture portion. An experienced trainer/facilitator offers added information and concepts as the group needs it. With each pass through the learning cycle, the participants' understanding of the story expands to include more details and adjusts with better appreciation of the original author's intended impact. Individuals' interpretations are tempered by the rich and varied perspectives of the entire group. And, the memory of the Bible portion is stored as vivid images organized by scenes, patterns that focus our attention, and much repetition.

Introduction

Jim and Janet Stahl are longtime members of Wycliffe Bible Translators, currently assigned to the Seed Company as International Orality Consultants.

Prior to working with the Seed Company, they worked in Vanuatu, developing mother-tongue translation and literacy courses that use competency-based training methods, including a translation course that was accredited by the Australian Training Authority. They have also implemented learning tools of dialogue and discovery as described by Jane Vella. In the early 2000s they served as training consultants for SIL International.

In 2007 they moved from Bible translation to Oral Bible Storytelling (OBS), having been invited by Seed Company to develop such storytelling methods to enhance the Bible translation process. Jim and Janet designed a community-based approach that includes training teams of mother-tongue Bible storytellers. The OBS training also includes mentoring regional trainers and story checkers. As a result, OBS has been used over a period of 17 years, and in more than 80 language communities around the world, many of whom have no Bible translated in their language.

The OBS approach that the Stahls developed involves six cycles that are offered over a period of two to three years. Each cycle starts off with a two-week workshop. During the two-week workshops, the storytelling participants work together as teams to experience, internalize, craft, tell, revise, practice, and get consultant help for six to eight Bible stories. The participants return to their home communities between the workshops with plans to tell these Bible stories in a variety of ministries and audiences, and to train others to tell these Bible stories like they were trained during the workshop.

OBS and Learning Approaches

Built-in to OBS are different pedagogical practices, five of which are described in this article.

1. Group/collaborative learning
2. On-the-job training
3. Experiential learning
4. Scaffolded learning
5. Competency-based training

The OBS approach is organized around on-the-job training. It involves much group learning, as four to six teams of about four people learn the Bible stories together. OBS involves competency-based training, which is tied to evaluating and assessing the team's progress, based on what they demonstrate on-the-job. OBS also focuses on group discovery, and experiential learning cycles. Having already discussed competency-based training in detail in a previous paper, the current chapter will describe the other four learning aspects.[1]

So, the OBS approach involves shared experiences and learning together in groups of four people on average. In order to demonstrate this and to help the reader/hearer experience what happens in an OBS project, the following is a transcript of a Bible story from Mark 1 as told by Janet Stahl. The story is about Jesus as he healed Simon's mother-in-law. It is likely familiar to the reader, which is okay. The goal is for the audience to hear it afresh, putting aside typical Sunday school lessons or teachings learned about Mark's gospel. The invitation is to listen to the story as told by Janet.

> Jesus and disciples had just been involved in a Sabbath Day service in the synagogue. And when the service was over, Jesus and his disciples, including James and John, left the synagogue and went to Peter and Andrew's house. And when they got there, the family informed Jesus that Peter's mother-in-law was gravely ill; she was sick in bed with a fever. And Jesus went to her and took her by the hand and helped her to sit up. And immediately the fever left her, and she was well. And she got up and began to serve.

> And as the Sabbath ended, people from that whole area brought sick family members and others who were possessed by demons to Peter's house, hoping that Jesus would heal them. In fact, the whole town or village of Capernaum showed up at Peter's house to see what was happening. Now, that's the gospel story from the gospel of Mark, chapter one.

If we were sitting together to hear this in an OBS workshop after the first hearing of the story, we would invite people to share the impact the story had on them, asking questions like the following:

- What images jumped out for you as you heard this story?
- What were the senses in you that were provoked as you experienced this story?
- And what other stories did this storytelling remind you of?

And we would invite everybody from the group to share the impact of the story.

---

[1] Janet & Jim Stahl, "Oral Bible Storytelling as Shaped by On-the-job Competency-based Training and Group Experiential Learning," (paper presented at Bible Translation Conference 2021, Dallas, TX, October 15-19, 2021). https://youtu.be/VeO8NQ552Kc

OBS and Group Learning

Some might share the vivid image of this this woman, gravely ill with a fever, lying in bed one moment, and in the next moment, up and perfectly well, able to move around and be part of the community. Or perhaps they might share their reflection on the relief that Peter's family would have experienced being so worried about his mother-in-law being very sick, and then suddenly, rejoicing that she was well again. Others might feel compelled to share their own personal story about being gravely ill, and wishing they had some magic pill, or some way to be to be made well again, and then the relief that they would feel once they were healed. They might have thought of other stories from the Bible in which Jesus healed others, like a leper, a blind person, or a woman that had been sick for 12 years.

This is all part of group learning. Everyone in the group comes with their own perspectives, their own backgrounds, their own experiences, their own talents, and skills. They all contribute by sharing from their own experiences and points of view. In the process, each member of the group has a broader experience of the Bible's story.

This is what Johnson and Johnson, from the University of Minnesota, describe as collaborative or cooperative learning.[2] Each team member shares from their own variety of skills, knowledge, talent, and experience, and in this way, enhances the group learning. Storytelling lends itself to group learning, because in order to tell the Bible story, one must have an audience. We use this kind of group learning to share the story and to give each other feedback and encouragement, to give reviews, and to share what was discovered through the learning experience.

Each part of the OBS process in the workshops involves a group learning experience. While internalizing the stories, the group gives each other feedback and explores the story for questions and new learnings. In this learning process the group develops a synergy, a team working style, cooperating with each other, knowing who has which particular expertise that the group can draw on, and reveling in the fact that together they can discover many new things, and become motivated to share their own experiences with the story.

Rather than group learning being considered as cumbersome and taking extra time, we have learned over the years that it is efficient. Furthermore, a group can learn many more stories that would be very difficult for one person to learn on their own. And, collectively, the group can remember the story

---

[2] Roger T. Johnson and David W. Johnson, *An Overview of Cooperative Learning*, eds. J. Thousand, A. Villa and A. Nevin, Creativity and Collaborative Learning (Baltimore: Brookes, 1994).

better than can one person. The other piece of group learning that adds to the overall learning experience is the sense of community developed within the teams and the large group. The participants not only work together, crafting the stories and giving feedback, they share their own stories that are thematically connected to the biblical stories, and they as a team rely on and learn from each other's expertise and talents. This relationship adds to the group motivation to learn and continue improving their storytelling.

OBS and On-the-job Training

Another aspect of the OBS training process is known as on-the-job training, which has the advantage for the team members of knowing where and how to apply what they are learning. The entire process is organized around workflow and not around academic or training exercises. And so, as the group might be learning this story about Jesus going to Peter and Andrew's house and healing Peter's mother-in-law, they would be discussing different ways to open and close this story. Telling this story to children would be different than telling it in a formal setting to adults. Making decisions about how to tell a story to different audiences is part of on-the-job training, and helps the participants prepare to return to their communities and share the stories as they need. From the start, they are learning to tell the Bible stories in their work teams in preparation for telling the stories in their own communities.

Since the stories involve Jewish religious practices and ancient concepts not familiar to many of the storytellers, there would be a discussion about things like what a synagogue or Sabbath day is. All learning related to the OBS approach is structured through the work process. As people confront new challenges and discover more questions and confusions, the facilitator adds that information and invites discussion. Adults generally want to know that the time, effort, and energy they put into learning something is going to have a benefit or a return for their role. So, in the OBS process, the group, while learning together, helps each other fulfill their roles as Bible story crafters and prepares them to train others to be Bible storytellers.

Neither Jim nor Janet Stahl are language and culture experts in the language areas where they conducted OBS training. However, the participants and local and regional staff bring that expertise with them. Much of the OBS process is to help the participants discover what they know intuitively and experientially about their own language and culture, and to apply what they discover to their telling of the Bible stories. They are also responsible for passing on what they learn as Bible storytellers to others in their home communities. In this way, the workshops are structured according to their workflow and the team members are able to replicate what they have done in the workshop in their various responsibilities in their community.

OBS and the experiential learning cycle

A third aspect of the OBS process includes the experiential learning cycle. In 1975, David Kolb and Roger Fry discussed the development of lifelong or continual learning.[3] For example, how does one continue to learn and improve as a storyteller, or stay current in their field of expertise? Kolb and Fry learned that people must go through this learning cycle to continually learn and adapt in each sector.

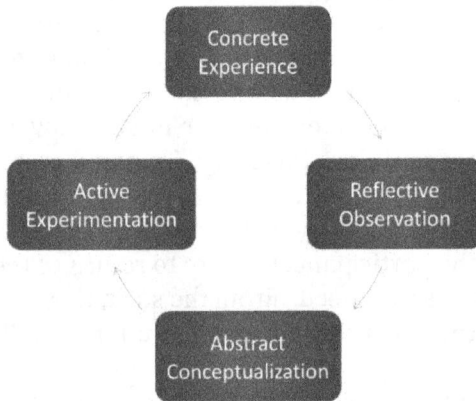

Figure 8. Learning Cycle

One can say that the concrete experience is doing the job of going out and telling Bible stories to various audiences. People learning to master the art of storytelling need to pause at regular intervals and reflect on what they're doing. They could ask themselves the following questions to help them reflect and improve as storytellers.

- Is the storytelling working?
- Where does my storytelling approach need improvement?
- What are the challenges?
- How do I address unique situations?
- Where am I having difficulty understanding the Bible story?
- Which parts of the story am I struggling to say smoothly or clearly?

---

[3] D.A. Kolb, *Experiential Learning: Experience as the Source of Learning and Development* (Englewood Cliffs: Prentice Hall, 1984), 32.

This is all part of mastering the craft of storytelling. To improve, the storytellers need to access new information, new abstract concepts, and learn new skills. And so, they need to continue to learn and develop within their field, and possibly from other fields, as appropriate to their job. Some of the new information may come from their peers who know the language well and can give feedback. Some new skills or abstract concepts may come from the trainers who have studied the Bible story and translation principles. Mastery also requires revising and experimenting, trying other ways of telling the stories, with various techniques, with newly learned information, thereby continuing their journey around the learning cycle. The OBS approach is organized around this experiential learning cycle. For each Bible story the teams are learning to tell, they may go through this learning cycle more than 20 times in a day.

Telling stories in small groups

Retelling stories   Concrete   More discussion
                         Experience

Revising the story   Active   Reflective   Giving each other
                      Experimentation   Observation   feedback

                      Abstract
                      Conceptualization

Learning a storytelling principle

Figure 9. The Learning Cycle with OBS

When Janet told the story from Mark 1, she invited the audience to enter a shared experience built around a concrete experience. She did not initiate the learning situation through an abstract conceptualization, which is where our formal education framework mostly asks students to enter the learning cycle. When students attend school, they take classes like math, science, language arts, and social science classes, all of which are organized by fields of study. In those classes there are controlled exercises that help students apply what they learned in controlled environments, and later, they are sent off into the real world. But most people do not learn as they would in a school classroom. That is not how real life works. Most people learn on-the-job, and start with a shared experience, and a concrete experience.

So, the audience hears the Bible storytelling together as a shared experience. In the OBS process, each day of a workshop starts with the telling of a Bible story and with the entire group reflecting on the impact of the story and what they might have heard newly or in a different way. But as the group participants repeatedly hear the story, they are asked discussion questions by the facilitator, such as:

- Where did the story take place?
- What does not make sense about this ancient story?
- Where do we find parts that are confusing?

Some people might rightly ask about the cultures of the Middle East during the time that Jesus lived on earth. They might ask, "If Jesus lived in a patriarchal society, why was Peter's mother-in-law living with him? Why wasn't she with her husband's family?"

These are questions that scholars ask and speculate about because the answers are not known, and the author only wrote what is in the text. Perhaps Peter's father-in-law had died. Or, possibly, Peter's mother-in-law did not have any sons to help her. And so, Peter and his wife took her into their house to live with them.

Somebody else may ask the question, "What did Peter and Andrew's house look like that the entire village of Capernaum would come to see what happened?" And so, a facilitator might bring pictures, line drawings, and illustrations of what a compound during Jesus' time might have looked like, with extended families living in smaller houses centered around a shared area. These drawings help the storytellers visualize what might have happened during this experience. After learning each new piece of information or abstract concept or skill, the facilitator asks the participants to reflect on this new bit of information and see how it changes their experience with the story and the way they will tell it.

Now, in Mark's Gospel, in the Koine Greek, one part of the story went something like this: "Jesus went to the sick mother-in-law, took her hand, and helped her to sit up. And immediately the fever disappeared. And she got up and deaconed [διακονέω]."

That Greek word *diakonos* (διάκονος), or deacon, is the one where we got (borrowed) our English term referring to someone serving in a church community. The deacon goes and helps people in the congregation and serves people in the community who are in need. Deacons connect people with the help and assistance that they might need, which, in this case, is Peter's mother-in-law. Mark tells us that Peter's mother-in-law got up and served/deaconed. Now some translations of the Bible say that she got up and prepared a meal, which is not likely, because it was the Sabbath, and that kind of work was done the day before the Sabbath. Mark tells us, immediately following her service, that others brought sick family members and those possessed by demons to Peter's house, hoping that Jesus would heal them.

Could it possibly be that Peter's mother-in-law did like a lot of women would do, sharing her story, going out and telling everybody the good news? "I was sick, and Jesus healed me. Now, I'm better." Did she invite others to come to see Jesus, that they, too might be healed? Is this Mark telling us that one of the first people to serve Jesus' movement was Peter's mother-in-law? It's quite possible.

In a typical OBS workshop day, we would go through this learning cycle many times with lots of repetition, different people telling the story, small groups practicing telling the story to each other, giving each other feedback on what they missed and what they might have added that maybe was not correct. Throughout the day, the participants would continue practicing different ways to tell the story and choose the ones that best fit their ways to tell a story, and that best fit the gospel of Mark.

OBS and Scaffolded Learning

The OBS process is organized as scaffolded learning, which is a learning strategy developed by Jerome Bruner as a method in psychology to help students break down what is needed to learn a new concept or task.[4] It is the principle of starting with the basics and adding more complexity as each piece is mastered. Scaffolding is closely related to the concept of the zone of proximal development described by psychologist Lev Vygotsky, focusing on what the learner is able to do with support from a teacher, trainer, or mentor.[5] An adage we learned in the Australian Certificate in the Workplace Training fits this philosophy, "I do it for you, we do it together, you do it for me, and off you go."[6]

So, as the OBS participant goes through the learning cycle, they confront more difficulties and need more information. The facilitator adds that information or new skills incrementally, rather than tackling the entire gospel of Mark with all its complexities at the very beginning. New information and skills are layered on as OBS participants need to address various issues. And as the storytelling participants continue around this learning cycle,

---

[4] D. J Wood., J. S. Bruner and G. Ross, "The role of tutoring in problem solving," *Journal of Child Psychiatry and Psychology* 17, no. 2 (1970), 90.

[5] M Diaz, Rafael M., Cynthia J. Neal, and Marina Amaya-Williams, "The Social Origins of Self-regulation," in *Vygotsky and Education: Instructional Implications and Applications of Sociohistorical Psychology*, ed. Luis C. Moll (New York: Cambridge University, 1990), 140.

[6] "7 Scaffolding Learning Strategies for the Classroom," University of San Diego, https://pce.sandiego.edu/scaffolding-in-education-examples/.

practicing, telling, and giving each other feedback, they are demonstrating that they are competent to do the job, to tell the Bible stories in their language communities, and to practice telling it for different kinds of audiences and groups. And so, the whole OBS group evaluates each participant's language and cultural expertise. They evaluate their communication in the vernacular language, and give constructive feedback to each other, helping each other choose just the right words, expressions, intonation, and gestures for telling the Bible story well, and using good and appropriate storytelling techniques from that language community.

Once the team is very familiar with the story and has had much practice telling and revising it, consultants and checkers join the team and help give feedback to ensure the fidelity of the story. Is the story consistent with the impact that Mark was intending as he told the story? What can be improved? The storyteller team then revises the telling of the story based on that feedback and further research they might need to do in their home communities.

Conclusion

We have purposefully implemented the four learning strategies described above: on-the-job training, group learning, scaffolded learning, and experiential learning in the development of the OBS approach so that it is both reproducible and adaptable to the workplace. We have also structured the training as competency-based, which also lends itself to being adaptable to the workplace and the individual storytellers' roles and ministries.

Telling biblical stories to each other can be a rich shared learning experience, and telling biblical stories in groups provokes rich imagery and ignites our senses, reminds us of other stories, both in our own lives and in stories we have learned of others and other times. Being part of a biblical storytelling experience helps us connect with these stories and learn from them.

OBS is a discovery process. It is iterative and involves active experimentation. The storyteller team members discover together through group learning dynamics, inviting each participant to bring their experiences, their own unique set of talents, and background experiences, and with the other members of the group, to learn and train each other, and improve their storytelling mastery.

References

"7 Scaffolding Learning Strategies for the Classroom." University of San Diego Professional and Continuing Education. https://pce.sandiego.edu/scaffolding-in-education-examples.

Kolb, D.A. *Experiential Learning: Experience as the Source of Learning and Development.* Englewood Cliffs, NJ: Prentice Hall, 1984.

Johnson, Roger T., and David W. Johnson. "An Overview of Cooperative Learning." In *Creativity and Collaborative Learning*, eds. J. Thousand, A. Villa and A. Nevin. Baltimore: Brookes, 1994.

Diaz, Rafael M., Cynthia J. Neal, and Marina Amaya-Williams. "The Social Origins of Self-regulation." In *Vygotsky and Education: Instructional Implications and Applications of Sociohistorical Psychology.* Edited by Luis C. Moll. New York: Cambridge University, 1990.

Schwarz, Roger M. *The Skilled Facilitator: Practical Wisdom for Developing Effective Groups.* San Francisco: Jossey-Bass, 1994.

Stahl, Janet. "Telling Our Stories Well: Creating Memorable Images and Shaping Our Identity." *Missiologv: An International Review*, XXXVIII, no. 2 (April 2010).

———. "Bible Storytelling and Healing Communities." *Global Forum on Arts and Faith* 5, No. 1. (2017). www.artsandchristianfaith.org.

———. "Scripture Engagement before Bible Translation: What Women Bible Storytellers Are Doing in South Asia and Ethiopia to Promote Healing in Their Communities." Presentation at the BT17, Dallas, TX, 2017.

———. "Translating a Written Text into a Well-Told Performance." Presentation at the BT19, Dallas, TX. 2019.

Stahl, Janet & Jim Stahl. "Oral Bible Storytelling as Shaped by On-the-job Competency-based Training and Group Experiential Learning." Presentation at Bible Translation Conference 2021, Dallas, TX, October 15-19 2021. https://youtu.be/VeO8NQ552Kc.

Vella, Jane. *Training Through Dialogue.* San Francisco: Jossey-Bass, 1995.

———. *Taking Learning to Task.* San Francisco: Jossey-Bass, 2000.

Wlodkowski, Raymond J. *Enhancing Adult Motivation to Learn: A Guide to Improving Instruction and Increasing Learner Achievement.* San Francisco: Jossey-Bass, 1993.

Chapter 9:
Acknowledging, Developing, and Fostering Christian Community through Story

Mackenzie Griffin

Abstract

Cultural narratives and histories play an integral role in guiding communities on how to thrive within their local environments. For Indigenous cultures worldwide, but especially across Turtle Island, story is deeply interwoven into daily life. Stories shape our understanding of reality and are fundamental in cultural, social, and ceremonial education. The Bible is full of stories, some of the most prominent being contained within the pages of Genesis. Unfortunately, Genesis theology is often lacking and too frequently begins with chapter three's focus on the fall and humanity's inherent sinfulness. However, a more holistic approach starts by acknowledging the goodness of creation and God's original intent for humans to live in treaty relationships with God, each other, and creation. By doing so, a fresh perspective is brought to the original story, reminding Christians of their foundational beliefs when engaging in evangelization and mission work. Missions should never force or expect cultures to assimilate into another to be considered worthy of the Christian identity. Rather, mission work should always be done in partnership with the community being supported. As Jesus addressed in the early days of his ministry, the Gospel is for all people. If that is indeed to be the case, then Christians must relearn what that phrase means. Mission workers must work to understand their personal cultural stories and origins while honoring the cultures they interact with to authentically acknowledge, develop, and foster new Christian communities that embrace their diverse God-given identities.

The Biblical Story Thus Far

The One at the Beginning opened their eyes. They stretched their arms out as far as they could, letting out a yawn so loud it filled the empty space around them. The One at the Beginning knew it was time to get to work. Still, she knew she had to be careful. Creation would take time and it would be worth the wait. It could not be rushed for it was a job that only Original One could do. He had to get it right.

So, rubbing his hands together, The One at the Beginning felt a twinge of excitement deep in his belly. Now Original One created the first thought, and

111

he merged his thoughts with the excitement he felt and all of his heart, creating the heavens and the earth.

Now, the earth was formless, a vast emptiness full of potential. Original One hovered over the waters, their spirit all encompassing. In their fingers they birthed light, using a small fire to separate the darkness from its opposite. Original One knew that the light was good, and she splattered the darkness with tiny twinkling lights called stars and a larger burning orb which Original One called the sun. Then, the One at the Beginning created the four directions which he used to guide the sky and the waters into their proper place. The sun passed from the east to the west and another day came and went. The sun's sister, the moon, rose in the sun's place and kept track of the time during the night. Together, the sun and the moon helped bring into existence the Twinnings. It was the idea that all things have a twin, a counter of sorts to maintain harmony and wholeness. The Twinnings, however, is not so much about opposition as the partnerships required for balance.

When the sun began to rise on the third day, Original One created the earth or First Mother, using the existence of the four directions and Twinness. The One at the Beginning gifted the Earth Mother the ability to produce vegetation and out from aki, the dirt, sprung all kinds of life. Trees shot into the sky making some of the area dense and sheltered. Sunlight shone through pockets called clearings. Shrubs, flowers, mosses, and all kinds of grasses covered the ground in soft squishy undergrowth. Still, forests, rocky mountains, foothills, and plains created a variety of terrain which the Animal People and the People-to-Be would soon explore. Knowing the Animal People would need something to eat, Original One created all kinds of fruits and vegetables, shrubberies and flowers to spring up from the earth. She allowed Nibi, the waters, to carve their place through the lands so there would always be access to the lifeblood of Creator.

After the vegetation was growing in all its splendor, The One at the Beginning knew it was time. They created creatures to roam the seas, skies, and land. Some animals walked on all fours, others on two-legs and still others used fins to swim or wings to fly. All Original One had created was beautiful in its difference. With proper tenderness and care, the Animal People would increase in number and the vegetation would continue to grow even when windstorms, fires, and floods ravaged the land or when the People-to-Be neglected their treaties. As she gazed upon creation, something stirred within Original One, but she couldn't quite place it, so she set to work on perhaps the most important task of all.

Original One knew creating human beings would take a very long time, but the One at the Beginning was patient, he was persistent. Original One dreamed and visioned and when it came time, she collected particles from the earth, fire, air, and water. She used the matter to form the being and breathed her spirit into them. With one touch of her fingertips to that first being's forehead she poured her thoughts and creative energy, every part of herself, into you or me.

Then, ever so gently, she lowered you, and I'll have you imagine yourself as the first human being, to earth. One look and Original One fell in love. The stirring she had first felt with the Animal People overtook her entire being. Her love for creation was unconditional, and with that, Original One took on a new name: The One Who Loves Us Unconditionally. Now, when The One Who Loves Us Unconditionally poured their thoughts into you, the knowledge of creating the universe was so expansive that the thoughts could not just fill your head but needed to flow into every part of your being. The thoughts made your fingertips tingle and your heart thrum, united with the Earth Mother. The thoughts surged down into your belly, hair follicles and feet. Not a single part of you was left untouched by love.

Though the journey to come was far from over, The One Who Loves Us Unconditionally saw all that she had made and rested a full day and night. She knew the importance of rest for her whole being. The physical, spiritual, intellectual, and emotional aspects of herself had been poured into creation. He knew that to continue being strong and powerful, he would need to sleep. It didn't mean he was giving up or displaying weakness. He knew rest was a part of the natural order of all things, and he would need to model it for creation.

One day, Original One called you over. He was so tall and magnificent that he knelt on the garden soil, so that he was level with your eyes. He gave you one long look and nodded once, assessing his creation, tenderness revealed in every crease in his body.

"I have a job for you, Little One, but it is a great task and I need to know you are ready for it."

You nod vigorously, your whole body vibrates. You can't keep still. "I am. I'd do anything for you."

There is a smile on Original One's face, and it fills you with a warmth that can't be contained.

"I want you to be my steward," he says. "Respect the land, the Animal People, and the Earth Mother. Take only what is given and you will continue to have water to drink and food to eat. You will grow strong and healthy, and creation will flourish under your watch."

"I can do that!" You proclaim, but The One Who Loves Us Unconditionally wasn't too sure. So, she decided to create partners. Soon, the land was teeming with people. The people cultivated relationships with one another and some even fell in love.

Life was beautiful. It was harmonious, but The One Who Loves Us Unconditionally knew that it could not always be this way. One day while you were tending the garden, he pulled you aside to give you and the others a warning.

"You must realize something, Little One. The road ahead will not be easy, and indeed you and the people will make many mistakes. There will be suffering and great unrest among the land and the people, but if you keep your treaty with me, I will never leave you or my creation alone. Heed my warning and trust me. Though my thoughts are yours, if you do not walk harmoniously with creation, you will not always have access to them, and it will bring great destruction."

You try to heed the warning, but you struggle to grasp what could be so dangerous about the creation you love so dearly. You go about your life, just like I do, growing selfish and prideful. We forget the warning The One Who Loves Us Unconditionally had given you and me.

Sure enough, Original One was correct. Though he had foreseen all that had and would happen, she loved her people too much. She had to give them a chance, allowed them to live on their own, so she took her place in the heavens. Although her spirit dwelled in and within creation, the people did not always see her. Occasionally, Original One would appear through visions to the people or the birds would come as messengers. He would correct and guide them, and when they forgot, he would make sure they'd remember. Though his power was immense, her grace was even more so. He was The One Who Loves Us Unconditionally.

Finally, after thousands of years, The One Who Loves Us Unconditionally came down from their home in the heavens and was reborn as a man. No, not so much a man, but a baby born in a manger among shepherds and donkeys in the little town of Bethlehem.

Confined to the constructs of time and space, the little innocent life known as Creator Sets Free was born into the community of a distinct tribal people. That tribal people, known as the Israelites, were born out of a promise The One Who Loves Us Unconditionally had made to a man known as Abraham many years ago. Now Abraham was faithful to God, so the Lord made a generational covenant with him, blessing him and the many nations that would be born out of that treaty.

Throughout the years, the Israelites failed countless times, but God had chosen them for a special purpose. He had chosen them to be the message bearers for the story of Creator Sets Free who was Jesus Christ. It was a story that every tribe and tongue would need to learn. It was the story about the One Who Would Bring Fulfillment.

Now Creator Sets Free was a great and powerful teacher, prophet, and healer. He was God incarnate. The Word made flesh. Fully God and fully man. Creator Sets Free realized that the people had become like a lost son. The son had tried to step out on his own, but he quickly blew his inheritance. He knew he needed to ask his father for help, but was too proud to do so. They were like Nanabush who had gotten himself into trouble again and needed to 'fess up to Creator. Creator, of course, was graceful with the broken and welcoming to the lost ones. His mercy stretched out like a blanket that covered the entirety of the land with spirit.

The brokenness of Creator's people made his heart fall on the ground. Creator Sets Free was the Great Chieftain that many others from all kinds of nations had tried but failed to be. He spoke only truth and was the epitome of the good values Original One had bestowed on humankind. Creator Sets Free grieved, flipped tables in righteous anger, and rejoiced with those who found new life. He was the incarnation of courage, respect, reciprocity, humility, honesty, wisdom, love, and kindness, the type of kindness requiring the embodiment of all other teachings. He was the Prince of Peace, faithful to Creator, gentle to the people and full of self-control. All these values were good things, and when the people expressed all of them, they walked in the ways of the Great Chieftain, but when they did not, the world shifted into turmoil.

Creator Sets Free came to restore balance and give abundant life back to the people. He came to bring justice to a world under duress, to speak truth and bring peace. The harmony at the beginning of the story was so muddled with darkness that for some it seemed unrecognizable. Humans were so unlike the shepherds or stewards they had once been called to be, but Creator Sets Free embodied grace and stewardship. The King tended to his flock, saving all who had fallen into darkness, and helped them remember the original treaty with themselves, creator, creation, and one another. Yet, education was not enough. The darkness needed to be paid for, and all things needed to be made right. There was only one act that could accomplish this task.

Sacrifice.

No, not the kind of sacrifice of burning deer on a fire or throwing meat into lake waters for safe passage. It was not a sacrifice of sweet-smelling aromas of sweetgrass and tobacco. It was a sacrifice only Creator Sets Free could accomplish. So, to make all these things happen, Creator Sets Free laid down his life for all of creation.

Now, the darkness thought it had won. The darkness was the expression of every great and powerful Trickster, the ultimate accuser who had spent every day of their miserable lives fighting the good that Original One had completed. Three long and cold days passed. The Accuser was giddy with excitement, and he had begun to plan out everything he would do now that he was the ruler. But then, Creator Sets Free did something crazy.

He rose from the dead.

The tomb which had kept Creator's body was blocked by a boulder so large no man could move it. Yet when the women of Jesus' time came to the tomb to tend to the body and perform the proper funeral rites, they found it empty. Creator Sets Free, then, appeared to his disciples so that they would know he had truly risen.

Creator Sets Free made himself the least of these and rose as the most powerful, wise, and loving being in all the universe. Creator Sets Free saved his people, leaving them with one last message.

"Come walk the Good Road with me."[1]

Today, we are all offered that same choice. Creator Sets Free is always reaching, always waiting for us to join the Good Road. All we need to do is step out in trust and love.

The "Why" and "Why Not" of Creation Stories

The story I've outlined above has one simple purpose. It is the Christian biblical creation story and Jesus' death and resurrection told in the Anishinaabe way. I image there are plenty of questions that might arise from the text. For example, "isn't God referred to in the bible as a 'he'?" "What is this description of 'the Twinnings' and movement?" The Biblical story does not have these aspects in the original story. Perhaps you are wondering if there is any truth at all to the story. Afterall, isn't the telling of Genesis literal? Is it the only worthwhile interpretation? For now, I'm going to ask you to set aside your wonderings, for the story I have told has one simple purpose. It is the story of Jesus and its connection to our Native way. To be Christian and Indigenous are not separate identities Indigenous people must bear. Indigeneity cannot and should not be denied or silenced, hidden or worshipped any more than any other culture or tradition. Indigenous peoples need a story of hope and healing. They do not need to embrace blind optimistic hope, but the kind that trusts in God's creating power and unconditional love to guide and support His people.

---

[1] Story written and created by Mackenzie Griffin through listening to the stories of Anishnaabe elders and knowledge-keepers such as Leanne Simpson and from the creation narratives in Genesis.

When Christians brought the gospel, it was under the guise of salvation, but it brought subjugation, colonialism, and genocide. Christians destroyed the land in the name of dominion, an apparent God-like calling. They forgot Christ's true intentions. Christians always speak about how the gospel is for all people, and if that is true, then Christians need to begin to show it.

The above story is a missional story that encourages Indigenous people, especially Anishinaabe people, to connect with the Jesus Way in their context. I open with this story to propose a reimagined Christian journey for North American Indigenous people. In my sharing, I hope that missions might begin to look different depending on the context, whether we are talking about Indigenous peoples or not, and that we remember to mirror Paul and Jesus in their radical enactment of gospel and mission.

The creation story I told draws on Indigenous naming traditions, Anishinaabe words for earth and water, Trickster characters, and the seven ancestor teachings. It blurs the line between sacred and fiction not to question the gospel or to sour its message. It is not intended to diminish the Good News in anyway, but to bring new life into a story that has been tainted by colonialism. There are mentions of God as genderless, and Adam and Eve not as abstract beings but as you or me. There is less attention to the fall and sin then there is to creation and wholeness. However, there is significant mention of balance and the need for harmony. Creator calls the people to live under a treaty or a covenant and when they fail, God helps the people to make it right. The story is not heretical or syncretistic, although I assume some people will label it as such, but it does allow Indigenous peoples to connect to the old words in a new way that is familiar to them.

Syncretism and Contextualization

The question Indigenous Christians are most often asked when they practice their traditional ways is whether it is syncretism. Indigenous ways are not to mix with Christianity. One cannot be both. If they are, they are syncretistic, and that is to be feared. Syncretism carries many connotations. For Western Christians, it means mixing two incompatible religious beliefs.[2] Pagan culture fraternizes with Christian doctrine and orthodoxy and becomes unrecognizable. The Jesus way is lost. The problem with labelling Indigenous traditions as syncretistic is that it often ignores where Western Christian theology itself has been impacted by culture.

Western Christians must remember their cultural stories and origins. *Pagan Christianity* explains that Western Christians no longer understand

---

[2] Richard Twiss. *Rescuing the Gospel from the Cowboys: A Native American Expression of the Jesus Way*, ed. Ray Martell and Sue Martell (Downers Grove: InterVarsity, 2015) 28-29.

where their traditions such as tithing, order of worship or the sermon originate.[3] The foundations of their faith are hidden by the label of orthodoxy, when their traditions are actually pagan. Viola and Barna make clear that "pagan acts" are not necessarily evil or wrong, but they are not rooted in scripture.[4] Rather, these practices and traditions stem from rituals picked up from neighbouring cultures.[5] As Paul speaks in many of his letters to the Gentile churches, not everything in culture is good, nor is it bad, but we must discern the difference. This discernment is known as contextualization and it is not syncretism, or at least not the kind that is to be feared. Contextualization is how one understands and lives out the gospel in their context.

The letter to the Galatians outlines the distinction between culture and gospel beautifully. The church in Galatia was struggling with religious leaders who believed that to be Christian meant one needed to be Jewish (Galatians 2:4, NIV). These religious leaders believed Gentiles must follow Judaic law, practice circumcision, and refrain from fellowship and eating with Jewish people. Paul states that all these Jewish qualifications were not required by the Gentiles because "God would justify the Gentiles by faith" due to his covenant with Abraham (Galatians 3:8, NIV). The law does not keep a person righteous, nor is it unholy. God gave the law to the Israelites to help them keep covenant and live into their call to be image bearers. Similarly, he gave Indigenous peoples oral stories and ceremonies to help them lie in harmony with one another, Creator, and the earth. Then, just over 2000 years ago, he came to fulfill his original promise to Abraham on the cross. Jesus' death and resurrection restores harmony to creation and reconciles relationships. His is a kingdom of now, and not yet.

In Galatians 2, Paul mentions a disagreement between the Jerusalem elders and himself, a similar encounter further described in Acts 15. In the Acts story, the apostles and elders concluded a heated discussion in agreement with one another and wrote a letter to a church in Antioch. They agreed that the Gentiles did not need to participate in circumcision but should "abstain from food sacrificed to idols, from blood, from the meat of strangled animals and from sexual immorality" (Acts 15:19-21, NIV). Now at first glance, one might read this and become confused. Didn't Peter receive a vision from God that declared all food clean? In Galatians 2 was he not later called out by Paul for refusing to eat with Gentiles because of his fear of the Jewish leaders who practiced differently? He was, but there is an important

---

[3] George Barna and Frank Viola, *Pagan Christianity?: Exploring the Roots of Our Church Practices* (Carol Stream: Tyndale, 2012), xxxi.

[4] Barna and Viola, *Pagan Christianity*, XXV.

[5] Barna and Viola, *Pagan Christianity*, XIV.

distinction here. God's creation is holy, it has been made clean by Jesus' death and resurrection. Although God gifted the people with animals to eat, he reminds them to be respectful of creation. A strangled animal or an animal sacrificed to a God that is not Creator is disrespectful and unnecessarily violent. It is why Indigenous peoples use every part of the body of an animal and pray to Creator, thanking him for sustenance and providence. Indigenous peoples know the sacred gift of creation and recognize our need for the earth to survive. So, Paul and the Jewish leaders ask the people to abstain from these activities for it kept them further from God and each other. In Galatians, Paul mentions one stipulation from the elders: that they never forget the poor, a matter already close to his heart (Galatians 2:10, NIV). These things were common in the surrounding culture but kept people from God.

Both the Acts and Galatian stories remind readers that salvation is not dependent on Jewish ceremony or tradition, but because of grace. All cultural activities require discernment through community, scripture, and spirit-leadings. Just like the Jewish people, the Gentiles in Galatia and Antioch were encouraged to contextualize the gospel in their communities. When Paul and Silas went to Jerusalem to meet with other elders, they wrestled with culture and faith. They had to decide how to honour different cultural traditions while remaining true to the teachings of Christ. These discussions led to the sanctification of some aspects of the Gentile culture such as no longer requiring circumcision, and rejecting other aspects such as sexual immorality.

Missions, Relationships, Unity, and Diversity

The above stories are both examples of how to deal with cultural conflict. According to Jacobs, there are four main responses to cultural conflict: rejection, absorption, syncretism, and sanctification.[6] Sanctification allows the Word of God to judge one's personal and communal relationship with Creator.[7] For Indigenous peoples, that means being allowed to wrestle with and judge their culture on their own terms. It means allowing them to be all of who they are and not hiding what makes them uniquely created beings. It also means Western Christians must understand their culture and origins. So often, North Americans don't know where they came from. They don't even know what it means to be Canadian or American, occupying a land that wasn't theirs to begin with and holding onto stereotypes that make their

---

[6] Adrian Jacobs, "The Meeting of the Two Ways," *Native and Christian: Indigenous Voices on Religious Identity in the United States and Canada*, ed. James Treat (New York: Routledge, 1996), 186.

[7] Jacobs, *Meeting*, 189.

nation unique, like apologizing a lot or recreating a Promised Land God had never intended. Woodley notes that we are all tribal people, and that we all Indigenous to somewhere.[8] Only when we understand our personal and cultural contexts can missions be truly impactful.

Missions. Let's pause for a moment and unpack the term. People are not targets and missions are not accomplishments. Missions are a deeply relational act. In Matthew 28:16-20, Creator Sets Free calls his disciples to all the nations. Not only does he call his disciples, but he instructs them to teach the nations how to "walk the road with [him]" (Matthew 28:19, FNV). In Acts 2:42-48, walking the road is further described as eating together, generous giving and relationship with all, despite difference because their commonality comes from God. Though Jesus' physical body does not remain on earth, his Holy Spirit remains with the people. God never forgets his people. So, we should not forget each other.

Even in Revelation, God clothes his people in grace. In 7:9, John wrote about a great crowd of people from every nation and language, tribe, and tongue, worshipping God. Knowing the answer, an elder asked John who the people were. John stated what he saw and the elder responded that these people had come from great suffering but remained faithful to God (Revelation 7:14). The Lamb of God, Jesus, declared that the people would never again suffer, and the Great Spirit would ceremoniously wipe the tears of every person away (Revelation 7:16-17). It is difficult to note just what suffering occurred to the people, but the diversity of this image always strikes me. Instead of uniting people so everyone is the same, God honours the multiplicity of creation. Not only that, but he acknowledges the difficulty of following Jesus and doesn't deny it but honours the struggle.

Many Christians have and will face persecution. Indeed, many non-Christians faced persecution in the name of Christ, and the story in Revelation feels eerily familiar for Native peoples. It is true that Indigenous peoples need to hear the Gospel story, but they did not need to experience the violence, persecution, and subjugation they faced when colonizers came. Missions in its purest form is an honourable one. It offers people the choice to believe and follow Creator God and the Son in making all things right. Missions should share the Great Story, yes, but it should not deny the current reality of a people. It should not strip away who Creator made them to be. Jesus calls them to walk the good road, not because of their sinfulness, but because they were created good. Yes, sin is present. It is imbalance and persecution, resource extraction and broken relationships between nations.

---

[8] Randy Woodley, "Decolonize Your Faith w/Dr. Randy Woodley," Dec. 28, 2021, in *Holy Heretics: Losing Religion and Finding Jesus,* produced by the Sophia Society, podcast, 10:39-10:41.

Sin is obvious to any marginalized person around, but they need to know their worth is not dependant on their use. God did not leave them to have their culture destroyed with the Doctrine of Discovery and a diseased Christian theology.

In the West, the Evangelical, Catholic, Protestant idea of mission was not biblical but born out of a "dysfunctional" and indeed, "diseased" theology.[9] It was a theology built on empire; one that transitioned from the suffering of the early church to exceptionalism and triumphalism.[10] No matter where one's ancestors originate, every Christian has a responsibility and a choice to walk the good road now, to follow the paths of the ancient ways and find rest for our souls (Jeremiah 6:16). Every Christian must actively discern the role of culture in their life. They must keep open minds and hearts and truly listen to people with different backgrounds from their own.

A Journey of One Little Not-quite-Native Girl and One Little Not-quite-missionary

Before we end, I want to tell two more stories to further understand contextualization and the importance of relationship in mission. The first is of the Masai people in Africa, told from the perspective of a missionary by the name of Vincent J. Donovan. He saw that the Masai had not changed their ways in thousands of years, and despite missionary efforts remained unfazed. He decided to throw out everything he knew about missions and forge a new path with the Masai people. This story is about community. It is what contextualization looks like in practice. Sanctification, discernment, and missions must be done the way the early church did it, not how humans have been taught to do it today.

The second narrative is my own, because if I'm going to talk about the importance of learning one's personal story in missions, I suppose I should do the same. Afterall, it is through my own personal journey that I have begun to educate myself in contextualization. Every Christian has a journey, and people are meant to journey together.

Now, if you didn't read the name at the beginning of this chapter and my bio, my name is Mackenzie Griffin. I am Cree and Saulteaux on my mother's side, but I grew up disconnected from my culture and community. I am English and Scottish on my father's side but am estranged from all of that too. My kinship to land and connection to story was mediocre at best. The last few years, I have only begun to reclaim them. It is a lifelong expedition.

---

[9] Mark Charles and Soong-Chan Rah, *Unsettling Truths: The Ongoing, Dehumanizing Legacy of the Doctrine of Discovery* (Downers Grove: InterVarsity, 2019), 21.

[10] Charles and Rah, *Unsettling Truths*, 59.

Growing up off-reserve in a small, white conservative town north of Edmonton, Alberta, I grew up colonized, not knowing there was any other way to be. While my mother is Indigenous, she never spoke about her culture or history, believing she was protecting her children by hiding all the difficult parts of her heritage. My grandmother went to Ermineskin Residential School, and although she speaks her language, she never passed it on to her children. She does not know how to love or share with her family, and has suffered with addictions for many years. From the ages of zero to eighteen, everything I learned about my Indigenous heritage came from my father. He took it upon himself to learn about his wife and children through university and cultural safety training. He works in social work and has had a passion for contextualization before I even learned of the term. My father encouraged me to find my voice in school and with my friends.

Unfortunately, my childhood education consisted primarily of white faculty members who knew nothing but a whitewashed history. My teachers and peers covertly encouraged me to bury my Indigenous identity or forced me and my siblings into caricatures of "Dead Indians."[11] My brother would often be called Chief or Big Eagle by his friends in an endearing, not-so-endearing way. I remember after the only class we had—and would ever have—on residential schools, a friend expressed her frustration in learning about Indigenous peoples. She'd already heard everything she needed to know about us. For Thomas King, "Dead Indians" are not deceased but are the kind of caricatures created from "collective imaginings and fears."[12] After years of assimilation and genocidal practices, the Indigenous peoples North Americans wished did not exist became characters they could play games with, make products out of, and turn into tourist attractions.

Alongside my education, my upbringing in a charismatic, conservative, Pentecostal church greatly impacted how I saw myself in the church and community. I felt called to be a pastor at the age of sixteen. I remember approaching my pastor for advice, hoping he could offer me some encouragement on my journey. He told me women could not be lead pastors. They may find roles in children's or youth ministry, but I would never stand at pulpit. Even my female youth leaders told me to consider other options. Was I really being called to be a pastor? Afterall, ministry could look like working in a dental office or serving at Sunday School. It didn't mean I had to speak from the pulpit. Maybe I should have heeded those words, but I couldn't shake it. I knew the Holy Spirit was calling me, but I felt stuck. I

---

[11] Thomas King, *The Inconvenient Indian: A Curious Account of Native People in North America* (Toronto: Anchor Canada, 2013), 53.

[12] King, *Inconvenient Indian*, 53.

internalized everything I was told I could not be. I am not a pastor if I am a woman. I cannot be Indigenous if I am Christian.

One of the biggest healing moments for me was when I heard an Anishinaabe creation story. It wasn't a Cree story, but my Saulteaux roots come from the Anishinaabe people and so it felt culturally adjacent. Hearing the words identified a hole I had not noticed before. When I heard Leanne Simpson talk about the First Man, or myself being lowered to the earth, I was filled with gratitude and peace. I could sense the Holy Spirit within every word she spoke. I knew God was present, I just didn't know how to explain that to others.

Moving to Kelowna, British Columbia, to attend university, I took as many Indigenous studies classes as possible. My first Indigenous literature class forced me to question my identity, the trauma I had buried deep inside, and called me home. The following summer, I practiced land meditations to connect to the earth and Creator. Then, in my third year, I was given the opportunity to research anything I wanted about Indigenous peoples. I researched identity. What did it mean to be Indigenous and Christian? It was there I realized how deep the internalized racism had gone and I realized there was no quick fix.

Even today, my journey continues. The first time I smudged I was so nervous. By that time, I knew that I would not go to hell for smudging, but I didn't know if I was doing it in a culturally appropriate or Christian way. No one had taught me how to smudge, and I felt uncomfortable with the lies I had grown up believing. Smudging is evil, it calls on spirits, and is idol worship. These assumptions are lies from the devil. Smudging, quite simply, is prayer. It is burning of sage, sweetgrass, tobacco or cedar, and letting the smoke lift our prayers to Creator. Sage, sweetgrass, tobacco and cedar are the four sacred medicines Indigenous peoples used in ceremony, instruction, and trade for generations. They each have different purposes, which can vary depending on the community, but all are healing.

Smudging allows me to focus on Creator and be intentional with my time. It allows the Holy Spirit to cleanse my whole being and the space around me with holy smoke. I feel at peace when I smudge, because I allow the Holy Spirit to work in me. I cast my anxieties on Him and trust that he takes my burdens. In Exodus 30:1, God commands Aaron to burn incense at an altar built of acacia wood. The aroma is pleasing to the Lord. I know that the smoke rising from my smudge bowl honours God. It is a way of finding harmony within myself and with Creator.

I am fully loved and fully cared for. I am worthy. Some people need to hear the truth in the grimmest of circumstances to really let it sink in. Repent or go to hell. Follow God or perish. Yet, there are others who have suffered enough. Some people must be taught first of shalom before sin is ever articulated. Since the Bible begins with creation, so must Christian theology start here.[13] God is the Creator, and human beings were made in the image of God (Genesis 1:27). Indigenous peoples need to be reminded of the goodness inside themselves, as well as the bad, and shown the unconditional love of Creator. The opening story of this article reminds Indigenous peoples that God so loved you or me. It is a very personal story because it is a story that is relevant today. God entrusts his people to take care of one another and the earth. Traditionally, Indigenous peoples understand the concepts of stewardship and the presence of evil, but do not have a word in their language for sin.[14]

The angle of repentance and individual sinfulness is not always the right perspective. Indigenous peoples have been taught for hundreds of years that their ceremonies and traditions are devil worship and their ancestral relationship to Creator is false. It is not that sin should never be spoken about, or else Jesus' death and resurrection rings hollow, but it is to say that sin must be communicated differently. Simply put, sin is broken relationship.[15] The goal of human beings is always to go back to that first covenantal relationship. Sin, without love, teaches nothing about salvation or the character of God, but sin with love instructs the people of God back to community.

It was with the Masai people that Vincent J. Donovan learned the lesson of love for all people. The Masai live virtually the same as they did pre-contact with their own systems of democratic government.[16] They are warriors and pastoralists with vibrant music and dance.[17] Although many missionaries have tried to bring the Gospel to the Masai, Donovan notes in a letter to his bishop that the relationship between missionaries and the Masai is "dismal" at best and "there is no likelihood" that they might receive Christianity by the current missionary effort.[18] Therefore, he proposes to be given a chance to try something new. In fact, after his first meeting with the people, he realizes that virtually everything he prepared to teach them needed to be reworked or

---

[13] Paul Schultz and George Tinker, "Rivers of Life: Native Spirituality for Native Churches," *Native and Christian: Indigenous Voices on Religious Identity in the United States and Canada*, ed. James Treat (New York: Routledge, 1996), 57.

[14] Schultz and Tinker, *Rivers of Life*, 58.

[15] Robert W. Jenson, *A Theology in Outline: Can These Bones Live?*, ed. Adam Eitel (New York: Oxford University, 2016), 75.

[16] Vincent J. Donovan, *Christianity Rediscovered* (Maryknoll: Orbis, 1995), 14, 16.

[17] Donovan, *Christianity Rediscovered*, 15-17.

[18] Donovan, *Christianity Rediscovered*, 13.

rejected.[19] Indeed, there was not language in Masai for Christian concepts such as person, creation, sin, grace, spirit, freedom, or immortality.[20]

In North America, Christians might note this as Christianese, or language that is not easily understood by people who have never heard or rejected the faith. If freedom in Christ is not conceptualized, then missionaries must work to find similar terminology within the Masai language. Whether through visualizations, stories, or actions, missionaries must do more than preach at a target. They must respect the culture of a people, acknowledging that all people can "reach salvation" through their own "customs and traditions".[21] One does not need to give up their culture to follow Christianity, but they must discern what parts of their culture are honouring and just to God and what must be left behind.

There will be bad and good things within every culture, but not everything about Indigenous culture is problematic, nor is everything honourable and good. The same is true for North American, African, or Israelite culture. In all things, there must be discernment, grace to make mistakes, and hope in the One who made it all.

What Good is All of This

So, what am I getting at? Is culture morally neutral or is it syncretistic? How might missions be contextualized and how does knowing your background help in education? In the West, the idea of missions is usually an exciting and prominent feature of the Christian movement. People go on missions, often to a country far from their own to teach their understanding of the gospel to a new or so-called unreached people group. Often, churches get caught up in the numbers. How many people can I save? How many souls can I win? They forget that it is not the people who do the saving, but Christ alone. Our actions are powerful. Walking with people in their contexts is more valuable than spewing Christianese and expecting others to understand. Discipleship is about more than just spreading the Good News. It is living it out through community and striving for shalom with all of creation.

Sometimes, the people Christians need to reach the most are in their communities. Sometimes, the stories that Christians need to understand are their own. Every single human being has biases and assumptions that they bring to the Gospel and their relationships. Whether Christians like it or not, they are shaped by time, location, and culture. I propose that in understanding our personal cultural stories, we can better understand the

---

[19] Donovan, *Christianity Rediscovered*, 21.
[20] Donovan, *Christianity Rediscovered*, 21.
[21] Donovan, *Christianity Rediscovered*, 23.

people we are trying to reach. Christians must understand the Bible, but that requires living it out. The Bible is only as good as the Christians who heed its words.

Indigenous peoples have a saying: "Listening requires that one hears with more than their ears. They must also hear with their hearts." The Christian life is an embodied experience. It is intellectual, spiritual, emotional, and physical knowledge lived out. Creator came to give abundant life, just as he came to wash away all the sins of the world (John 10:10). Abundancy is life lived now. It does not mean everything about a culture, or the world is good. It just means living with a truth inside you that cannot help but spread with every interaction.

Bibliography

Barna, George, and Frank Viola. *Pagan Christianity?: Exploring the Roots of Our Church Practices.* Carol Stream: Tyndale, 2012.

Charles, Mark, and Soong-Chan Rah. *Unsettling Truths: The Ongoing, Dehumanizing Legacy of the Doctrine of Discovery.* Downers Grove: InterVarsity, 2019.

Dickson, Courtney, and Watson Bridgette. "Remains of 215 Children Found Buried at Former B.C. Residential School, First Nation Says | CBC News." CBCnews. CBC/Radio Canada, May 29, 2021. https://www.cbc.ca/news/canada/british-columbia/tk-eml%C3%BAps-te-secw%C3%A9pemc-215-children-former-kamloops-indian-residential-school-1.6043778.

Donovan, Vincent J. *Christianity Rediscovered.* Maryknoll: Orbis, 1995.

Indigenous Governance. *IGOV Indigenous Speaker Series - Leanne Simpson's "Dancing on Our Turtle's Back." YouTube*, 2013. https://www.youtube.com/watch?v=28u7BOx0_9k&t=1902s.

Jacobs, Adrian. "The Meeting of the Two Ways." *Native and Christian: Indigenous Voices on Religious Identity in the United States and Canada,* edited by James Treat, 184–190. New York: Routledge, 1996.

Jenson, Robert W. *A Theology in Outline: Can These Bones Live?* Edited by Adam Eitel. New York: Oxford University Press, 2016.

King, Thomas. *The Inconvenient Indian: A Curious Account of Native People in North America.* Anchor Canada, 2013.

NCTR. "Residential School History." National Centre for Truth and Reconciliation, October 26, 2021. https://nctr.ca/education/teaching-resources/residential-school-history/

Schultz, Paul, and George Tinker. "Rivers of Life: Native Spirituality for Native Churches." *Native and Christian: Indigenous Voices on Religious Identity in the United States and Canada.* Edited by James Treat, 56–67. New York: Routledge, 1996.

Twiss, Richard. *Rescuing the Gospel from the Cowboys: A Native American Expression of the Jesus Way.* Edited by Ray Martell and Sue Martell. Downers Grove: InterVarsity Press, 2015.

Chapter 10:
Bible Education Through Tajik Orality

Enoch Wan & Timothy Hanuk

Abstract

Recent years in the orality movement reveal an emphasis on narrative for Bible education, but what about spoken poetry? Can we think seriously about the practice of poetry for Bible education? For the Tajik in Central Asia, the habitual speaking of poetry encompasses much more than an ode to human feelings. Through the lens of relational interactionism and with a goal of transformational change, this paper shows a contextualized strategy for Bible education among Tajik oral learners.

Introduction

Tajiks' pervasive practice of poetry brings a unique twist to the subject of orality. From a first-grade child reciting poetry for his class, to ladies gathering in villages in preparation for a wedding, oral poetry in relational interactions touches deep within the heart of a Tajik. Considering this saturation of poetic utterances, we endeavor to discover what Bible education might look like in the Tajik cultural context. We, therefore, venture to present a contextualized strategy for Bible education for Tajik believers who are oral learners.

This paper is the collaborative efforts of Enoch Wan, director of PhD/EdD/DIS programs at Western Seminary, and Timothy Hanuk (a pseudonym), EdD candidate at Western Seminary. For the sake of clarity, several terms are defined as follows:

Bible Education: The relational formal/informal/non-formal process of intentional learning from the Bible in the interactive convergence of God, people, and the Bible toward development/enrichment in a learner's knowledge, attitude, and actions.

Contextualized Strategy: "The efforts of formulating, presenting and practicing a plan of action for the Christian faith in such a way that is relevant to the cultural context of the target group in terms of conceptualization, expression and application; yet maintaining theological coherence, biblical integrity and theoretical consistency."[1]

---

[1] Enoch Wan, "Jesus Christ for the Chinese: A Contextual Reflection," *Global Missiology*, Contextualization, Oct. 2003, http://ojs.globalmissiology.org/index.php/english/article/view/439/1132

Orality: "A preferred way to hear, process, remember, and communicate with the human voice as the primary medium. Orality includes multiple media, such as storytelling, poetry, music, visual arts, drama, and dance."[2]

Tajik: An ethnic/linguistic people group from Central Asia of Persian background.

Tajik Poetry: An oral and literary work in the Tajik language as well as ancient Persian which normally includes rhyme (*kofiya*), meaning (*mazmon*), and meter (*vazn*) as stylistic features.[3] This includes Tajik poems (*sher*) as well as proverbs (*masal*). In this paper we use both "poem" and "proverb" under the umbrella term of "poetry" because of ethnographic research.[4]

Ethnography of Tajik Oral Culture and Oral Learners

Below is an ethnographic description of Tajik oral practices of poetry in a region of Tajikistan.[5] We endeavor to show that Tajik oral practices of poetry reveal an extensive cultural pattern in terms of their interactions and relationships. This is a brief description of Tajik oral practices of poetry, followed by the introduction of major themes within Tajik oral practices.

Ethnographic Description of Tajik Oral Practices of Poetry

We divide descriptions of oral practices of poetry into six categories to show the extent of Tajiks familiarity and practice in speaking poetry in everyday life and circumstances. We see the Tajik practice of poetry within childhood development, within festivals, within religious practices, within family, and within community.

Poetry from Childhood to Adulthood

From early childhood through university, students' use of poetry in education is pervasive. From the ethnographic research data, three

---

[2] Tom A. Steffen and William Bjoraker, *The Return of Oral Hermeneutics: As Good Today as It Was for the Hebrew Bible and First-Century Christianity* (Eugene: Wipf and Stock, 2020), 317.

[3] Additional resources on the form and structure of Tajik/Persian poetry: J. T. P. de Bruijn, *Persian Sufi Poetry: An Introduction to the Mystical Use of Classical Persian Poems* (London: Routledge, 2013); Jeannine Marie Heny, "Rhythmic Elements in Persian Poetry" (PhD diss., University of Pennsylvania, 1981); Julie Meisami, *Structure and Meaning in Medieval Arabic and Persian Lyric Poetry: Orient Pearls* (Routledge, 2003).

[4] Ethnographic research shows a blurred distinctions with *sher* and *masal* characterized in the Tajik practice of poems and proverbs. We incorporate both poems and proverbs together because of the interchangeability of the terms, the occasion and usage of *masal* and *sher*, and the authority given *masal* and *sher* in Tajik culture.

[5] For security concerns, the name of the region of the research is not included in this paper. We have also changed the names of all involved in the ethnographic research.

reoccurring themes emerge on both adult perspective of childhood oral education as well as observable patterns of children in formal and informal education settings. Before we outline the themes of tradition, mental capacity, and wisdom, we give an apt example of common occurrence of young children reciting poetry. During an evening with some Tajik neighbors, I engaged in conversation with their two younger daughters, Munisa (5 years old) and Shukria (3 years old). I asked the girls if they had a poem to tell me.[6] Munisa, who has yet to be in any school, stood up straight and recited a poem about winter that was fourteen lines long. Shukria, who had trouble pronouncing words, quoted me a different poem, which also followed the same pattern.[7] Neither of these girls have had any formal schooling. They learn poems from their mother and sisters with the expectation to say poems on demand.

The first reoccurring theme of adult perspective of childhood oral education is that learning poetry bonds students with their tradition, giving them a sense of connectedness to Tajik identity. Timur says, "Knowing poetry has become a habit and tradition for us."[8] Hasan says, "Children learning poetry is very important in Tajikistan. If we look at Tajik history, we are very rich by our Tajik poets and traditions. It is the habit and the tradition of Tajiks to write and say poems, so we shouldn't lose this tradition and habit." Students in lower grades memorize simple age-appropriate poems, while students in secondary schools may be required to memorize one or two pages of poetry a week. For example, much of the content in Tajik language class is found in the learning of poetry. One teacher said to me, "We need to learn about Rudaki.[9] If a commissioner comes and asks a student to quote a poem from Rudaki, and if a child can't, the commissioner might say, 'What! Are you not Tajik? You don't know a poem by Rudaki?'" This teacher outlines cultural expectations while hinting at Tajik identity.

Second, Tajik adults believe that poetry aids a child's ability to learn even into adulthood. It exercises the capacity for the child to think and grow in

---

[6] It is common to ask this question of children in Tajikistan.

[7] Additional resources on the form and structure of Persian poetry: 1) J. T. P. de Bruijn, *Persian Sufi Poetry: An Introduction to the Mystical Use of Classical Persian Poems* (London: Routledge, 2013). And 2) Jeannine Marie Heny, *Rhythmic Elements in Persian Poetry* (PhD diss., University of Pennsylvania, 1981). And 3) Julie Meisami, *Structure and Meaning in Medieval Arabic and Persian Lyric Poetry: Orient Pearls* (London: Routledge, 2003).

[8] Timur, Hasan, and all other individuals quoted in this paper without specific citation are Tajik people who participated in the ethnographic research through personal conversation and interview.

[9] Lived during the Samanid Empire in the 9th and 10th centuries, he is considered the father of classical Persian literature. See: Sassan Tabatabai, *Father of Persian Verse: Rudaki and His Poetry* (Leiden: Leiden University, 2016).

knowledge. Faridun, speaking of memorizing, says, "This increases his mental capacity for learning...If he memorizes a lot, he will be able to study a lot (be educated). It is a good practice for his mind." Takmina says, "It is important for improving outlook and getting wisdom...their memory capacity will grow." "If they learn a sentence, they quickly forget it, but if they learn a poem, they memorize it," Adina adds. Growing in knowledge is growing in the ability to memorize poetry. The two are intricately connected. Memorizing gives the student the foundational tool of his/her ability to learn.

It is common in both cities and large villages in this region for mothers to send their children, ranging from 3 to 6 years old, to daycare-type preschool. In preschool, teachers focus on children reciting poetry. In one ethnographic interview, Alima said to me, "Kids learn more poems in preschool than in formal school. All they do is memorize poetry." Teachers quote short poems and tell the children to repeat the words. One teacher told me, "If a child learns poetry when he is young, he will improve his overall ability to learn other things when he gets older."

Third, there is the strong belief that a child will grow wiser through poetry. Poetry teaches wisdom, which all children need. Sabr says, "This is important...the children's speech will get better, they will grow wiser. If each one of them want to become an educated person, or they want to take part in the parties, it is important to know poems." Mavzuna says that a child learning poetry disciplines the child for life into adulthood. Mariam asserts, "Poetry plays the main role in their life, they will learn how to respect and obey their elders." Muisafed, who teaches at the local University, explains that in his physics classes he teaches the students about life situations. In relating life to physics, he says that he uses poetry over fifty percent of the time. "Poetry is like explaining, but something that touches the hearts of my students more quickly," Muisafed proposes.

Within Festivals

Tajiks esteem using poetry within various festivals. From weddings to Islamic holidays, people young and old alike quote the poets. "When people say poetry the holiday goes better," one lady said to me after she quoted a poem about Presidents' Day." The use of poetry for festivals, holidays, and major events comes to the forefront of the lips of Tajik people. Take marriage ceremonies for example. Marriage ceremonies are an important part of Tajik culture. Shohin says that a wedding will not be good if poetry is absent. A Tajik wedding event can encompass up to eight separate ceremonies. Within these ceremonies poetry is pervasive. Tajiks recite poetry at the *vecher*[10] ceremony of the wedding event, for example. In the summer of 2022, my wife and I attended a *vecher* at a restaurant with 150+ people. At the beginning of the party the emcee welcomed everyone by quoting 5 poems. After a series of songs with people dancing, the emcee would talk and quote more poetry in a rhythmic fashion, emphasizing certain words and pauses in certain places. There is rhythm and meter to her quoting the poetry. For example, she said many poems which included an A,A,B,A metered pattern.[11] Further, during the wedding event every person who gave their public congratulations quoted poetry as part of their speech.

The holiday of *Navruz* is arguably the biggest holiday of the year.[12] The city and villages organize events often with music and speeches to celebrate this historic holiday. Speeches inevitably include the quoting of poetry. New life in the spring or something new is often the theme of the speeches. For the *Navruz* celebration in a nearby village, people gather each year for a three-day event in a predetermined place at the base of the mountain, sit in family groupings and picnic in the spring warmth. Both in family groupings and in formal speeches over a loudspeaker, poems of spring fill the air.[13] In my ethnographic interviews, every person told me that *Navruz* would not be *Navruz* without poetry, that it would have no meaning apart from poetry.

Within Religious Practices

The practice of poetry in religion reveals itself in Tajik culture. All the great Tajik/Persian poets were Muslims and wrote poetry from that perspective. The quoting of their poetry both shapes and reinforces the religious perspective. For example, during Friday mid-day prayer time at the central Mosque in this region, one can hear from the street the *Mullah* giving his Islamic sermon. Within his message, to the men gathered at the Mosque, he uses poetry mixed with his instructions for life as a good Muslim. Islamic preaching is reinforced by short proverbs and poems by the prophets.[14]

---

[10] *Vecher* is a borrowed Russian word meaning 'evening' or 'night,' as the *vecher* ceremony happens in the evening.

[11] The musical pattern of the traditional trumpets (*karniz*) at this *vecher* followed the same rhythmic pattern, A,A,B,A.

[12] *Navruz* means new day. It is the spring solstice on March 21.

[13] Example of this in Tajikistan in general is Tajikistan President, Imomali Rahmon, speech with poetry: *Таҷлили Ҷашни Наврӯз Дар Душанбе / Церемония Празднования Навруза в Душанбе (2018) Full HD* (VarzishTV, 2018), https://www.youtube.com/watch?v=bohsDgO4ZWo.

[14] Compare Ben Gatling's research in which he shows poetry during religious ceremonies. Benjamin Gatling, "Post-Soviet Sufism: Texts and the Performance of Tradition in Tajikistan" (Ph.D. product, Ohio State University, 2012).

Mariam discloses to me the role the poets play in formulating beliefs. She says,

> All poetry written by a poet is...always beneficial, and they only show the right path. A poet only says that a good person should have good behavior and actions. They show the right way, before God, to act toward other people, and they show the way of Satan will lead to regret.

Mariam places her faith in the poets communicating the right and wrong path. The poets, at least in part, provide a guidebook or a standard of how one ought to live within community.

Prayers can have poems in them. Faridun says that sometimes in prayer people may say poetry because it expresses something of their hearts' desire. Takmina explains that the great poet Rumi[15] wrote poems of prayers to God and that these are good to use when praying. In a conversation with Shohin, he outlines a prayer with poetry.[16] He says that if you know this poem, the effect of prayer is greater with God. These examples show the blending of faith in poetry to both formal Islam as well as colloquial practices within an Islamic paradigm.

Within Family

The practice of speaking poetry to one another extends into everyday family life. Ikrom and Alima went walking one evening with their two older daughters. During the stroll, Ikrom started saying a poem and Alima finished it. They asked their girls to identify the poet of that poem. The girls asked them to say the poem again, which they did. Both girls hesitated, not knowing the answer. Alima, lightly scolding, says, "Oh you haven't been reading your poets!" Then Ikrom and Alima quoted the poem again and told them it was the poet Firdausi.[17]

Nabijon expressed his enjoyment of speaking poetry in the home context. He says, "My father tells me a lot of poems. Sometimes when we sit together and have breakfast, my father will quote from great poets like Rumi or Hofiz." While sitting in Mahina's house having dinner, she reminisced of how, when she was younger, her mom would quote poetry and make Mahina learn poems, saying, "We must keep the poems with us so that they will not be

---

[15] Compare Jalāl al-Dīn Rūmī (Maulana) et al., *The Sufi Path of Love: The Spiritual Teachings of Rumi*, ed. William C. Chittick (Albany: New York Press, 1983).

[16] *Lohato ilo ali ilo saif ilo zulfikor, Har baloe har kazoe pesh oyad dur kun parvardigor.* There is none strongest than Ali, his sword is sharpest, In whatever happens take away any misfortune. (translation mine). The first half of this poem is in Arabic the second half is in Tajiki.

[17] A famous Persian poet from the late 10th Century.

134

lost." Of course, people do not speak poems in every situation; family life is not like that. Stories, instructions, and even arguing all happen, but the usage and value Tajiks place on poetry within the family context is significant.

Within Community

Moving outside the family context, Tajik practice of poetry extends to community interaction. One summer my family and I spent some time in a remote mountain Tajik village. My wife gathered with a group of village ladies to remove the shells of apricot seeds, in preparation for a wedding. Several ladies gathered around a large pile of apricot pits and the shelling began. For three hours the ladies shelled these pits. During this entire process the ladies played a game. One lady would say a poem and the ending letter of that poem would be the beginning letter of the next poem. Quoting poetry continued continuously for three hours. When we relayed this story to Alima sometime later, she said, "Oh yes, we play the same game in our village too. People gather for whatever work is needed and we quote poetry to one another for a long time...it helps you from getting bored."

When I asked Eson if he could remember anyone saying a poem to him this week he said, "My wife said one to me the other day, my former classmate told me a poem and my friends spoke poetry to me as well...I can remember five people who told me poems this week." He goes on to say,

> Spiritually I receive joy from poetry...this life comes once, so I must pass it joyfully. You should help someone, so you should know many poems and proverbs, so that people would listen to you. When people listen to the radio, they listen to music, poems, and proverbs. When you give life advice by saying a proverb, other people would like to listen to you. The people who listen to you once will have a desire to listen to you again and again.

For Eson, and others, community interaction is intertwined with poetry.[18] It happens in the interactions people have with one another. Poetry is a pastime, a means of entertainment, a challenge, and a community event.

Oral-preference Tajik Patterns

In this second part of the paper, we introduce four major themes within Tajik oral practices of poetry. From the ethnographic data, these themes include, *foridan, ta'lim, fikri chukur,* and *tojik.* Before we address these four

---

[18] The following interview of university professors shows Tajik preference of poetry: "Гапи Озод: "Тоҷикон Шоирона Фикр Мекунанд" ВИДЕО," Радиои Озодӣ, accessed March 29, 2021, https://www.ozodi.org/a/31171403.html.

themes, it must be emphasized that Tajik oral practices of poetry are first and foremost relational. Oral-preference Tajik learners practice poetry from a shared experience posture. Though there are books of poetry published, the memorizing, communicating, and passing of poetry happens in the context of relational interactions. Most Tajiks in this area interact with poetry orally with other people. Therefore, the DNA embedded into each of the following themes is relational oral interactions.

Foridan

Foridan is the first and probably the most obvious ethnographic theme in Tajik oral practices of poetry. It means to please, to bring pleasure, to sooth, to benefit, to enjoy, and happiness. This theme stands strong as Tajiks talk not only about weddings, but also things of beauty, family, community, encouragement, and more. Poetry both causes pleasure and is an inner heart response to pleasure.

"When guests came to my house, I was so pleased that I said this poem (quoting a poem by Mirzo Tursinzoda). Sometimes when you are so happy you just say a poem and that is the best thing you could say," Marcida explains. For Marcida the sudden arrival of friends to her house has a pleasurable effect upon her. There was no planning or preparation for oral exercise. It was a poem she had memorized years ago, but now with pleasure in her heart the poem surfaces. Pleasure produces poetry, but it also has a reverse role. Poetry produces pleasure. On a different occasion Marcida explains, "Poems make you happy." Speaking poetry, then, is both affectual and effectual. When Nozanin gave birth to her fifth girl, the women who knew her quoted poetry for her to support the pleasantness of a new girl. Having a son in Tajik society is important. A son is the future of the parents as they enter old age. When the community saw that Nozanin produced no boys, they said poetry to her to create happiness within her heart. Mualimjon states plainly what the community had done to Nozanin saying, "We say poems to make someone happy." As Eson mentioned in a separate conversation, "I get pleasure from poetry, it lifts my heart." Mavzuna says, "When you use a lot of proverbs and poems, this will please people. For example, when guests come to my house, I say poetry to them. So, my guests rejoice and are happy with me...you see, you can transfer feelings in a poem." With many other examples, Mavzuna relays this theme of speaking poetry for pleasure within the context of others.

Nurijon says, "You can express whatever you want to in a poem, for example at a wedding you could say,

"Eh arusi nozanin bar hona bakhtovar shavi,
Bar yori hud as sidki dil dilbar shavi."

"Oh, beautiful bride, may you bring happiness to this house,
May the service from your heart be loved." (Translation mine.)

"So, it means," she explains, "I wish you happiness and other good things.
So, this brings beauty in the party." Nurijon's connection of beauty as a
pleasing or soothing element is preeminent with Tajik oral practices of
poetry. Marsida also describes quoting a poem to a new bride as a
pronouncement of blessing over her. Blessing is improved through poetry.
Beauty, goodness, and blessing are words people use in association with the
bringing of pleasure to others through poetry. The way in which people
communicate poetry brings a strong pleasurable element into community.

From early childhood, kids are taught the correct way to speak a poem.
There are certain vocal influxes and pauses in speaking poetry. How loud or
how quietly is important in communicating the essence of the poem. While
the poem itself is of an artistic nature, speaking poetry is equally artistically
important. Beauty is communicated by how one says poetry. When Munisa
quoted me a poem about Spring, she stood erect, arms to the side, eyes
straight ahead with her voice loud and clear. The common word people use
about how to speak poetry is *hushrui* (beauty). Invariably the connection of
speaking *hushrui* to others hearing the poem is *foridan*. Conversely, when a
poem is poorly spoken, one might hear the comment, "*nameforad*" which
means, "It does not give pleasure." At Ruhi's wedding the emcee held a
similar posture, yet communicating with head movements, voice intonations,
and body posture the emotion found in the poem. When I commented to a
friend the beauty at which emcee spoke, he replied, "Yes, she brings
happiness to others."

Ta'lim

The next theme from the ethnographic data of Tajik oral practices of
poetry is *ta'lim*. *Ta'lim* can mean teaching, training, or instruction. People
use poetry for *ta'lim* with one another. There are many subjects included in
the practice of teaching, training, or giving instruction with poetry. As many
have stated, "There is a poem for everything." However, in this paper, I only
show *ta'lim* from topics in faith, in right behavior within community, in
relationships, and in character qualities. When giving *ta'lim*, Tajiks inevitably
reveal something within their value paradigm. These four categories address
intended communication focuses within *ta'lim*.

In Faith

The oral practice of poetry trains Tajiks in issues of faith. By faith I am referring to their beliefs and practices within the Tajik version of Islam. As mentioned in earlier in this paper, Persian and Tajik poets were Muslims, and their poetry reflects that faith. This is why there are some *Mullah*'s in this region who easily use poetry. However, their faith is not merely communicated within the walls of the mosque, but within the conversations in any given day. Tajiks use poems to teach issues of faith. Consider the simple *masal*, spoken often in this region, "*az hudo barakat az odam harakat*," (translation: "from God comes blessing, from man comes effort"). Much could be said on settings in which people use *masal*, but for our purposes we focus on the faith topic in the *masal*.[19] Blessing comes from God. Blessings are always connected with the physical world. It refers to God giving tangible things related to wealth. God's role is blessing. Man's role is effort. As a man tries, God gives blessing. Therefore, man's role before God is effort. Mualimjon tries to practice his prayers five times a day, attends the mosque when he can, tries to fast during the month of fasting, *ramazon*, prays for the dead, and generally tries to be a good Muslim. Mualimjon, whom I have sat with many times, did not tell me that the Qur'an or the Hadiths teach people the right way. He told me that poetry shows the right way to live.

In Right Behavior in Community

Tajiks practice poetry for right behavior in community. Sitting with Shohin at a restaurant on the main road in the city, he explained to me that people are drawn to right actions through poetry. Poems teach people the right path. He then relayed a story of a teacher in the city who constantly mocked village people, insulting them in their simple ways. Shohin spoke a poem about how a scorpion strikes not because it is a bad insect, but because its nature is to strike. The teacher challenged Shohin saying, "Are you calling me a scorpion?" Shohin replies, "I am only telling you what the poet says." Shohin then said to me, "Maybe he won't repeat his mistake after I told him the poem about scorpions. Maybe he will stop mocking village people." He emphasized the perspective that communicating poetry actually trains people. Shohin did not agree with the actions of this fellow teacher. He exhorted him to stop mocking, but he did it in an indirect way of poetry in hopes it would affect change.

In Relationships

Tajiks practice poetry in training about relationships. Managing the web of relationships is vital to the future. For Tajiks, a key relationship and

---

[19] I am giving the most common interpretation of this *masal*.

devotion is with one's mother. There are countless poems about mothers. Faridun said to me, "If children learn poems about mothers, it teaches them to love their mothers." There are poems about one's homeland, which Nurijon says are meant to "Awaken your sense of love towards your country." These poems express metaphors and terms of feelings and responsibilities in relationship to others. For the Tajik, those feelings in the poems are intended to bring inspiration inciting one's network of relationships. They are useful for the Tajik as they both shape and strengthen the importance of relationships within community.

In Character Qualities

Tajiks speak poetry to one another in both affirmation and affecting character qualities. For the Tajik, poetry helps form positive character qualities such as loyalty, courage, generosity, persistence, bravery, patience, peacefulness, and more. As Sabr was reminiscing about her days in school she said, "We learned a lot of life lessons from poetry in school. I remember my Tajik literature teacher explained the meaning of poems for us so that we would grow in good character traits." For Sabr, poetry, as communicated by her teacher, built positive attributes and temperaments which carried her into adulthood.

Fikri Chukur

The next major theme in the practice of poetry we classify as *fikri chukur*. This literally means deep thinking. Practicing poetry becomes the practices of pondering and philosophical thinking. It is meditative while bringing forth wisdom.[20]

First, practicing poetry incites people to meditation. To put it another way, experiencing poetry causes thinking deeply on a subject. Hasan's uncle is a poet and is currently compiling a book of his own poems. His relatives think of him as a smart philosophical thinker because he puts his ideas into the place of deep thinking, poetry. Rasheed says, "Knowledge is learned from poems. There are some poems that are so beautiful and have deep meanings. Some poems have eternally deep meanings, they don't age, they are about life." Faridun shows, in a poem he spoke, how poetry gives rise to deep thinking. The *sher* follows:

---

[20] Not included in this paper is the third aspect of *fikri chikur*, many meanings. A Tajik hermeneutical paradigm sees poetry as having multiple meanings. Each person experiencing the poem is to develop their own meaning. This discovery of one's own meaning aids to philosophical thinking. Annemarie Schimmel proposes that a level of ambiguity is intended in Persian poetry. See: Annemarie Schimmel, *A Two-Colored Brocade: The Imagery of Persian Poetry* (Chapel Hill: UNC, 2004), 3.

Shush, shush in yak chizi bemaza,
Baroi haivon yakjoi gust bemaza.
Mo meguyem ki az shush shush nahta,
Beh az dumbai nasiha.

Lung, lung is a tasteless thing,
For an animal, a piece of tasteless meat.
We say not the lung, the lung,
It is better to have advice from the tail. (Translation mine.)

He goes on to say that if you had a lung to eat you would not eat it. However, if you had a tail, which is the choicest piece of fat on the sheep, you would gladly eat it. The advice from the tail, which is not there, is that you are only left with a lung to eat. Faridun says, "It is better to have lung than nothing." Thus, this poem with the use of vivid metaphors encourages thinking about gratitude.

Marcida once said to me, "You know who a smart person is by how they use poetry. Smart people know poems and how to use them." Another Tajik friend told me that when he reads the 13th century Persian poet Rumi, he must have a dictionary, because there are words he does not understand, and he must think a long time on them to discover meaning. He said that if a poem is so simple it does not have respect. "Poetry is communicated in language slightly difficult to understand, so that you will think through the poem," he continues. "However, poetry is also rhythmic to help you memorize. Poems force you to think through words and those words have meaning to them." For Rashid, Hasan, Faridun, Marcida, and others, poetry is meant to be meditative. Tajiks use poetry not only for pleasure and instruction, but for pondering the things of life.

A repeated word in understanding *fikri chikur* is *khirad*. *Khirad,* and its synonyms, means wisdom.[21] The oral practice of poetry is for the obtaining of wisdom. Closely related to *ta'lim*, wisdom includes knowing a good meaning of a poem and speaking it. Wisdom includes people's perceptions on intelligence (*madani*), on being learned (*ma'rifat*), and knowledge (*donnish*). Mansur, in speaking about poetry in relation to students, says, "Every poem has a deep meaning...students should be able to know their mother tongue well, if they know more poetry, they can bring examples in life by saying poetry and proving themselves true." Mansur made connections between the deep meaning of poetry and students' knowledge of their own language through poetry and the use of poetry in life situations. Wisdom, for the Tajik, is obtained through knowing and using poetry. Rasheed confesses that

---

[21] Wisdom is also understood as *hikmad*.

poetry makes one wise. Sitting with Ikrom one evening over a meal he tells me,

> Poems have a huge influence on people, they guide a person's heart in the right way. Poems discipline us. People show their knowledge by poetry. Poems show people's knowledge; and in my opinion, people's influence is greater the more poetic they speak. Poems are very effective. A wise and knowledgeable person is obvious, it is one who knows and speaks poetry well; and people listen to him.

Therefore, when Tajiks speak poetry, the consensus is that they speak wisdom. Especially, poetry regarding faith and life situations. The more you can recall the words of the poets, the more wisdom you possess and share in the community.

Tojik

Tojik is the last major theme emerging from ethnographic data of Tajik oral practices of poetry. This deals with identity. There are two ways to look at identity within Tajik oral practices of poetry. Tajik identity as a people, and Tajik identity within the people. First, see Tajik identity as a people.[22] Tajiks are keenly aware that to be Tajik is to practice poetry. Who they are and what they become, as a people, stems from a heritage of speaking poetry. The practice of poetry is an embracing who they are as a people. And with that comes a sense of togetherness. Poetry, as Tajiks see it, is a Tajik community experience.

Sitting one afternoon over tea, Alijon said to me, "You, in America, have your tall buildings and factories...Tajiks, we have the poets." Alijon, in thinking about America, speaks of a production orientation, but when thinking about Tajik people he speaks of a historical past and yet present identity. Firuzjon says, "We see who our ancestors were and our homeland...We learn our culture from poetry."

The second aspect of identity in Tajik oral practices of poetry is an identity within the people. This refers to one's status, reputation, and role in community. How one is viewed in their community is important. For the Tajik, their place in the community impacts their family and extended relatives within that same community. How one is viewed, whether real or perceived, by that community is vital. The training of children in poetry and then the appropriation of what they learned from childhood stands as a

---

[22] Good ethnographic resource on Tajik identity and patron/client relationship: Hafiz Boboyorov, *Collective Identities and Patronage Networks in Southern Tajikistan* (Berlin: Lit Verlag, 2013).

motivator for continuing poetry. Takmina points out that if you are a person that can speak much poetry your reputation grows and people think well of you, thinking that you are a wise person. "We work hard to learn poetry, and when we know it, we say it in different places and situations, and we will be respected more by other people. But if we cannot learn a poem by heart, then people will criticize us that we cannot even learn a poem," Nabijon explains. A person and his family's status are motivations for a good reputation in the community of relationships.[23] Jamshed says that it is what others think about you that is important. Yes, there are those, like Rahim, who confess to not knowing much poetry. He, for example, knows that his status is just that of a farmer. He recognizes and regrets that he did not do the work of learning poems when he was younger. And he praises and holds people in high regard who know and use poetry. For the Tajik, the status and reputation within community is connected to the practice of poetry.

Summary

In this section we provide a description and major themes with Tajik oral practices of poetry. The research shows dynamic cultural oral patterns supporting pervasive practice of poetry across the scope of Tajik relational interactions.

Contextualized Strategy for Bible Education

In this section, we provide a contextualized strategy for Bible education for believing Tajik adult oral learners. In this we explore pedagogy and criteria, which then informs the various features of this strategy. Finally, we conclude by proposing procedures and activities for Bible education in the Tajik cultural context.

Pedagogy in Tajik Culture

In formulating a contextualized strategy for Bible education for the Tajik we now look at pedagogy in Tajik culture. Pedagogy in Tajik culture is both relational and orally poetic. This "Relational Oral Poetic Education" (ROPE) is reflected within the ethnographic research, highlighted in the previous section.

---

[23] Both in my ethnographic research and literature Tajik culture shows a high level of collectivism as defined in: Geert Hofstede, "Cultural Differences in Teaching and Learning," *International Journal of Intercultural Relations* 10, no. 3 (January 1, 1986): 307; Also see: Colette Harris, *Muslim Youth: Tensions and Transitions in Tajikistan.*, Westview Case Studies in Anthropology (Boulder: Westview, 2006).

The ethnographic research points to three reoccurring themes on both adult perspective of childhood oral education as well as the observable patterns of children in various settings. The value and practice of poetry in childhood learning is seen through the lens of tradition, mental capacity, and wisdom. Relational oral poetry is an educational theory and method for the Tajik. From early childhood, adults expect children to speak poems. The first few years of school, and even pre-school, focus largely on the oral reciting of poems. Because reciting poetry does not require being able to read, they use it as a method in the preschool level. Sometimes the poems are portions of larger poems that the child will learn to their full extent in later years. By using poetry orally to teach many things to children, society is training spoken poetry as a valid method of learning.

ROPE is also clearly seen in the four themes within Tajik oral practices of poetry. Not in that adults go to school and have a teacher with a book. Those things characterize formal school, not adult practices in learning. When I asked if adults try to learn new poems, many people said that they really do not try. Later, I realized that they were equating "trying" with the memorizing they did as school children. People speak poetry to one another in a variety of situations and circumstances. Participating in people speaking poetry is how they learn new poems. One man told me, "If I want to remember the poem, I ask him to repeat it…then after about four or five times I remember it." Tajiks believe that from early on in life, speaking poetry trains people to remember. Tajiks often equate being an educated person with knowing many poems. Rahim confessed that he is not very smart because he did not memorize many poems. Intellect is bonded to knowledge in poetry. As mentioned above, when adults inquire about a child's learning, they will often ask the children to quote poetry. Mavzuna said to me, "This is how poetry trains you, the poet Loik, in one of his poems, says that Tajik poetry clearly communicates your thoughts to people." Her point is that poetry trains a person in communication with others and then how to communicate your thoughts to people.

Tajik oral practice of poetry is *ta'lim* (training) in that it provides an educational theory. For the Tajik, poetry gives birth to cognitive retention as it leans on the social interactions and communal experiences in the process of learning. Poetry is used, as seen above, in forming and influencing one's faith, behavior, network of relationships, as well as character qualities. These occasions are situational, in that as the events of life shift so does spoken poetry. Because ROPE is situational, it provides an immensely practical platform for learning.

Practicing poetry with one another also brings a sense of *foridan* (pleasure). People speak poetry as a result of "pleasure" and speak poetry to bring about "pleasure." Many Tajiks speak of poetry on a spiritual level in connection with their inner experiences and attitudes. Positive affective feelings surround the oral practice of poetry in such a way as to aid in change of attitude and behavior. *Foridan* impacts the feelings aspect in the dynamic of learning.

ROPE is supported by the Tajik cultural theme of *fikri chukur* (deep thinking). Practicing poetry provides not only a formulating and strengthening of their Islamic faith, but it also reveals a philosophical framework. Tajiks ascribe authority to their poetry. They believe in it. They believe that it makes one ponder on knowing both the metaphysical and the physical. The logic they employ from poetry is not based on a system of propositions, but pictorial, metaphorical, rhyming, oral art. This logic then informs their choosing a wise path and then acting on it. It spans and satisfies both the philosopher and farmer, as the mind ponders things and the hand keeps to the plow.

ROPE is strengthened through being *Tojik*. Tajiks' heritage grounds itself in the poets and their poetry. Their method of education is historic and consistent with how they identify themselves. This sense of identity as a people and within the people reinforces their sense of belonging. Identity impacts their thought process and decisions as a communal people.

The themes listed above as well as Tajik use of poetry within family, community, religious practices, and festivals all support relational oral poetic learning as a practiced educational theory in Tajik society. Figure 10 below visualizes the contributions of ethnographic research to educational theory.

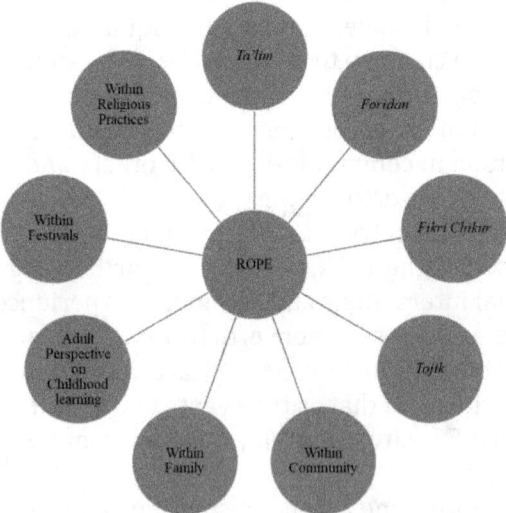

Figure 10. Tajik Relational Oral Poetic Education with Context Research

Criteria for Formulating a Strategy

The ethnographic section above provides a cultural starting point for a paradigm in formulating a contextualized strategy for Bible education for Tajik oral learners. The next step in this formulation is to identify criteria for this strategy (see Figure 11). The bottom of the pyramid shows both the theoretical and theological foundation for the strategy. The colors in this section of the pyramid are both blue and green, showing two bases for the strategy. The next section is a mixing of blue and green to get the teal color, signifying congruency for the framework. It also has a dark border showing a structure in order to build the strategy. The pyramid structure follows this framework.[24]

The top half of the pyramid of criteria for a strategy for Bible education consists of five distinct points. First, the criterion asks, "What are the goals for this strategy?" Are these goals clear and consistent with both the foundation and framework? This touches on understanding the anticipated change for the strategy.[25] Second, the "Process" shows the key elements for accomplishing the goals. We are not talking about the details of the strategy at this point, but of the process for the goals. The third criterion is pedagogical confluence. This criterion brings a multi-disciplinary educational aspect into the strategy. The main question, "Is there pedagogical confluence and is it congruent?" Fourth, we move to asking the question of where the contextual relevancy lies. The question is, "In what ways are the goals, process, and pedagogy relevant contextually?" In this we incorporate context and consequence of a particular group of people. Fifth, when we look at a pyramid our eyes naturally go to the top, the point in the pyramid. It is what makes the pyramid complete. It is what is most seen. This last criterion, "Procedures and Activities," is what is most visible in the strategy because it informs what we do in order to accomplish the goals. The key question is, "What are the procedures and activities, and do they fit the rest of the criteria?"

---

[24] These two foundational building blocks ideas for criteria are taken from: Enoch Wan, "Narrative Framework for Relational Transformational Change" (Evangelical Missiological Society National Conference, 2021); Enoch Wan and Jon Raibley, *Transformational Change in Christian Ministry*, 2nd edition, Relational Paradigm Series of CDRR (Portland: Western Academic, 2022) 9-24.

[25] See the middle of Vella's pyramid framework: Jane Kathryn Vella, "The 8 Steps of Design," Global Learning Partners, https://www.globallearningpartners.com/resources/shareable-resources/.

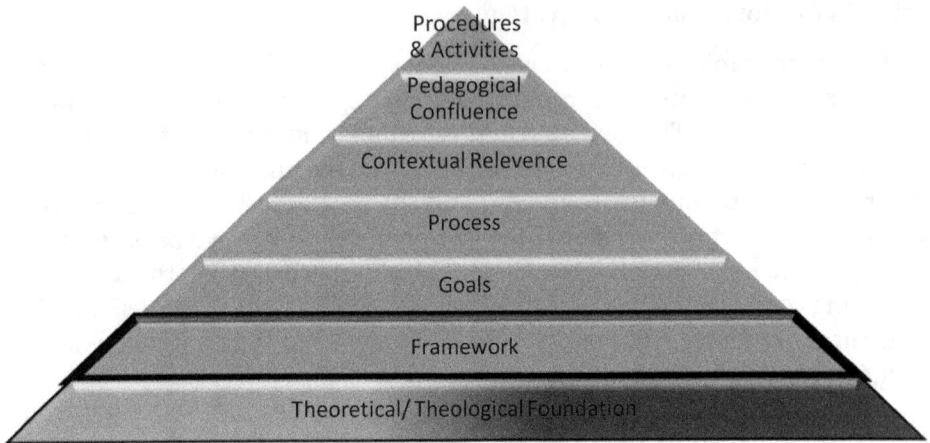

Figure 11. Criteria for Bible Education Strategy

Contextualized Strategy for Bible education

In the final section, we outline a contextualized strategy for Bible education for Tajik believers who are oral learners. In the figure below, the left-hand column lists the criteria for formulating a strategy. This coincides with Figure 11. The right-hand column lists the answers to the criteria questions.

The first four criteria are developed more fully in other articles and books; therefore, we only mention these four in brief here. The last three require more attention, providing the foci of this paper.

Strategy Criteria	Relational Orally Poetic Bible Education Strategy
Theoretical/Theological Foundation	Relational Realism
Framework	Relational Interactionism
Goal	Relational Transformational Change (Being, Belonging, Becoming)
Process	Relational Transformational Growth: God's Person → God's Scripture, God's People – Oral use of poetic forms of Scripture
Contextual Relevance	Cultural Patterns – ROPE
Pedagogical Confluence	ROPE, Kolb adapted model, Psalm/Prov edu. method
Procedures &Activities	Resource Development, Transformational Gatherings, Situational Oral Bible Poetry, Encouragement & Challenge

Figure 12. Relational Oral Poetic Bible Education Strategy for Tajik Learners

146

Relational Realism

Relational realism, as previously defined, is the theoretical/theological foundation in formulating ROPE.

Relational Interactionism

Relational Interactionism is an interdisciplinary approach for building theory and implementing practices such as ROPE. The figure below is an ontological description for ROPE.

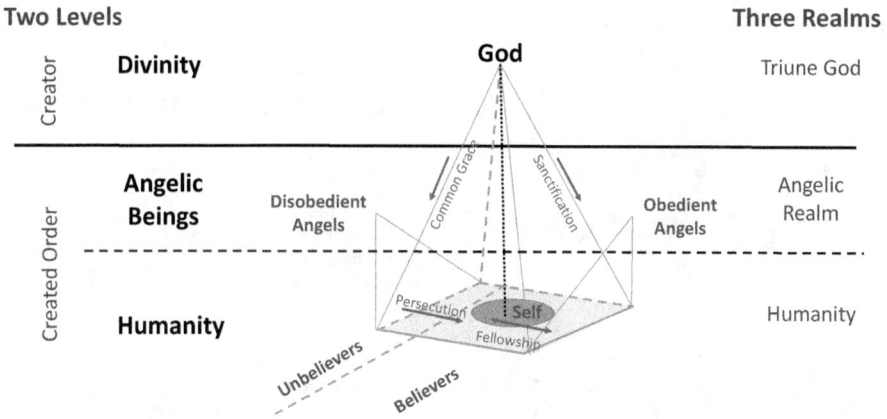

Figure 13. Macro Perspective of "Relational Interactionism"

Relational interactionism is a framework that helps understand how socio-cultural reality is formed, preserved, and changed through dynamic, repeated, and meaningful interactions between personal Beings/beings. The relational process that occurs between interactions helps create and recreate relational network, create perceived meaning, and perform functions.

In contrast to functionalism and conflict theory, symbolic interactionism emphasizes the micro-processes through which people construct meanings, while relational interactionism emphasizes the micro- and macro-processes through which the relational reality of complex networks is dynamically formed, maintained, and changed.

Relational interactionism comes from an interdisciplinary perspective of theology, anthropology, sociology, psychology, missiology, linguistics, and communication sciences. It is a study of the way that cultures are formed and social worlds of relational networks are created through interaction between personal Being/beings at micro- (individual) and macro- (institutional) levels.

147

How then does orality interact with relational interactionism? The dynamism for transformational change originates from the Triune God and channels through transformed Christian teachers/trainers, impacting oral learners by way of interaction, process, and experience (BELONGING: God working among us) in the relational learning process. The transformational change of "being" (i.e., in terms of spiritual, cognitive, affective and attitudinal) and "doing" (i.e. behavioral) is positive, blessed, and God-honoring. In contrast, transgressional change (dark forces against us) is the consequence of impact by the kingdom of darkness, leading to decline and even death. Figure 14 provides a visual diagram of orality and the paradigm of Relational Interactionism.

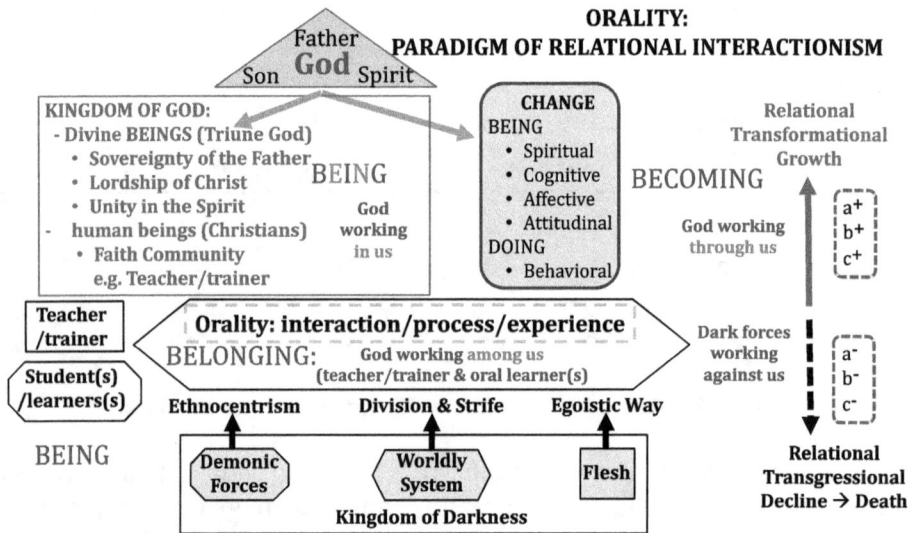

Figure 14. Orality and the Paradigm of Relational Interactionism

Relational Transformational Change

The third criterion encompasses goals in the strategy. The goal seeks clarity on anticipated changes. Relational Transformational Change is our goal. It is the dynamism of change, originated vertically from the Triune God and ushered in horizontally, through the process of interaction between transformed godly leaders and followers, leading to Christ-like character and Spirit-guided sanctification multi-dimensionally (i.e., spiritual, moral, social, behavioral dimensions at personal and/or institutional levels).[26]

---

[26] Enoch Wan, "Relational Transformational Leadership: An Asian Christian Perspective," *Asian Mission Advance*, April 2021, 2–7.

Figure 15 shows the state (i.e. three phases of transformational change: being → belonging → becoming) and process (with vertical and horizontal directions) of transformational change.

Being: All human beings are vertically connected with the Triune God: the Christian teacher/trainer by special grace (being transformed), and non-Christian oral learners by common grace (without transformation).

Belonging: When they interact within the context of the oral learning process, the Christian teacher/trainer is the conduit of God's transformational power impacting oral learners, whether they be Christian or non-Christian (vertical + horizontal).

Becoming: Positive change (transformational growth) is the consequence of relational interaction (vertically and horizontally), connected with the Triune God in the context of the Kingdom of God (*ecclesia* and *koinonia*), whereas negative change (transgressional change—decline/death) is the consequence of the negative impact from the kingdom of darkness (see Figure 15).

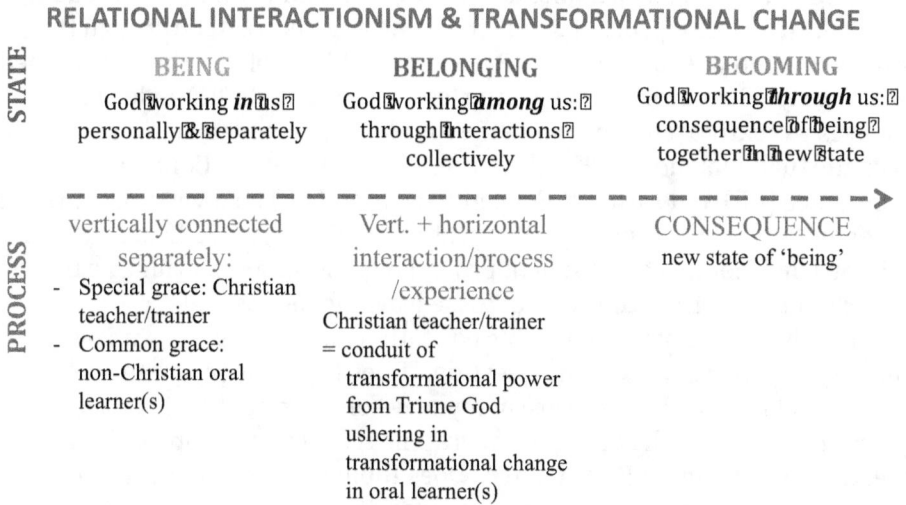

RELATIONAL INTERACTIONISM & TRANSFORMATIONAL CHANGE

	BEING	BELONGING	BECOMING
STATE	God working *in* us: personally & separately	God working *among* us: through interactions collectively	God working *through* us: consequence of being together in new state
	- →		
PROCESS	vertically connected separately: - Special grace: Christian teacher/trainer - Common grace: non-Christian oral learner(s)	Vert. + horizontal interaction/process /experience Christian teacher/trainer = conduit of transformational power from Triune God ushering in transformational change in oral learner(s)	CONSEQUENCE new state of 'being'

Figure 15. Relational Interactionism and Transformational Change

Relational Transformational Growth

The fourth criterion is 'Process.' Relational Transformational Growth is the process of "becoming" in the children of God (with *imago Christi*), brought about by the Spirit of God through the Word of God in the context of the faith community of God (*koinonia* and *ecclesia*) to the glory of God based on the *missio Dei* of the Triune God.[27] The Christian is progressively becoming conformed to the image of Christ. The Spirit of God receives all credit for transformational change, and yet He chooses to use His Scripture and His people (Prov. 1:1-7). In light of God's tools for transformational change in his children (His people and His Scripture), this process for the Tajik faith community includes the experience of the oral use of poetic forms of Scripture.

Pedagogical Confluence

The fifth criterion we examine is "Pedagogical Confluence." This multidisciplinary approach to formulating a strategy seeks pedagogical confluence. This strategy shows a congruency of three essential domains of study: andragogical theory, Bible based educational method, and cultural context learning theory/method.

In andragogical theory we select, and slightly adapt, the widely used and respected Experiential Learning Theory (ELT) championed by David Kolb. Learning is a process which includes feeling, watching, thinking, and doing. Kolb calls learning a process in which "knowledge is created through the transformation of experience."[28] Based on the ELT, Kolb further researched a learning style inventory, in which the learner constructs "Knowledge that involves a creative tension among the four learning modes that is responsive to contextual demands."[29] Kolb's four learning modes are Concrete Experience (CE) and Abstract Conceptualization (AC) on a vertical continuum of perception, while Reflective Observation (RO) and Active Experimentation (AE) on a horizontal continuum of processing. He shows learning as the process and pattern of the cycle of these learning modes.

Since this strategy is about Bible education and not discipleship or ministry in general, we ask the question, "Does the Bible promote an educational method?" There are many ways one can approach answering this question. In light of the above ethnographic research, we approach this question by examining Bible poetry. Does Bible poetry promote a learning method? Scripture is indeed useful for teaching and training in righteousness as God uses his Word for our transformation. The following paragraphs unfold portions of Bible poetry amalgamating with a relational interaction ELT. We also survey how the book of Proverbs promotes ROPE ideas.

---

[27] Enoch Wan, "Rethinking Urban Mission in Terms of Spiritual and Social Transformational Change" (Virtual, October 26, 2021).

[28] David A Kolb, *Experiential Learning: Experience as the Source of Learning and Development* (Englewood Cliffs: Prentice-Hall, 1984), 41.

[29] Alice Kolb and David Kolb, "The Kolb Learning Style Inventory—Version 3.1 2005 Technical Specifi Cations," *Experience Based Learning Systems, Inc* (January 1, 2005): 2.

In the previous section, we described ROPE within the Tajik context. Elements of this educational theory/method show integration with both ELT as well as Bible poetry to help further our pedagogical confluence.

Kolb brings to light what Psalms and Proverbs show, namely that learning is an experiential process. From the pedagogical foundation and framework above we know that learning is a relational interactive process (Relational Interactionism). Thus, we qualify Kolb's experiential process to incorporate relational experiential idea (see Figure 16).

We select two Bible passages (Psalm 48 and Proverbs 24:30-34). They are helpful in showing the confluence in describing and displaying the very things Kolb reveals in CE, RO, AC, and AE. Due to time and space, we will only briefly discuss Psalm 48.

Psalm 48:1-8 coincide with CE. There is an attention on the feeling here, in which the Poet uses metaphor to enhance the mood. He uses the contrasting emotions of seeing the beauty of Zion with the terror of the enemies.

Psalm 48:9 brings to light RO. Notice the communal response of thinking together on God's lovingkindness as displayed in Him being in the midst of His temple. This promotes the discussion of the experience of seeing God's presence.

Psalm 48:10-11 prods the listener to think, AC. There is an appeal to logic here: as is...so is. Notice, also, the appeal to God's attributes to help understand the situation of why praise is fitting in considering the presence of God as well as the enemies.

Psalm 48:12-14 appeals to AE. This encourages a return to the first few verses in the Psalm as one participates again in experiencing the grandeur of God's presence in Zion. However, this time the goal is to apply those experiences by interacting with the next generation.

The rope encircling the ELT model shows ROPE (see Figure 16). In doing this, we show how ROPE incorporates the four learning modes. As Tajiks practice poetry for *ta'lim*, for example, they engage in CE. This is both relational and situational. Practicing poems happens in a wide range of situations. Childhood learning lays the foundation of memorized poems. Adult learning often reaches into that memorized database to engage in the social activity of a situational issue or topic being experienced in the moment. Learners, both listeners and speakers, actively engage in concrete experiences through oral art.

When Tajiks practice poetry for *fikri Chikur*, for example, they are thinking and talking about meaning with others in community—RO. The oral poetry enables one to bridge the gap of one's understanding and experiences, as together listeners and speakers involve themselves in poetry. This also touches on AC as ideas or concepts are brought into the process, often through metaphor, to help understand situational circumstances or problems. Poetry is used situationally, bringing a form of logic into the life experience.

In Tajiks practicing poetry for *foridan*, we see the testing stage of AE. The Tajik, knowing conceptually that oral poetry brings pleasure, seek to use poetry for this purpose. Mavzuna then speaks poems to her guest to bring about pleasure. The experience of poetry stays alive as it not only produces *foridan* for an individual, but also as one shares his/her experiences.

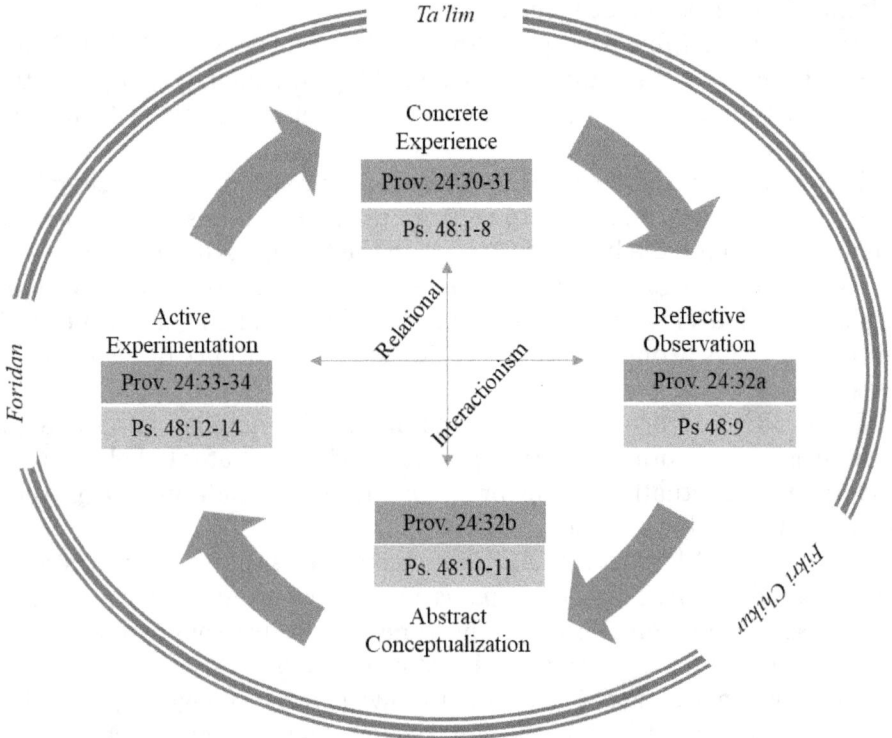

Figure 16. Pedagogical Confluence: ELT, Psalm/Proverbs, ROPE

We propose that not only do Psalms and Proverbs show congruency with ELT, but also show an oral learning proposition. Psalms and Proverbs inform us of oral propositions to enhance learning. This we call, "POEM METRICS." This is an acronym for the oralized learning being Poetic, Orientation of present to future, Emotive, Metaphorical, Meditative, Experiential, Traditional, Relational, Instructive, Cyclical, and Spiritual.

In Figure 17, the two middle columns give examples of POEM METRICS. The right-hand column shows how ROPE intersects with the learning procedures from Psalms and Proverbs. For example, look at the proposition of "Tradition." Proverbs 4:3-4 speaks of a man reminiscing of when his father taught him. This shows a tradition of passing along what you have learned. Psalm 78:2,4 speak of a man communicating in an oral art for the purpose of passing along wisdom to the next generation. The Psalmist, using the plural form, says that they will pass along to their children the works of the Lord. Tradition is emphasized. In ROPE we see learning happening from an identity of being people who speak poetry. A recognized history of oral poetry in learning attests to a traditional idea.

For a second example, look at the proposition of "Cyclical." Proverbs 14:5 with Proverbs 19:5 is an example of the cyclical nature of proverbial teaching. Both passages say the same thing: a false witness is one who is a liar. One proverb says a very similar thing to another. It is repetitive. Psalm 78 tells a condensed story of narrative passages in the Old Testament but does it in poetry. This is a retelling of story showing us a cyclical nature to teaching. ROPE reveals repetitive characteristics. Not only in memorizing, but in the constant quoting of learned poems in a variety of situations. We show these brief examples to show confluence with Bible propositions in learning with Tajik ROPE.

POEM METRICS	Proverbs e.g.	Psalm e.g.	ROPE
Poetic	1:5-6	78:1,2	Uses Poetry
Orientation present to future	2:3-5	78:5,6	Adult perspective on Child Edu.
Emotive	14:13	78:18-21	Foridan
Metaphorical	6:20-23	78:13,15,16...	Nature of poetry
Meditative	24:32	78:8	Fikri chikur
Experiential	23:29-35	78:3	Situational
Traditional	4:3-4	78:2,4	Historic, Tojik
Relational	2:1-22	78:1,4	Communal
Instructive	15:32	78:1,7	Ta'lim
Cyclical	14:5 with 19:5	78:6,7 78:8-72 poetic story	Repetitive
Spiritual	1:6-7	78:4	Faith incorporated

Figure 17. Pedagogical Confluence: Psalm/Proverbs Learning Propositions with ROPE

Procedures and Activities for Bible Education Strategy

The last and most visible part of a strategy for Bible education for Tajik believers are procedures and activities. We organize the procedures and activities into categories for furthering Bible education for the Tajik believer. These categories include resource development of poetry, transformational

153

gatherings, utilizing situational oral Bible poetry, and encouragement/challenge.

Resource Development

If Tajiks are going to involve themselves with ROPE from Bible poetry, there first needs to be resource development. This category incorporates dependence upon the Holy Spirit (Vertical). The first category we divide into two phases.

Phase One: Resource Development Initiation. The first phase in this category in procedures and activities is for us, the foreigners, to initiate the development of various Bible resources to aid in transformational change. A topical collection of Bible poetry in Tajik forms a resource database for furthering education. Topics include, but are not limited to, touch on identity as being part of the family of God, Bible *ta'lim* of believers for life and godliness, *foridan* passages, reflective thinking and explicit wisdom passages (*fikri chikur*), behavioral and character qualities, relational aspects, and faith as followers of Jesus. The second resource is a set of lessons in understanding how Bible poetry is constructed with an emphasis in Psalms and Proverbs. The third resource is initiation of a plan for adults to use Bible poetry in, with, and for the children. This will first be poetry that coincides with the Tajik alphabet. This also includes topics from the above topical collection with a target elementary age group.

Phase Two: Resource Development Together. The second phase encourages community dialogue over resources for practicing Bible poetry. The first phase is about initiating while the second phase is about incorporating Tajik believers into the process. This we do in conjunction with church leaders. We first seek adaptation/completion of the above resources. Next, we, as a learning community, initiate a theological guidebook of Bible poetry. In this we discuss topics of importance and relevance to Tajik believers. Last, based on the above resources, we perform audio recordings of Bible poetry, with an emphasis on reading in a Tajik poetic manner. With these audio recordings we make culturally engaging YouTube video clips, memes, and a website of oral Bible poetry.

Transformational Gatherings

The second category in procedures and activities for Bible education strategy is Transformational Gatherings with believers. This category incorporates pedagogical confluence. The second category also includes two phases.

Phase One: Gathering local believers for special poetry events. This phase encourages identity and learning in community. Sunday church gatherings already have their own liturgy. Changing things within the Sunday gatherings will be from influence. The special poetry events provide an open flexible format to encourage interaction with poetry for CE, RO, AC, and AE. These special poetry events include interactive lessons about understanding Bible poetry, Tajik value of poetry integrating with Bible value of poetry, as well helping moms teach Bible alphabet poetry to their children.

Phase Two: Gathering Tajik Christian poets. This encourages identity, creativity, and unity in the Tajik church. This phase, with the foundation of prayer for Spirit guidance, aims to find and gather Tajik believers country-wide to both present ROPE with local church engagement in ROPE and to envision future collaboration for the Tajik church.

Situational Oral Bible Poetry

The third category in procedures and activities for Bible education strategy is utilizing situational oral Bible poetry. This category requires two essential ingredients: memorization with intentional speaking of Bible poetry, and prayer. We see this in two phases. First, seeking to model ROPE for those believing Tajiks we influence, we use the above resources to put to memory Bible poetry for an array of situations. Then, we use Bible poetry as situations arise, with prayer for Spirit guidance. Second, after overcoming initial inertia of putting to memory and speaking Tajik Bible poetry, we challenge others in the community of Tajik believers to follow our example. Together we continue intentionally growing in ability to memorize and speak Bible poetry to one another.

Encouragement and Challenge

The fourth category in procedures and activities for Bible education strategy is encouragement and challenge. Related to situational oral Bible poetry, our emphasis in this strategy is encouragement and challenge through relational interactions with God and others. Along with the third category, this encourages Being, Belonging, and Becoming. ROPE is profoundly interpersonal, so is Relational Interactionism. There must be an emphasis on encouraging and challenging others with a personal relationship with God through Jesus Christ (vertical relationship). This is done, in part, through communing with God together through poetic expression. Memorizing the Lord's prayer from Matthew 6:9-13 provides a good starting point. An emphasis on prayer with Tajik believers while using poetry helps encourage this relational dynamic. This also incorporates challenging Tajik believers to relationship with God through Bible poetry.

The encouragement and challenge also happen on the horizontal level. In this, we encourage and challenge the crafting of new poetry based on Bible truths and passages. This also includes dialogue with key leaders regarding the new Bible translation project to reflect more poetic style in translating poetry.

Conclusion

In this paper, we provided a summary of the results of recent ethnographic research showing Tajik people's overwhelming oral use of poetry in everyday life. Following the ethnographic description of Tajik oral practices of poetry, we identified the oral preferences of Tajik learners then proposed a contextualized oral strategy for Bible education for Tajik believers.

Bibliography

"The 8 Steps of Design." *Global Learning Partners.* Accessed July 31, 2018. https://www.globallearningpartners.com/wp-content/uploads/migrated/resources/8_Steps_of_Design.pdf.

Chittick, William C. *The Sufi Path of Love: The Spiritual Teachings of Rumi.* Reprint edition. Albany: State University of New York, 1984.

Kolb, Alice and David Kolb, "The Kolb Learning Style Inventory—Version 3.1 2005 Technical Specifications," *Experience Based Learning Systems, Inc* (January 1, 2005).

Kolb, David A. *Experiential Learning: Experience as the Source of Learning and Development.* 1st edition. Englewood Cliffs: Prentice Hall, 1983.

Steffen, Tom & William Bjoraker. *The Return of Oral Hermeneutics: As Good Today as It Was for the Hebrew Bible and First-Century Christianity.* Eugene: Wipf and Stock, 2020.

Wan, Enoch. "Jesus Christ for the Chinese: A Contextual Reflection." *Global Missiology* (October 2003). http://ojs.globalmissiology.org/index.php/english/article/view/439/1132.

———. "Narrative Framework for Relational Transformational Growth." Paper presented at Evangelical Missiological Society National Conference, Dallas, TX, September 2021.

———. "Relational Transformation Leadership - An Asian Christian Perspective." *Asian Missions Advance* (April 2021).

http://www.asiamissions.net/relational-transformational-leadership-an-asian-christian-perspective/.

———. "Rethinking Urban Mission in Terms of Spiritual and Social Transformational Change." Virtual: Missiological Society of Ghana/WAMS Biennial International Conference, October 26, 2021.

Part 3: Oral Leadership Training

Chapter 11:
A Graduate Program for Orality Missiology

Cameron D. Armstrong

Abstract[1]

The year 2022 will go down in history as a landmark year for the Orality Movement. In 2022, the Asia Graduate School of Theology – Philippines and the International Orality Network partnered together to launch the world's first accredited graduate program in orality studies from a missiological lens. Program Director Cameron D. Armstrong reviews how orality experts came together to tweak a ThM/PhD curriculum designed to produce contextual studies in orality missiology. The chapter then discusses critical program objectives, core competencies, and characteristics of students admitted to the first cohort.

Introduction

At the north end of Woodstock Road in Oxford sits an old Anglican church transformed years ago into a graduate institute for mission education. On a sunny day in late September 2019, I walked through the wooden arch doors and met two men unfolding banners for our conference. Mark Overstreet and Charles Madinger, whose names I often read in International Orality Network literature, struck me immediately as both erudite and humble. I told them how honored I was to meet them, to which Overstreet replied, "We are all just servants of the King." Now, over three years later, my opinion of these leaders remains unchanged.

The subject of that conference in September 2019 concerned "Orality in Europe." Although I previously interacted with several leaders connected with the International Orality Network (ION), I had yet to attend an ION event personally. When I was invited, then, to come to Oxford and address a plenary session on my research concerning orality in Romania, I was more than willing. By that point, I was in the writing phase of my own dissertation

---

[1] This chapter is adapted from an article in the *Journal of Asian Mission.* Cameron D. Armstrong, "A Graduate Program for Orality Missiology," *Journal of Asian Mission* 23, no. 2 (2022): 87-101.

research at Biola University.[2] My talk at the conference drew from both my dissertation research and further research concerning how Romanian millennial university students prefer to learn, offering implications for theological education in Romania and beyond.[3]

At the conclusion of the conference, Madinger approached me about being part of a global Zoom conversation among theological educators concerning how orality studies helps Bible schools and seminaries train leaders for the 21st Century. The group met monthly beginning August 2020. We met monthly and gleaned the best from global scholars throughout Asia, Africa, South America, and Australia. In our monthly meetings, we shared research, best practices, frustrations, and prayer requests. These meetings, led by Overstreet, were a genuine source of joy and hope for all of us during the height of pandemic woes.

In January 2021, Madinger, representing the global leadership team of ION, asked me to sketch out an initial draft of a ThM/PhD curriculum in Orality Studies from a missiological perspective. "Sure," I responded. I brought my draft before the monthly Zoom group, which by then included several first-rate scholars well-versed in curriculum design, and we began tweaking the curriculum. We all enjoyed the process. Little did I realize how this process would change the direction of my life. These leaders from around the world agreed that motivating other seminaries to adopt orality studies into their curricula would require at least one highly respected institution demonstrating how it might be done.

Many leaders from the early 20th century worked to introduce orality content into higher education. Walter Ong launched a research center at Saint Louis University. James Slack and Grant Lovejoy of the International Mission Board encouraged Southern Baptist seminaries to offer at least one course in orality and Bible storytelling. Charles Madinger introduced a five-course curriculum at the University of Kentucky, which was later adapted for Christian university contexts. Romer Macalinao started an orality training program for Wycliffe Bible Translators in the Philippines. Other universities like Biola, Oklahoma Baptist, and Houston Baptist also began teaching courses in orality. Yet no institution had successfully introduced a graduate program in orality missiology.

During our meeting the following month, Filipino scholar Romerlito Macalinao announced that his institution in Manila agreed to take on the program. As Dean of the Asia Graduate School of Theology – Philippines

---

[2] Cameron D. Armstrong, "Finding Yourself in Stories: Romanian Theology Students' Experience using Oral-Based Teaching Methods" (PhD diss., Biola University, 2020).

[3] Cameron D. Armstrong, "Orality Reality: Implications for Theological Education in Romania and Beyond," *Transformation* (2022).

(AGST) and a leader within ION, Macalinao was overjoyed to bring us this news.[4] Macalinao, Madinger, and Overstreet tapped me to be the ION spokesperson in conversation with the seminary hosting the program, Asian Theological Seminary (ATS) – one of the eight member schools of the AGST consortium regularly sharing courses and faculty. I was surprised at their confidence in me but our meetings went well and ATS voted to officially become the host school in March. Then, in late April 2021, Madinger offered me the role of the Orality Studies Program Director. Taking the position would mean transitioning from Bucharest, our home of nearly a decade, to Manila.[5]

Our transfer to join the IMB team in Manila was a long process. Nevertheless, my family and I boarded our plane in Bucharest and landed in Manila at the end of March 2022. The initial cohort of ThM/PhD Orality Studies students launched August 1. This chapter is the story of how scholars came together to tweak the curriculum for the world's first graduate degree in orality missiology. After detailing our curriculum development, I discuss key program objectives and core competencies. The chapter concludes by discussing the ideal student, the type of students enrolled in our initial cohort, and the kinds of contextual studies to be produced by these burgeoning orality scholars.

Curriculum Design

Designing the Orality Studies Program (OSP) curriculum was an adventure from the start. As I wrote elsewhere,

Orality is an action discipline within missiology, albeit one that deserves further scholarly attention. Grounded in the lived experiences of the

---

[4] Macalinao first introduced the idea of AGST spearheading an orality program at an International Orality Network Consultation on Theological Education in Hong Kong, held June 11-13, 2013. See Romerlito C. Macalinao, "The Case of Asia Graduate School of Theology," *Orality Journal* 3, no. 2 (2014): 31-36.

[5] At first, my wife and I did not think remaining with IMB would be possible. As an organization whose primary task is church planting, we thought my theological education-specific role would not fit IMB's strategy. We knew God was clearly calling us but were unsure how this might look logistically. Still, my IMB supervisors encouraged me to contact Grant Lovejoy, Director of Orality Strategies for IMB. Grant made multiple phone calls and emails on my behalf to IMB personnel in the Philippines and Southeast Asia. These leaders all agreed that our transitioning to the Philippines could be highly strategic, especially in helping reengage the Filipino Southern Baptist seminaries. I would personally like to thank the many IMB leaders from Europe, Asia, and IMB Headquarters in Richmond, Virginia, for believing in us and helping us through this process.

majority of the world's peoples, orality takes seriously identity and learning preferences and calls educators to creative action.[6]

As I began drafting a curriculum, then, I knew potential professors and students must glean from their specific ministerial contexts to produce collaborative research. Courses, teaching, and learning must move toward a particular point in which learners not only feel, but *are*, better equipped to reach and teach oral peoples for Christ. If such is the goal, curriculum ought to demonstrably move students both cognitively and experientially toward that end. Such a goal mirrors the premise of Wiggins & McTighe's *Understanding by Design,* in which they state, "A curriculum is more than a traditional program guide, therefore; beyond mapping out the topics and material, it specifies the most appropriate experiences, assignments, and assessments that might be used for achieving goals."[7] Wiggins & McTighe then go on to explain the concept of "backward design," where curriculum designers first identify desired results, then determine acceptable evidence, and finally plan learning experiences and instruction. This process is "backward" in the sense that curriculum is often designed first with its topics and courses and later by its intended results.[8]

The first question presented, then, is this: What are the intended results of a graduate program in orality studies? Given the nature of orality as a concept among learners who prefer spoken rather than written communication who live "within the 'story' of the community," an orality studies curriculum for cross-cultural ministry workers should be multidisciplinary.[9] This is especially true if over 80% of the world's peoples rely on spoken rather than written communication.[10] Yet what exact disciplines orality covers is a difficult question. Charles Madinger posits seven disciplines based on the communication strategies of Jesus in what he terms a "holistic model of orality:"

---

[6] Cameron D. Armstrong, "Conclusion," in *New and Old Horizons in the Orality Movement: Expanding the Firm Foundations,* eds. Tom Steffen and Cameron D. Armstrong. (Eugene: Pickwick, 2022), 275.

[7] Grant Wiggins and Jay McTighe, *Understanding by Design,* 2nd ed. (Alexandria, VA: Association for Supervision and Curriculum Development, 2005), 6.

[8] Wiggins & McTighe, *Understanding,* 18.

[9] Samuel Chiang, "Editors Notes," *Orality Journal 1* (2012): 7.

[10] Grant Lovejoy, "The Extent of Orality: 2012 Update," *Orality Journal 1* (2012): 12. "To the extent that people rely on spoken communication instead of written communication, they are characterized by 'orality.' There are degrees of orality, depending on whether someone relies on spoken language totally or less than totally" (12).

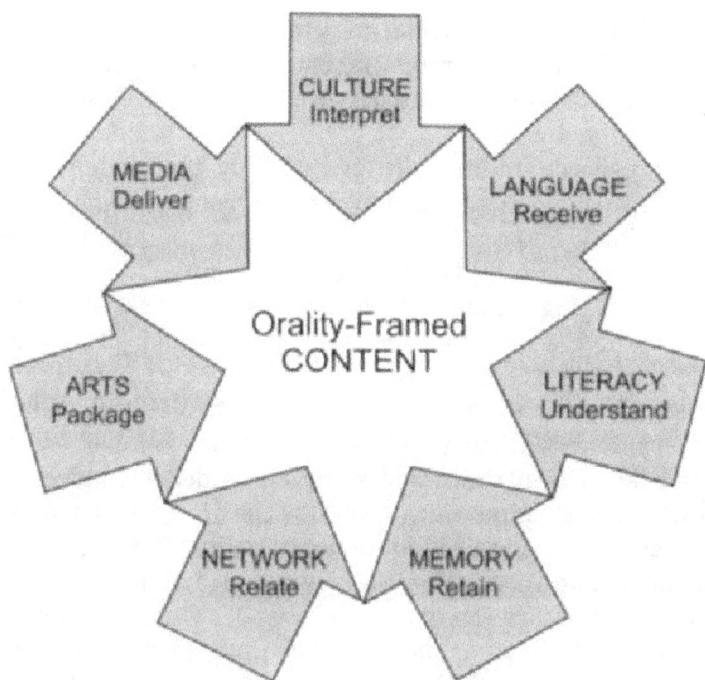

Figure 18. Madinger's Diagram of Orality-Framed Communication[11]

This conceptual framework is a missiological application of the orality Jesus modeled. A graduate program in orality studies, therefore, must consider how orality as a framework can practice each of these disciplines to multiply our fruitfulness in communicating the Good News.

Further, when one considers training pastors, missionaries, clergy, chaplains, and all other forms of religious workers, the various forms of theological education are in view.[12] The International Orality Network estimates that over 90% of the world's seminary-trained religious leaders

---

[11] Charles Madinger, "Coming to Terms With Orality," *Missiology* 38 (April 2012): 205. An updated version can be found in Charles Madinger, "The Power of Orality," in *Voices from the Margins: Wisdom of Primal Peoples in the Era of World Christianity,* Jangkholam Haokip & David W. Smith, eds. (Carlisle: Langham, 2022).

[12] Judith and Sherwood Lingenfelter remind that, in forming educational curricula in cross-cultural settings, educators should also note the "hidden curriculum," which they define as the unexpressed, culturally based learning that surrounds the "stated curriculum." Judith E. Lingenfelter and Sherwood G. Lingenfelter, *Teaching Cross-Culturally: An Incarnational Model for Learning and Teaching* (Grand Rapids: Baker, 2003), 28. For oral learners studying in the majority of the world's theological education institutions, the "hidden curriculum" asks the learner to adapt to the highly literate culture of the institution's founders and leaders.

utilize highly literate models while ministering in the world's churches.[13] If 80% of the world's peoples prefer oral communication, but over 90% of the world's ministers favor highly textual teaching and delivery models, the gap becomes glaringly obvious.[14]

PhD-level research traditionally favors highly literate delivery models that produce dissertations usually read by a small group of highly literate scholars in one's field. Rarely does a dissertation break out of this mold. What we are after with the Orality Studies curriculum is a combination of oral and literate methods: maintaining the highest levels of academic research while utilizing oral-based methods as much as possible. The end goal, after all, is to equip ministry leaders to better reach oral learners in their contexts.

After our initial rounds of jostling and critiquing, editing and tweaking, we opted for several introductory and elective courses followed by four academic tracks. The introductory courses provide all students, regardless their chosen track, a glimpse into several of the disciplines upon which orality touches. These courses are Foundations of Orality; Theology of Mission; and Culture, Context, and Worldview. Following the introductory classes, students will choose three courses from a list of six elective courses. The four academic tracks offer further specialized courses, each culminating in a supervised practicum. Included also in the curriculum are several research courses, including Qualitative Research, Literature Review, and Dissertation Proposal.

---

[13] International Orality Network & Lausanne Committee for World Evangelization, *Making Disciples of Oral Learners* (Lima, NY: Elim, 2005).

[14] Further, Lynn Thigpen, citing a 2012 study published by the Program for the International Assessment of Adult Competencies, points out that only two percent of students in the world's theological education institutions are able to read at levels high enough for successful understanding. Lynn Thigpen, *Connected Learning: How Adults with Limited Formal Education Learn*, American Society of Missiology Monograph Series 44 (Eugene: Pickwick, 2020).

ThM/PhD in Orality Studies		
48 units total		
Required Courses (9 units)		
Foundations of Orality		
Theology of Mission		
Culture, Context, and Worldview		
Elective Courses (9 units)		
Choose three from the following:		
Oralities of Scripture		
Discipleship in Oral Contexts		
Oral Hermeneutics		
Orality and the Arts		
Oral Pedagogies and Philosophies		
Orality and Bible Translation		
Concentration Tracks (9 units)		
Choose one of the following concentrations:		
Narratology		
Narrative Theology		
Narrative Preaching		
Practicum		
Ethno-Arts		
Arts for a Better Future		
Proverbs and Folklore		
Practicum		
Church Planting		
Disciple Making Foundations		
Christian Spiritual Formation		
Practicum		
Bible Translation		
Translation History, Methodology, and Technology		
Quality Assurance and Special Needs Translation		
Practicum		
Research Courses (21 units)		
Qualitative Research (3)	Comprehensive Exam (0)
Literature Review (3)	Dissertation Proposal (3)
	Dissertation Research and Writing (12)

Figure 19. Curriculum of ThM/PhD in Orality Studies

Initially, our program totaled 60 units. Such was within the proposed number of units for a research-based doctoral degree in the Philippines to be accredited by the Commission on Higher Education (CHED). Yet, largely due to the Covid-19 Pandemic and the global shift to online learning, CHED loosened their accreditation standards in several areas. One of these updates significantly reduced the required units for doctoral degrees. We then opted to reduce our program to 48 units.[15] All told, students should be able to complete the program within five to six years.

Ideal Candidates

After designing the curriculum, our next step was to discern the type of ideal candidate. While we had certainly hashed out this discussion prior to our final curriculum draft, I had not yet put our thoughts on paper. I began adapting an accreditation application template given me by Macalinao, which afforded the opportunity to verbalize the competencies of the program. Some of this program description is reproduced here.

The Master of Theology and Doctor of Philosophy with specialization in Orality Studies provides academic formation to those called to Christian service through the church, the academy, and mission in nonprofit settings. The ThM/PhD in Orality Studies equips Christian leaders to research ways theological content can be better delivered and embodied to serve the world's oral reliant peoples. This program pairs the world's orality experts with Majority World practitioners to ensure instruction is contextual, applicable, and diverse.

We deliver the Orality Studies Program in a modular format with online courses and two-week on-campus residency components. Coursework will be completed by taking up to half of the program online, as well as part-time. For the in-person courses, content will be delivered in blended formats at AGST/ATS in Manila and the AGST/ION partnering Extension Campuses.[16] This is the *only* ThM/PhD program in Orality Studies anywhere in the world, and the flexible learning model makes it possible for students to study without relocating from their ministry locations to Manila.

---

[15] The ThM/PhD in Orality Studies falls under what CHED refers to as a "Straight Masters-Doctoral Program." In such a program, students must still pass a comprehensive exam, publicly defend their dissertation, complete practice-based research, and publish at least one article in a peer-reviewed journal. Commission on Higher Education, "Section III.C.1 "Straight Master's-Doctoral (SMD) Program," CHED Memorandum Order No. 15, 2019, 9. In addition to CHED accreditation, the Orality Studies Program is also accredited by the Asian Theological Association (ATA). Similar to the American Theological Association in North America, ATA accredits theological institutions across Asia.

[16] These Extension Campuses will launch in the next few years.

Three core competencies drive both the types of students and professors composing ideal candidates for the orality studies program. In other words, our desire for participants in the Orality Studies Program is broken into three overarching goals. These three components are:

1. Examine the role and significance of orality through cultural analyses with the aim of biblically and meaningfully engaging culture.
2. Explore key presuppositions, developments, and future directions of orality missiology.
3. Publish original missiological research in the learner's chosen field on topics such as ethnodoxology, narratology, church planting, and leadership development among the oral majority.

Aiming for the highest academic levels of scholarship, Orality Studies scholars will be guided by leading global experts through the latest academic and field research methodologies and techniques. Combining academic reflection and quality mentoring, students craft contextualized research projects on orality studies and mission. Students then present these projects through intensive symposia and tutorials taught by orality experts. Our vision is the same as that of the International Orality Network: every oral communicator freely following Jesus.

I am thrilled to offer the lineup of professors willing to teach in our program. Most of these first-rate scholars joined our Zoom discussions from August 2020 – May 2021. The table below offers our faculty matrix, their educational qualifications, and the courses they will teach.

Name	Educational Qualifications	Subject Assignment(s)
Cameron Armstrong *Program Director*	Ph.D. Biola University	Foundations of Orality Practicum
Romerlito Macalinao	Ed.D. Asia Graduate School of Theology	Orality and Bible Translation
Erik Aasland	Ph.D. Fuller Theological Seminary	Proverbs and Folklore
Ezekiel Ajibade	Ph.D. Nigerian Baptist Theological Seminary	Narrative Preaching
Uday Balasundaram	Ph.D. Asbury Theological Seminary	Christian Spiritual Formation
Grant Lovejoy	Ph.D. Southwestern Baptist Theological Seminary	Disciple-Making Foundations
Charles Madinger	Ph.D. University of Kentucky	Foundations of Orality Introducing Narrative Theology

Name	Educational Qualifications	Subject Assignment(s)
	D.Min. Fuller Theological Seminary	
Roce Madinger	M.A. University of the Philippines	Orality and the Arts
Jay Moon	Ph.D. Asbury Theological Seminary	Discipleship in Oral Contexts
Mark Overstreet	Ph.D. The Southern Baptist Theological Seminary	Oralities of Scripture
Tom Steffen	D.Miss. Biola University	Oral Hermeneutics
Lynn Thigpen	Ph.D. Biola University	Oral Pedagogies and Philosophies

Figure 20. Th.M./Ph.D. in Orality Studies Faculty Listing

Each of these scholars, all highly published in their fields, are committed to equipping students to reach the Oral Majority for Christ. Moreover, they believe in seeing leaders from and working in the Majority World rise to the highest levels of the academy, recognizing the influence a doctoral title can bring. To be able to speak into culture-shaping circles, often high academic titles are the key. We are honored that these men and women are offering their resources to join us in this endeavor.

With the help of these colleagues and the hardworking staff of ATS in Manila, we asked students to meet the following requirements for admittance.

- MDiv or MA
- 3 References (Pastor, Ministry partners, Academic)
- 3 years cross-cultural ministry experience (preferred)
- Writing Sample in English (Thesis or equivalent)
- Completed Application

By God's grace, eight students have been accepted into the initial cohort of the Orality Studies Program. Each of these cross-cultural workers came highly recommended by ministry leaders connected to the International Orality Network. While I will not divulge their names, I will mention the countries in which the students live: Zimbabwe, Ghana, Nigeria, Vietnam, Philippines, Indonesia, and Oman. Each January, students will gather for two weeks of face-to-face classes in Manila.

Conclusion

Nearly 30 years ago, Christian historian Mark Noll sparked a lively conversation concerning the lamentable state of modern evangelicalism. Noll's *The Scandal of the Evangelical Mind* boldly claims, "The scandal of the evangelical mind is that there is not much of an evangelical mind."[17] Evangelicals, he claimed, had lost their foothold in influential cultural spheres because they knowingly sacrificed intellectual engagement with the world for a kind of revivalism that calls believers out of the world entirely. As a result, evangelicalism itself is at stake. Writes Noll,

> In the history of the church, Christian movements of long-lasting significance regularly have involved thinking at the most serious and most comprehensive levels. To be sure, such movements almost never arise because of intellectual efforts as such. Much more often they come into existence out of deep inner response to God's grace. Yet as such movements develop, they show great concern for the way in which Christians view the world at large. They are vitally interested in the Christian mind…They all promoted serious learning as an offering to the Lord.[18]

Although Noll has in view here the evangelical movement at large, these conclusions may also be applied to the modern-day Orality Movement. Growing from a mission movement among tribal groups in the Philippines in the early 1980s, the Orality Movement has now "come of age" to be embraced by missionaries in both rural and urban settings, as well as among lesser and more educated people groups.[19] However, many scholars and institutions of theological education still view orality with suspicion, dismissing the movement as a "passing fad" that cannot truly disciple believers.[20]

---

[17] Mark A. Noll, *The Scandal of the Evangelical Mind* (Grand Rapids: Eerdmans, 1994), 3.

[18] Noll, *Scandal*, 44.

[19] For the definitive history of the Orality Movement to date, see Tom Steffen, *Worldview-Based Storying: The Integration of Symbol, Story, and Ritual* (Richmond: Rainmaker, 2018). For the shift toward urban settings and more highly educated groups, see Tom Steffen, "Orality Comes of Age: The Maturation of a Movement," *International Journal of Frontier Missiology* 31 (Fall 2014): 144-145. See also the use of oral strategies in urban churches in the United States in Avery T. Willis & Mark Snowden, *Truth That Sticks: How to Communicate Velcro Truth in a Teflon World* (Colorado Springs: NavPress, 2010).

[20] See, for example, John Piper's critique of the orality movement. John Piper, "Missions, Orality, and the Bible," https://desiringgod.org/articles/missions-orality-and-the-bible. I responded to Piper's critique in Cameron D. Armstrong, "The Efficiency of Storying," *Evangelical Missions Quarterly 49* (2013): 322-328. Even more recent is Nehrbass, who repeats Piper's claim that orality cannot lead to serious analysis of Scripture. Kenneth Nehrbass, *Advanced Missiology: How to Study Missions in Credible and Useful Ways* (Eugene: Cascade, 2021), 248-249.

What is needed is no less than an academically and theologically robust platform that showcases orality scholarship of the highest order. Such is what we are advancing with the Orality Studies Program. If indeed the locus of Christianity is shifting southward, scholars from the Majority World will shape Christianity's future.[21] We believe that our graduates will lead the way.

Passing through the doors of the Anglican church in Oxford that afternoon in September 2019 was, for me, symbolic. I'll never forget the warm greeting I received from ION leaders Charles Madinger and Mark Overstreet, who evidently had already considered me for the future Program Director role and kept tabs on my growth as a junior scholar. Thus began an orality journey whose future looks bright. I pray that as we launch the Orality Studies Program, orality scholarship will be taken seriously by the academy, innumerable churches will be planted and established, and God alone will get the glory.

Bibliography

Armstrong, Cameron D. "A Graduate Program for Orality Missiology." *Journal of Asian Mission* 23, no. 2 (2022): 87-101.

———. "Finding Yourself in Stories: Romanian Theology Students' Experience Using Oral-Based Teaching Methods," PhD diss., Biola University, 2020.

———. "Orality Reality: Implications for Theological Education in Romania and Beyond." *Transformation* (2022).

———. "The Efficiency of Storying." *Evangelical Missions Quarterly 49* (2013): 322-328.

Chiang, Samuel. "Editors Notes." *Orality Journal* 1 (2012): 7-10. Commission on Higher Education. CHED Memorandum Order No. 15. 2019.

International Orality Network and Lausanne Committee for World Evangelization. *Making Disciples of Oral Learners.* Lima, NY: Elim, 2005.

Jenkins, Philip. *The Next Christendom: The Coming of Global Christianity,* 3rd edition. New York: Oxford, 2011.

Lingenfelter, Judith E. & Sherwood G. Lingenfelter. *Teaching Cross-Culturally: An Incarnational Model for Learning and Teaching.* Grand Rapids: Baker, 2003.

---

[21] Philip Jenkins, *The Next Christendom: The Coming of Global Christianity*, 3rd ed. (New York: Oxford, 2011).

Lovejoy, Grant. "The Extent of Orality: 2012 Update." *Orality Journal* 1 (2012): 11-39.

Macalinao, Romerlito C. "The Case of Asia Graduate School of Theology." *Orality Journal* 3, no. 2 (2014): 31–36.

Madinger, Charles. "Coming to Terms with Orality: A Holistic Model." *Missiology* 38 (April 2010): 201-213.

———. "The Power of Orality." In *Voices from the Margins: Wisdom of Primal Peoples in the Era of World Christianity.* Edited by Jangkholam Haokip & David W. Smith. Carlisle: Langham, 2022.

Nehrbass, Kenneth. *Advanced Missiology: How to Study Missions in Credible and Useful Ways.* Eugene: Cascade, 2021.

Noll, Mark A. *The Scandal of the Evangelical Mind.* Grand Rapids: Eerdmans, 1994.

Piper, John. "Missions, Orality, and the Bible." Desiring God. November 16, 2005. https://desiringgod.org/articles/missions-orality-and-the-bible

Steffen, Tom. "Orality Comes of Age: The Maturation of a Movement." *International Journal of Frontier Missiology* 31 (Fall 2014): 139-147.

———. *Worldview-Based Storying: The Integration of Symbol, Story, and Ritual.* Richmond: Rainmaker, 2018.

Steffen, Tom & Cameron D. Armstrong, eds. *New and Old Horizons in the Orality Movement: Expanding the Firm Foundations.* Evangelical Missiological Society Monograph Series 14. Eugene: Pickwick, 2022.

Thigpen, Lynn. *Connected Learning: How Adults with Limited Formal Education Learn.* American Society of Missiology Monograph Series 44. Eugene: Pickwick, 2020.

Wiggins, Grant & Jay McTighe. *Understanding by Design.* 2nd edition. Alexandria, VA: Association for Supervision and Curriculum Development, 2005.

Willis, Avery T. & Mark Snowden. *Truth That Sticks: How to Communicate Velcro Truth in a Teflon World.* Colorado Springs: NavPress, 2010.

Chapter 12:
Training Expository Preachers Among Oral Learners by Embracing the Literary Diversity of the Scriptures

Joshua J. Montague

Abstract[1]

Most of the world's Christian preachers communicate to a congregation that is largely made up of oral learners. However, the homiletics instruction that is committed to a faithful preaching of the Scriptures has largely grown out of and been directed toward Western, print-learning cultures. This paper appeals for a shift in homiletics education among oral learning congregations from a logic-driven, linear sermon form toward sermon structures that more closely mirror the nature of the actual biblical text. While logic-driven, linear preaching does resonate well with some NT letters, the genres of narrative and poetry make up the vast majority of the written biblical communication. Furthermore, the Bible (even the more didactic NT letters) was written primarily to oral learners. It was written to be communally and audibly heard more than individually and silently read. This paper argues that encouraging preachers among oral learners to conform sermons to a didactic system of propositions is less effective than an alternative approach. Rather, understanding and communicating within the diverse literary forms of Scripture itself will create more effective channels of communication within oral learning cultures. Oral learning calls for preaching narratively and poetically because Scripture itself originally communicated narratively and poetically to oral learners. Westerners involved in the homiletical education and training of oral learning pastors and congregations must help their students understand the literary diversity of Scripture and use it as a means to communicate to oral learning congregations.

Introduction

If your desire is to get a group of evangelical ministers into a knock-down, drag-out argument, ask them what makes a sermon "expository." If your desire is to get a group of missiologists into an argument, ask them what makes a group of people "oral learners." Definitions and descriptions of both

---

[1] This paper is a distillation of a central chapter of my dissertation submitted to Western Seminary (Portland, OR) entitled *Expository Preaching among Oral Learners: Toward a Narrative Expository Sermon.*

abound *ad infinitum* in homiletics and missiology. For the purposes of this essay, I define expository preaching as "the public proclamation of the Christ-centered gospel from the Old and New Testament Scriptures."[2]

In a perhaps overly basic sense, oral learners are those who learn, understand, and trust information delivered through personal, audible communication as opposed to a more impersonal printed or digital communication. Estimates vary, but a common assertion that 70% of the world's population are primarily oral learners seems to be generally accepted.[3]

This juxtaposition creates a significant problem for someone committed to expository preaching as a critical element of the local church's worship and maturity: most expository preaching training does not engage in a robust understanding of oral learners and vice versa, most work among oral learners does not develop expository preachers. Western print learners feel the need to continuously reduce Scripture to simple propositional statements. We impulsively and compulsively must concretize abstract concepts. We cannot help but oversimplify the complex.

Interaction with the global church and numerous groups of oral learners has caused me to ask significant questions regarding hermeneutical and homiletical training. Preaching (and the education of preachers) in an oral context must include an understanding and retention of the stylistic, rhetorical differences of the literary genres of Scripture because the Bible—in its varied forms—was written to be read aloud to and with oral learners. Retaining some of this stylistic form in the sermon will allow the preacher to communicate the truths of Scripture more effectively to oral learner congregations.

---

[2] This is a modified version of Jonathan I. Griffiths' definition, "the public proclamation of God's word," (*Preaching in the New Testament: An Exegetical and Biblical-Theological Study*. New Studies in Biblical Theology 42. Downers Grove: IVP Academic, 2017, 17). My definition inserts a Christocentric assumption about the Scriptures and clarifies the meaning of "God's word" as the sixty-six books of the Old and New Testaments. My dissertation spends considerably more time explaining and clarifying this definition. The difference between expository preaching and preaching in general is the inextricable rootedness in, and exposition of, the Scriptures. Merriam-Webster defines "preaching" as "a religious discourse delivered in public usually by a member of the clergy as part of the worship service" ("Sermon." *Merriam-Webster.com Dictionary*, Merriam-Webster, https://www.merriam-webster.com/dictionary/sermon. Accessed 10 Nov. 2023.)

[3] Avery Willis, et al., "Lausanne Occasional Paper, No. 54: Making Disciples of Oral Learners" (2004), accessed on 19 June 2023, https://lausanne.org/content/lop/making-disciples-oral-learners-lop-54#11.

The Bible's Literary Diversity

The diverse forms in which Scripture was written provide various literary forms that naturally communicate to oral learners. Central Asian oral communities use poetry and proverbs to communicate and share community values. African communities share stories to communicate truth and lead to moral conclusions. In various oral communities, memorizing genealogies is critical for a community to know its past and ancestry. The Bible itself contains these forms. Old Testament historical books and New Testament Gospels are delivered through story or narrative. The psalms and much of Old Testament prophecy are delivered through Hebrew poetry with its characteristic imagery and parallelism. The temptation, especially for the Western preacher, is to pull these texts out of their literary genre and "propositionalize" them.[4] Our cultural communication forms, especially among formally trained pastors, naturally steer us toward a near-compulsive orientation toward propositional summary statements. It is striking, and even unsettling to us, that there is no Aesopian moral after a psalmist's poem. Our need to propositionalize yearns for these straightforward statements. Occasionally, the author or editor of narrative books steps out of the narrative to explain[5] or instruct, and there are clear instances of the New Testament authors making theological and moral conclusions from the Old Testament narratives.[6] The point here is that the Bible was delivered—and retained—in forms that inherently resonate well with oral cultures. If the original intention of the Bible's authors was to communicate to their oral learning audiences,[7] understanding and even retaining some faithfulness to

---

[4] That is, turn them into didactic, propositional statements. I prefer the term "propositionalize."

[5] See, for instance, Mark 1:1–3. Mark sets up the initial story of John the Baptist (1:4–11) and the entire Gospel with a non-narrative prologue summary statement and a quotation from Isaiah's prophecy. Of course, Mark is not the only example of this. John's famous prologue (1:1–18) precedes the narrative with a pseudo-narrative that is more theological statement than storytelling. John also breaks the fourth wall at the conclusion of his Gospel (21:25).

[6] A clear example of this can be found in 1 Cor. 10:1–12. After remembering the Israelites' failures at Massah and Meribah, the apostle Paul propositionally concludes, "Now these things happened to them as an example, but they were written down for our instruction, on whom the end of the ages has come. Therefore let anyone who thinks that he stands take heed lest he fall" (1 Cor 10:11–12; unless otherwise noted, all Scripture quotations are from the ESV). The original narrative can be found in Exod. 17:1–7, which is pure historical narrative. Even so, Paul calls this "instruction." The implication is that communication is not required to consist of propositional statements (or even explained with propositional statements) to be instructive. Narrative (along with other genres) instructs.

[7] See John H. Walton and D. Brent Sandy, *The Lost World of Scripture: Ancient Literary Culture and Biblical Authority* (Downers Grove: IVP Academic, 2013) for an extensive exploration of the oral learning culture of both the Old and New Testament original audiences.

the very form of a passage's genre in the delivery of the sermon will provide a pathway for those seeking to preach and teach among today's oral learning audiences.[8]

This "literary form-based preaching" is not a novel concept.[9] What has not been thoroughly explored are the implications and opportunities this form of expository preaching brings to the field of orality and the difficulties present in communicating the "whole counsel" of Scripture to oral learners. Grant Lovejoy's 2001 article points in this direction with his conclusion that in order to preach to oral learners, "[an] obvious first step...is to utilize biblical narratives as texts and *retain those texts' narrative character* and values in story form."[10]

Retaining some of the literary form of poems, proverbs, narrative, law, letter, song, apocalypse, parable, prophecy, or wisdom literature gives the preacher an expository vehicle for delivering the ancient truth of Scripture to a modern, oral audience. Many oral cultures already rely on communicative forms like narrative, poetry (including song), proverb, or genealogy. Reducing these forms to didactic propositions (as so many preachers are taught to do) loses more than just the form. It loses a communication channel

---

[8] Quoting R. P. Carroll's article "The Hebrew Bible as Literature—A Misprision?" (*Studia Theologica* 47, 77-90), Stephen G. Dempster helpfully cautions that "the Bible 'was never received as sacred scripture because of its literary merit." Dempster argues, though, that it must be heard, read, and studied with an understanding of its literary nature. "A linguistic insight to the rich diversity of genres found within the Bible and their hermeneutical implications is extremely important. A parable should not be read like the narration of an historical event, a poem in the Psalms like a chronicle from Kings, a vision in Daniel as a literal story. Moreover, what drives the literary approach is the need to get not just the little texts right but also the big Text, or what C. S. Lewis called 'the overall message.'" Stephen G. Dempster, *Dominion and Dynasty: A Theology of the Hebrew Bible*, New Studies in Biblical Theology 15 (Downers Grove: IVP Academic, 2003), 24.

[9] Authors such as Robert Alter and Leland Ryken have written extensively on the literary interpretation of Scripture. Thomas Long's *Preaching and the Literary Forms of the Bible* (Philadelphia: Fortress, 1989) began to wrestle with the implications of this approach for the preaching of the text. Mike Graves and Jeffrey Arthurs have written subsequent volumes exploring this concept in further detail (Mike Graves, *The Sermon as Symphony: Preaching the Literary Forms of the New Testament*, Valley Forge: PA: Judson Press, 1997; Jeffrey D. Arthurs, *Preaching with Variety: How to Re-Create the Dynamics of Biblical Genres*, Grand Rapids: Kregel, 2012).

[10] Lovejoy, "'But I Did Such Good Exposition,'" 30 (emphasis added). Lovejoy earlier provided an expanded view of genre-based preaching styles in Grant Lovejoy, "Shaping Sermons by the Literary Form of the Text," *Biblical Hermeneutics*, ed. Bruce Corley, Steve Lemke, and Grant Lovejoy, (Nashville: Broadman & Holman, 1996), 318–39. Unfortunately, the majority of missiological literature on orality has overwhelmingly focused on narrative and storytelling as the key to unlock communication. This is important (and I will later argue for narrative as a dominant, even controlling, form for the sermon), but it is not the only form of communication for communicating with oral learners.

for the preacher to speak the truth of God's written word among an oral audience.

Using the Literary Forms of Scripture to Faithfully Preach to Oral Learners

In general, homiletics instructors have relied on print learner methodology in the preparation, organization, and delivery of sermons. As the church has grown among oral learners and homiletics instructors have engaged with oral learner preachers, the methodologies taught have not adapted to the communication styles and needs of oral learning congregations. We are trying to fit our square pegs into round holes.

Those who have written on preaching the literary forms of Scripture have primarily written within the context of Western print learners,[11] but the prepackaged delivery system of the literary genres of Scripture are extremely helpful among oral cultures. Pushing toward more diverse styles of preaching, Long challenges preachers to ask five important questions in their sermon preparation:[12]

1. What is the genre of the text?
2. What is the rhetorical function [intended impact] of the genre?[13]
3. What literary devices does this genre employ to advance its rhetorical effect?
4. How in particular does this text under consideration, in its own literary setting, embody the characteristics and dynamics of Question 3?

---

[11] Western culture is amidst a shift from a print learning culture to a visual learning culture. The difference between print, visual, and oral learning will need to be explored by those preaching and teaching in Western cultures. Important to note here is that oral learners are not visual learners. As Western culture shifts away from a modernist, print learner culture, the traditional didactic, propositional forms of expository preaching will have less and less convictional authority among postmodern listeners. Writing nearly thirty years ago, Timothy A. Turner warns that "People who acquire a taste for TV prove unlikely to develop the capabilities needed to hear preaching." [*Preaching to a Programmed People* (Grand Rapids: Kregel, 1995), 21]. Turner also states that "pictures tend to by-pass conscious analysis and elicit direct emotional responses without prior listening and reflecting" (29). Understanding this transformation toward a visual learning culture, which is now light years ahead of what was happening in Turner's Day, Zack Eswine, *Preaching to a Post-Everything World: Crafting Biblical Sermons that Connect with Our Culture* (Grand Rapids: Baker, 2008), writes, "Reason alone is not enough . . . [Postmodern listeners] also need to see the resonance between the biblical world and our own. . . . [K]nowledge of the truth comes in the form of relational contact over time" (16-17).

[12] Long, *Preaching and the Literary Forms of the Bible*, 24.

[13] Note that this is the function of the "genre" not just a portion of the text.

5. How may the sermon in the new setting say and do what the text says and does in its setting?

Long's fifth question is the key homiletical question. This question is similar to a common definition of expository preaching wherein the sermon's main point must match the main point of the text.[14] Long adds to this by asking whether the *intent* of the sermon matches the *intent* of the text in its setting. Long is arguing here not for the purpose of the text reduced into a propositional statement, but the *intended effect* of the text within its actual genre. This does not suggest that employing the genre and form of the biblical text is as simple as rereading the text.[15] It does assume that the form itself communicates something.[16] According to Fred Craddock, the "form" (or genre) of the sermon "shapes the listener's experience of the material. As one can walk into a room and anticipate by the arrangement of the furniture what experience lies ahead, so does the shape of a presentation affect the listener."[17] Therefore, the preacher must think through that communication channel and bring in the genre's intended effect (Long's "rhetorical function").

Jeffrey D. Arthurs, a staunch advocate for expository preaching, urges pastors to consider preaching with variety in accordance with the genres of Scripture, arguing, "The defining essence of an expository sermon lies primarily in its content, not its form."[18] While still retaining what he sees as a necessary reduction of any text to a single, focused propositional idea, Arthurs suggests that the form of the sermon should vary as the preacher exposits different genres of Scripture. "Why preach with variety [of form]? The primary reason…is because God, the Great Communicator, uses variety."[19] A critical, and perhaps forgotten, secondary reason might be because the original audiences to whom the Great Communicator was communicating learned through these various communication forms.

Preaching in forms that more closely mirror the literary genres of Scripture seems to hold an important piece of the homiletical puzzle for

---

[14] Authors such as Haddon Robinson in *Biblical Preaching: The Development and Delivery of Expository Messages* (Grand Rapids: Baker Academic, 1980), David R. Helm in *Expositional Preaching: How We Speak God's Word Today* (Wheaton: Crossway, 2014), and Bryan Chappell in *Christ-Centered Preaching: Redeeming the Expository Sermon* (Grand Rapids: Baker Academic, 1994) all make such an argument.

[15] Though I would argue for much more. See Paul's command to Timothy in 1 Tim. 2:13. "Devote yourself to the public reading of Scripture, to exhortation, to teaching."

[16] Too often advocates of discerning and using the structure of a text in determining meaning remove the text from its original genre into an outline of propositions.

[17] Fred Craddock, *Preaching*, 25th anniversary ed. (Nashville: Abingdon, 1985), 173.

[18] Arthurs, *Preaching with Variety*, 16.

[19] Arthurs, *Preaching with Variety*, 30.

expository preaching among oral learners. Not every genre will be equally impactful for every oral culture. Some cultures will connect with genealogies, others with narrative, some with poetry, and others with proverbs. What is being proposed is that the vehicle for clear, transformative, expository preaching has already been provided in the very literary forms of Scripture.[20]

The Bible's literary genres are diverse and could include extensive sub-categories. Realizing that not every category can be deeply examined in a project of this scale, it is helpful to focus on three predominant literary categories: narrative, poetry, and (propositional, yet relational) letters, and to consider some of the characteristics of these genres which naturally appeal to oral learners.

Expository Preaching among Oral Learners from a Narrative Text

Narrative texts dominate the pages of Scripture from the Old Testament historical books to the New Testament Gospels and the book of Acts.[21] "The prominence of the narrative genre in the Bible is related to the Bible's central message that God acts in *history*. No other genre can express that message as well as narrative." Narrative is inherently active and engages, intrigues, captivates, and describes through its literary characteristics.

Humans live out stories every day filled with conflict, tension, resolution, character development, drama, and plot. Above these individual narratives, though, the biblical narrative primarily tells the story of God within and throughout history. While there are many identifiable characters and situations, the main character throughout the Scriptures, sometimes seen (as in Genesis 1, for example) and sometimes unseen (as in the book of Esther), is always God. The Bible is first and foremost the *narrative* of God, seen in the retellings of many smaller narrative sections.[22]

Literary genres are characterized by different elements. While an English poem may have a particular rhythm or rhyming scheme, a novel or news article does not capitalize on these elements in the same way. While more

---

[20] One might ask, "Then why preach at all? Why not just read the text?" While the text itself is both inspired and powerful, there is a need for explanation, discussion, and application in "sermonic" form. See Neh. 8:8 for an early example of explanation accompanying public reading: "They read from the Book of the Law of God, making it clear and giving the meaning so that the people understood what was being read" (NIV).

[21] Sidney Greidanus, *The Modern Preacher and the Ancient Text: Interpreting and Preaching Biblical Literature* (Grand Rapids: Eerdmans, 1998), 188, emphasis original.

[22] Individual narratives (Abraham, Moses, David, Jesus, Paul, etc.) not only dominate so many of the pages of the Bible but an overarching narrative plot also propels the greater Christ-centered storyline forward.

detailed analyses of narrative literature are readily available,[23] this study will mention seven elements.

Plot

First, narratives contain a plot. Arthurs defines plot as "the causally linked chain of events in a story that moves from disequilibrium to resolution."[24] Situations, characters, and locations change as the story advances. Often this movement involves a significant amount of *tension*. Think of David being stared down by the giant Goliath or Jesus taking his last breath on the cross at Calvary. There is an element of tense uncertainty in these stories, especially if you imagine hearing them for the first time. In biblical stories, this tension comes in all shapes and forms. Adam is alone. Will he find a companion like the animals have? The human race is completely wicked. How will God judge and save if Noah is the only righteous man left? Will Isaac die at the hands of his father, Abraham, or will God intervene?[25] Situation after situation of disequilibrium being resolved, or in some cases continuing in agonizing fashion while a promised final resolution is awaited.[26]

Greidanus points out that "the plot in Hebrew narrative [generally] moves at a faster pace than that of modern narration. This rapid pace is the result of short sentences, a lack of detail, and the absence of extended character development."[27] This is also (generally) true of New Testament narratives, though portions of John's Gospel and the book of Acts are exceptions. If this is generally true, the interpreter or preacher should pay attention to moments when the plot slows down or where extensive dialogue is inserted. When a fast-moving plot slows down, something is happening that the author wants the hearer to catch his or her breath, listen carefully to, and ponder. The hearer should be on the alert for these moments of surprise. Narrative authors (and therefore narrative preachers) will play off this element of surprise in a plot. Good stories keep an audience on the edge of their seat.

Character

The literary element of character presents itself in two different ways. First, the hearer is meant to *identify* with characters in a story. Long notes,

---

[23] The works of Robert Alter and Leland Ryken have already been mentioned as eminently helpful.

[24] Arthurs, *Preaching with Variety*, 68.

[25] As my kids say, "Spoiler Alert! God intervenes."

[26] Throughout the Old Testament, the listener wonders whether Israel will ever have a truly righteous king, an eternal priest, or a faithful prophet. This is, of course, resolved in the person and work of Jesus.

[27] Greidanus, *The Modern Preacher and the Ancient Text*, 205.

"When we identify with a character in a story, whatever happens to that character happens to us at the level of imagination."[28] The hearer is meant to experience and feel the situation, tension, and concerns of the characters in a story. Second, the hearer should notice the *development* of the characters throughout both small and extended stories. According to Lovejoy, "Unlike modern writers, biblical writers say surprisingly little about their characters' motives and psychological states."[29] This can frustrate a modern, Western reader, and the temptation exists to insert personal experiences, motivations, and feelings into the characters of a biblical narrative (e.g., "Isaac must have been angry with his dad"). While a sense of wonder and contemplation is certainly justified when hearing a story, caution should be taken not to add one's own projections to inspired Scripture.

Narrative literature creates a sense of identification for the hearer. Arthurs states that "Narrative, like all art, universalizes particular experience. Characters carry a freight of meaning larger than themselves."[30] Characters often represent something more than themselves. Moses intervenes on behalf of the people. David serves as a representative king who foreshadows a future King from his line. Job's suffering stands in the place of the hearer's suffering, and his questions become our questions.[31] While the hearer may find a sense of identification with individual characters and situations, the greater identification may be toward the fulfillment of the Scriptures, Jesus Christ.

Dialogue

A third element of biblical narrative is dialogue. Narrative is not just descriptive action. Characters speak and think, and a significant portion of the Bible's text is used to convey those words or thoughts. Alter even goes so far as to claim that "everything in biblical narrative ultimately gravitates toward dialogue."[32] Quite often those surprising moments of the narrative

---

[28] Long, *Preaching and the Literary Forms of the Bible*, 75.

[29] Lovejoy, "Shaping Sermons by the Literary Form of the Text," in Corley, Lemke, and Lovejoy, *Biblical Hermeneutics*, 328.

[30] Arthurs, *Preaching with Variety*, 73.

[31] Ultimately, the Bible's Christ-centered answer to these questions should become our answer.

[32] Robert Alter, *The Art of Biblical Narrative* (New York: Basic, 1981), 180, quoted in Greidanus, *The Modern Preacher and the Ancient Text*, 201. Note, for instance, the simple dialogue spoken by the Roman centurion after the death of Christ in the gospel of Mark: "Truly this was the son of God" (15:39). The dialogue is the climax of the story and reveals a conclusion from the described events.

slowing down are found in dialogue, which comprises "nearly fifty percent of the biblical narrative."[33]

Dialogue does not stop the movement or plot of a story. Quite often dialogue includes or enhances tension, progression, conflict, and resolution: "the quoted word carries the story's freight of meaning, yet the dialogue is compressed and crafted so that every word tells."[34] For a highly relational oral culture, examining and highlighting dialogue between characters is deeply important and meaningful.

Repetition

The fourth element of narrative is repetition, which will be considered more fully in our discussion of poetry. Narratives also repeat words, phrases, places, motifs, and themes both to emphasize a point ("Simon, do you love me?") or to serve as a rhetorical cue for the reader. While repetition is used most often to emphasize or give importance to a part of the story, at times the hearer-reader will be surprised that expected repetition does not occur. This cue as well should cause the hearer-reader to slow down, consider the difference between expectation and reality, and understand the significance of that moment.

Imagination

A fifth element is imagination. Stories (whether true history or mythological fables) are told so that the hearer enters the narrative emotionally and mentally. This has already been somewhat explored earlier with regard to tension and character identification, but it is worth reemphasizing that stories are meant to, in some part, be relived in the listening experience of the hearer. Stories were meant to be felt. Biblical stories at times will add descriptive detail for the sake of coloring in the story so the hearer can imagine in a fuller sense. Rahab's scarlet cord (Josh. 2:18) is likely just a literary detail to help the hearer imagine the scene with a (literal) splash of color. It does not have to be a theologically obscure precursor to the blood of Christ. Stories were meant to be "re-lived" by those listening.

Providence

A sixth element of narrative literature is more theological in nature. Throughout the narratives of Scripture, God's providence is portrayed. Even

---

[33] Arthurs, *Preaching with Variety*, 73.
[34] Arthurs, *Preaching with Variety*, 73.

in scenes where God, in a particular frame, is not one of the "characters" or is not represented by one of the characters, the scene as a whole will undoubtedly reveal the presence of God, for the human characters act out the scene against the backdrop of God's promises, God's enabling power, God's demands, and God's providence.[35]

Whether the situation for the humans in the narrative may be comfortable or difficult, whether there is suffering or prosperity, victory or defeat, God is always seen as providential. The sovereign and triune God is the main character in the entire biblical narrative and his providential hand is always directing.

> Biblical writers were historically oriented, but—and this is a crucial exception—they did not have a notion of history as "one damned thing after another." They saw history as grounded in the control and providence of God; therefore, history could not be told as a random series of disconnected events.[36]

The Bible is a connected story ultimately culminating in the triumph of Jesus.

Heroic Stories?

One final element is related to the priority of God's providence. It is often tempting to portray many biblical narratives purely as inspirational or exemplary heroic stories. However, the hero of each individual story and the hero of the grand story is the providential and merciful God. When human characters triumph, it is the Lord's hand that triumphs. When human characters suffer, the Lord is not absent but is redeeming that suffering for his glory and the good of his people. Biblical narratives are stories of the greater glory of God and not simply the heroism of its deeply flawed and sinful human characters.

This sampling of some of the elements of biblical narrative shows that faithfully preaching a biblical narrative means remaining faithful at least to the spirit or intention of the writing and this includes retaining—at least in part—the mode of the text's delivery. Narratives should be preached narratively.[37] A sermon on a biblical story should at least capture the sense of the plot and tension of the story throughout the entire sermon. The preacher should not stray far from a story-like feel.

---

[35] Greidanus, *The Modern Preacher and the Ancient Text*, 199.

[36] Long, *Preaching and the Literary Forms of the Bible*, 68.

[37] I have found Calvin Miller's *Preaching: The Art of Narrative Exposition* (Grand Rapids: Baker, 2006) to be the most helpful resource on this task. Chapter 4 of my dissertation, "The Narrative Expository Sermon: Bringing Expository Preaching into Oral Learner Cultures" gives more explanation of narrative exposition.

This approach of narrative preaching should be undertaken with care and wisdom. The charge Paul gives Timothy is to "preach the word" (2 Tim. 4:1). That word is often contained within a narrative. A faithful sermon from these texts will retain much of the feel and form of the original story.

Expository Preaching among Oral Learners from a Poetic Text

Approximately a third of the Bible is poetic in form. This includes, of course, the Psalms, but also much of Old Testament prophecy, various songs and poems set within narrative books, and even poems within some New Testament didactic letters or the Gospels. When preaching biblical poetry, Western preachers are tempted to quickly leave the genre behind and explain and propositionalize the poem. Poems, however, are not didactic explanations. To use Long's excellent definition, "Psalms are poetic liturgical prayers."[38] By very nature, they are meant to be sung, and ideally sung corporately. This creates trepidation for the preacher trained to simply explain and apply the text through a monologue.[39] Long considers this and states, "The reluctance to employ a literary form intended for one purpose as the basis for another activity (here, musical prayer as the basis for preaching) indicates both a recognition that psalms possess special literary and functional qualities and a respect for those qualities."[40]

If poetry, however unfamiliar to Western preachers, is to be preached faithfully, attention must be given to some of the critical elements of biblical poetry. We will explore six elements of biblical poetry, the understanding and utilization of which will help the faithful preacher deliver a faithful sermon from the poetic passages for both oral and literate audiences.

Musical

First, poems (and the Psalms in particular) are meant to be sung within the congregation of God's people, even though the written Scriptures we have today do not have musical notation or chord charts.[41] The Bible as it stands

---

[38] Long, *Preaching and the Literary Forms of the Bible*, 44.

[39] Many (if not most) of us are lousy singers.

[40] Long, *Preaching and the Literary Forms of the Bible*, 44.

[41] The Reformed tradition has a great tradition of psalm-singing and other modern artists are continuity this legacy. Listen, for instance, to Shane & Shane's album *Psalms* (Inpop, 2002) or Sovereign Grace Music's *Psalms* (Sovereign Grace Music, 2008) for excellent examples of musical recordings of various psalms. Multiple contemporary artists are working to put the entire Psalter to music at The Psalms Project (https://thepsalmsproject.com, accessed 14 September 2023). Using the work of artists like these in corporate worship is highly recommended as a way to honor the form in which biblical poetry was originally intended to

today is a written page with plain text, and subsequently poetry is often read much like prose. The original score, while hinted at in many superscriptions, has been lost to antiquity. Poetic music, however, naturally conveys a mood and can be happy, sad, somber, celebratory, or a myriad of other emotions. This was the original—and should be the ongoing—intention of biblical poetry.[42]

Arthurs reminds us that "music is very powerful rhetorically and…the biblical poets intended their poems to be accompanied by music."[43] Oral cultures, like those of the Old and New Testaments, would have had a large tradition of song.[44]

Even though the actual melodies cannot be replicated, the mood can still be discerned from the text of the psalm itself. The psalms contain moods and tones that match a significant range of the emotions of the human experience. From joy to sorrow, peace to anger, fear to gratitude, there is almost always "a psalm for that."[45] The preacher of the psalms should seek to discern the mood through reading, listening, studying, and meditating on the text of the psalm. As a sermon is delivered, the overall mood of the sermon should faithfully match the mood and tone of the psalm. If it is a psalm of lament,

be utilized. When preaching on a particular psalm, ideally that song should be corporately sung before, during, or after the sermon. The tradition of singing the Psalter runs deep throughout Christian history, from Jewish synagogues to the early church to the Protestant Reformation and in contemporary worship music, songs have been sung corporately. Christopher Ash provides an excellent starting point for the church leader seeking to incorporate psalm singing into their worship gathering (Christopher Ash, "Be Adventurous: Sing the Psalms," The Gospel Coalition, June 7, 2020, https://www.thegospelcoalition.org/article/sing-psalms/).

[42] As I write this, my Spotify app is playing a lively little ditty called "The Sailor's Bonnet" by a band called The Gloaming. As the fiddle quickly dances through a series of happy notes, my own mood has begun to match the cheerful tone of the song ("The Sailor's Bonnet," Spotify, track 6 on The Gloaming, *The Gloaming*, Brassland, 2013).

[43] Arthurs, *Preaching with Variety*, 57.

[44] See Box, *Don't Throw the Book at Them*, 29. Christopher Ash provides an eminently helpful discussion regarding Jesus praying the Psalms: "Jesus is the great singer of the Psalms; it is His voice we hear praying, lamenting, teaching, and praising. The Psalms are Christian Scripture." Christopher Ash, *Teaching Psalms. Volume One: From Text to Message* (Ross-shire, Scotland: Christian Focus, 2017), 38. Tim Keller states, "The psalms were Jesus's songbook. The hymn that Jesus sang at the Passover meal (Matthew 26:30; Mark 14:26) would have been the Great Hallel, Psalms 113–118. Indeed, there is every reason to assume that Jesus would have sung all the psalms, constantly, throughout his life, so that he knew them by heart. It is the book of the Bible that he quotes more than any other." Tim Keller, *The Songs of Jesus: A Year of Daily Devotions in the Psalms* (New York: Viking, 2015), ix.

[45] While training a group of Pakistani church leaders, I discovered that they had a great deal of the psalms committed to memory via song. Questioning them, I inquired if they could sing a psalm if I gave any number between 1 and 150. In the end, they could sing any of the 150 psalms on cue. This sort of knowledge of the psalms *through* song is not uncommon among oral learners.

preach (and sing) with a tone of sorrow and even grief. If it is a psalm of thanksgiving, preach (and sing) with a tone of joy and a smile on your face! Oral learners learn through song. It is no coincidence that the Bible is filled with songs.

Imagery

Contained within the text of their songs, the psalmists employ frequent imagery. Shields, towers, trees, rocks, pits, green pastures, still waters, paths, valleys of death, rods, a staff, tables, oil, and cups symbolically represent a truth about God, his ways, his covenant, and life with him.[46] A majority of the time, the psalm does not even attempt to explain or define the symbolic imagery, leaving the poetic imagery to stand alone. It is left to the imagination and contemplation of the listener. As Long states, "Psalms operate at the level of the imagination."[47]

In order to use these poetic images to stir the imagination, psalms employ literary techniques like metaphor and simile. Literary critic and Bible scholar Leland Ryken explains these techniques this way:

> Metaphor and simile place immense demands on a reader. They require far more activity than a direct propositional statement. Metaphor and simile first demand that we take the time to let the literal situation sink in. Then we must make a transfer of meaning(s) to the topic or experience the poem is talking about.[48]

Arthurs describes poetry's function as "using concrete nouns and verbs to create a picture of abstract ideas."[49] According to W. Jay Moon, oral learners "learn best when teaching is connected to real events, people, and struggles of life."[50]

---

[46] An incredibly valuable resource when exploring poetic imagery in Scripture is Leland Ryken, James C. Wilhoit, and Tremper Longman III, eds., Dictionary *of Biblical Imagery* (Downers Grove, IL: IVP Academic, 1998). This work not only wrestles with the intended meaning of an image but traces the use of a symbolic image throughout the entirety of the Scriptures.

[47] Long, *Preaching and the Literary Forms of the Bible*, 47. While training a group of Pakistani pastors to understand and communicate biblical poetry, my excellent and enthusiastic interpreter kept accidentally using the word "imagination" instead of "image" or "imagery." As time went on, I grew to appreciate the beautiful (and completely understandable) mistake. Imagery is meant to make the listener imagine things. In the end his (providential?) mistake helped the class understand poetic imagery more fully.

[48] Leland Ryken, *How to Read the Bible as Literature...and Get More Out of It* (Grand Rapids: Zondervan Academic, 1985), 95.

[49] Arthurs, *Preaching with Variety*, 46.

[50] Moon, "Teaching Oral Learners," 146.

The learning process of oral learners and the process of understanding the meaning of a poetic image seem to be at odds. Imagery is often concrete. A shield (like that referenced in Ps. 3:3) is a real, understandable thing. The understanding of a literal shield is rarely the issue. The problem is that the concept of a shield needed to be moved to an abstraction for meaning to be transferred as an attribute of God. The "transfer of meaning(s)" is what takes significant time and mental energy, but perhaps that is part of the poet's intention in using symbolic images. Arthurs states that images push toward three rhetorical effects. Imagery (1) "sparks the imagination," (2) "foster[s] identification," and (3) "aid[s] memory."[51]

Poems are not meant to be *quickly* read, understood, and applied. They are meant to stick with the listener, even more so when set to music. They are meant to be contemplated, chewed on, mulled over, repeated, and ultimately internalized. For this reason, Arthurs suggests that preachers use literal, physical images when possible and appropriate. Bring a lamp or a basket or a shield with you into the pulpit.[52] That image will stick with readers. Laurence Perrine states that "[poetry's] purpose is not to soothe and relax, but to arouse and awake, to shock into life, to make one more alive."[53] Imagery wakes people up.

Repetition

Repetition is found in many genres and used in many ways throughout the Scriptures. Hebrew scholars use the term parallelism to describe a central feature of Hebrew poetry. A line is stated, then restated in a slightly new way to highlight a new image or make a comparison, or a contrasting line is used to feature a difference.[54] David opens the third Psalm in such a manner:

O Lord, how many are my foes!
    Many are rising against me;
many are saying of my soul,
    there is no salvation for him in God. (Ps. 3:1-2)

---

[51] Arthurs, *Preaching with Variety*, 46–47

[52] Use wisdom and be cautious if preaching on Prov. 28:15: "Like a roaring lion or a charging bear is a wicked ruler over a poor people." Sometimes a picture is worth a thousand bears.

[53] Laurence Perrine, *Sound and Sense: An Introduction to Poetry* (New York: Harcourt, Brace, Jovanovich, 1977), 3-4, quoted in Long, *Preaching and the Literary Forms of the Bible*, 45.

[54] Much more could be said and explored regarding the intricacies of parallelism in Hebrew poetry, but that is beyond the scope and purpose of this paper. Any decent commentary on Psalms or introduction to the Old Testament will have an extensive discussion of this aspect of Hebrew poetry.

The first two lines are incredibly similar while the third and fourth lines together say a similar idea, but with more information. The repetition is striking...and often frustrating to Western readers.

Repetition is not just found in the literary technique of parallelism. Consider the refrain at the end of each verse in Psalm 136: "for his steadfast love endures forever." Why would the psalmist repeat this a total of twenty-six times in this psalm alone? Arthurs is once again helpful, stating that "[i]f you want the congregation to slow down, meditate, ponder, and turn the prism this way and that, try doing what the Bible does; use parallelism."[55]

Hebrew poetry is unashamedly repetitive. While Western readers might grow weary at this technique, oral learners expect and deeply appreciate repetition. In a culture where words are not preserved on a printed page or digitally archived, the hearers must remember the spoken words in order to retain the thoughts and ideas expressed. When preaching biblical poetry—or any text for that matter—among oral learners, do not be afraid to repeat ideas, themes, sentences, and words to an extent that often seems unnecessary for Western preachers.

Collective Use

When reading or studying biblical poetry, remember that the psalms were written to be sung *collectively* as God's people gathered to worship. These are not texts designed for a solo reader. Many of the psalms use a header to instruct a musician on the melody or instrument arrangement. Paul admonished the first-century church with these words: "Let the word of Christ dwell in you richly, teaching and admonishing one another with all wisdom, singing psalms and hymns and spiritual songs, with thanksgiving in your hearts to God" (Col. 3:16). In his letter to the Ephesian church (a collective group, not an individual), he writes, "be filled with the Spirit, addressing one another in psalms and hymns and spiritual songs, singing and making melody to the Lord in your heart" (Eph. 5:18b–19).

The psalms were meant to be sung, but *they were meant to be sung to each other within the local church.* Of course, there is benefit in reading them alone (preferably aloud), but they serve as a songbook for the worship of God's people. The psalms are indeed poetry and the elements of Hebrew poetry need to be considered when in the psalms, but they were poems meant to be sung. The psalms are poetic songs.

---

[55] Arthurs, *Preaching with Variety*, 54.

Expository Preaching among Oral Learners from a Propositional,[56] Relational[57] Letter

The bulk of the New Testament books are letters from the apostles to churches, groups of churches, or individuals. Once again, Arthurs's definition is particularly helpful: "An epistle is a letter designed for wide circulation that addresses current issues and revives personal relationship."[58] Notice that while a biblical letter does have a specific recipient like the Galatians or Titus, they were designed for wider circulation. Paul instructed the Colossian church to have the letter addressed to them in their situation sent down the road to Laodicea and read in that church. A letter to the Laodiceans, which has been lost to antiquity, was supposed to come to the Colossians and be read in their church (see Col. 4:16). Arthurs's definition also points out the personal relationship behind each of the biblical letters. The letters served to connect people who were geographically separated and revive or maintain a personal relationship. In Arthurs's words, "Epistles substitute for the personal presence of the author...Through epistles, the apostles reached out to touch the fledgling church."[59]

Relational (or the Narrative Context)

Bearing that critical aspect of New Testament letters in mind, the first element of this literary genre to highlight is its relational nature. James Cox points out that "a vibrant story lies just beneath the surface of many an epistle."[60] I would add that in those epistles where the "vibrant story" is not "just beneath the surface," it is lurking in the depths and can be found with a bit more thought and study. At some level, each biblical letter is "narratival." While it may not be a story in and of itself, it is set in the context of a story within the first century church.

In the preaching of the New Testament letters, it seems that the pulpit has become dominated by the proposition. There is merit and good reason for this since the letters contain many propositional statements. Paul, Peter,

---

[56] Steffen's term is "thought-organized" in "A Narrative Approach," 88.

[57] I realize there is a sense of overcomplexity in the heading of this section. "Propositional" as well as Steffen's term "thought-organized" highlight the logical, linear nature of the letters but is then contrasted with the deep relational nature of letters, originating from a real, historical person (even if unnamed) and intended for real, historical people. This relational characteristic is easily lost in studying the letters. In preaching among oral learners, this relationality is critical to retain. Hence the complex heading.

[58] Arthurs, *Preaching with Variety*, 152

[59] Arthurs, *Preaching with Variety*, 153.

[60] James Cox, *Preaching* (San Francisco: Harper & Row, 1985), 155, quoted in Greidanus, *The Modern Preacher and the Ancient Text*, 335.

John, and James do indeed utilize an abundance of propositional statements. However, there is also narrative text embedded in some letters, along with other genres. Paul will burst out in exclamatory and poetic worship from time to time, but the content of the letters is overwhelmingly filled with propositional statements.

Furthermore, those statements are not spoken into a non-relational void where biblical scholars and theologians then generalize and summarize them. They are not headings in a volume of systematic theology. They are set in the narrative context of a vibrant story. Paul has likely founded that church, prays for it, knows many of its people by name, and longs to be with his friends. In some cases, we are told the "vibrant story." The Corinthians are facing all sorts of difficult situations and need apostolic wisdom. The Philippian church faces disunity. Euodia and Syntyche are not getting along.[61] They need apostolic instruction. Greidanus states, "Listening to a letter without being aware of its historical situation has been likened to hearing only one side of a telephone conversation."[62] The relationship or historical situation (the "story" of a letter) is critical in understanding and communicating New Testament epistles.

Arthurs's caution is helpful here: "Remembering that the epistles address specific occasions will preserve us from theological myopia, that is building a system on a portion of the epistles' rich doctrine or even on a single metaphor."[63] He goes on to say, "We should think of Paul and the other letter writers as practical, not systematic theologians. Their theology is…theology at the service of particular needs."[64] In other words, the apostolic writers wrote a *relational theology* in their letters.[65] The "story" of this relationship needs to permeate any proposition in the preaching. This practical and relational theological understanding brings a didactic letter into a narrative context. While the letters are not written stories,[66] they are set within a relational story and the story of the establishment and expansion of the early church. If the narrative context is not easily discerned within the letter itself,

---

[61] See Phil. 4:2. This difficult situation of disunity can be discerned by reading not just this verse but the entire letter.

[62] Greidanus, *The Modern Preacher and the Ancient Text*, 327.

[63] Arthurs, *Preaching with Variety*, 155.

[64] Arthurs, *Preaching with Variety*, 155.

[65] My use of "relational theology" is not to be confused with a different sort of relational theology advocated by open theists. My use of the word "relational" describes the author-recipient relationship. For an excellent and doctrinally orthodox understanding of the relationship between God and his people, see J. Scott Duvall and J. Daniel Hays, *God's Relational Presence: The Cohesive Center of Biblical Theology* (Grand Rapids: Baker Academic, 2019).

[66] Of course, there are exceptions like the first chapter of Galatians or the letter to Philemon.

searching the book of Acts may fill out more of the relational picture and help the preacher see the occasion for this letter. Even in the letters, expository preaching can—and I am arguing, *absolutely should*—incorporate narrative while remaining faithful to the original intent and form of the letter. Ignoring the relational situation, which may be between author and hearer, between hearers, or between God and his people, removes a critical element of the biblical letter. It removes an aspect critically important in communicating among oral learners.

The Flow of an Argument

The authors of biblical letters made propositional statements. These statements string together to build an argument, seeking to convince an audience of a truth or persuade them to action. In order to discern those statements and arguments, it can be helpful to study the grammar, syntax, and the definition of words. The knowledge and study of New Testament Greek can aid in following the flow of Paul's argument. However, oral learners rarely have access to a translation reliable enough to embark on this sort of detailed and nuanced exegetical study.[67] Many oral cultures have the Scriptures translated into their language, but the translation work is often at the level of dynamic equivalence (at best). In fact, many languages only developed a written language when the process of Bible translation began. Even if the translation is accurate, oral cultures do not have a history of studying written literature. The Bible might be the only book translated into their language. Therefore, the preacher or trainer of preachers needs to be cautious as individual words and grammar are studied. Those words and grammatical sense are not always carried over as the Bible is translated into the languages of oral cultures.

Instead of individual words, consider studying the text in terms of units of thought and tracing the flow of a letter's argument through larger blocks of

---

[67] A few years ago, while teaching in rural northern Uganda among a group of Acholi speakers, our Bibles were opened to 2 Tim. 3:16 as we began to think about the nature of God's written Word. One instructor asked the class, "Who breathed out the Scriptures?" The answer, of course, from the text is clearly: "All Scripture is breathed out by God." However, our class, in increasingly loud and unified voices kept saying, "The Spirit breathed out Scripture." This may be theologically true, but it is not what the text says. So, we assumed that the group was making a theological conclusion. Pressing in on what the text *actually* said on the page, the students dug in and kept answering with "the Spirit." Come to find out, their printed Acholi pages actually had something akin to "All Scripture is breathed out by God's Spirit" written on them. This is but one anecdotal example of the frustration when specific and detailed language analysis is attempted within cultures who have an oral learning tradition and a less-than-fully accurate translation of the Bible.

text.[68] Look for narrative-like tension in text. Galatians 3:1–3 provides a clear example of this narrative-like tension within a didactic letter when Paul writes:

> O foolish Galatians! Who has bewitched you? It was before your eyes that Jesus Christ was publicly portrayed as crucified. Let me ask you only this: Did you receive the Spirit by works of the law or by hearing with faith? Are you so foolish? Having begun by the Spirit, are you now being perfected by the flesh?

While parsing words may be impossible, seeing and following a few sentences is more of a reasonable expectation. In the passage above, following those units of thought shows a clear narrative-like tension. The listener is asking, "How will this resolve?" When the connection between units of thought is seen, a sort of plot can be discovered in a didactic letter. An initial situation can be discerned, a problem introduced, tension (further description of the problem) grows, a solution is proffered, and resolution is achieved at the letter's end. Incorporating this sort of "narratival" plot in a sermon on the New Testament brings story back into the thought-organized, relational letter. As we have seen, story is an element of communication deeply helpful in communicating among oral cultures.[69]

Repetition

Poetry is not the only biblical genre to capitalize on repetition, whether it is individual words, themes, or phrases. A classic example is 2 Corinthians 1:3–7 (emphasis added):

> Blessed be the God and Father of our Lord Jesus Christ, the Father of mercies and God of all *comfort*, who *comforts* us in all our affliction, so that we may be able to *comfort* those who are in any affliction, with the *comfort* with which we ourselves are *comforted* by God. For as we share

---

[68] Bible versions like the New International Version translate the original language using an approach of "dynamic equivalence." Seeking to use modern language and avoid the "woodenness" of word-for-word translations, dynamic equivalence strives for readability. At times, this will result in a translation methodology that resembles what is argued for here, capturing blocks of text larger than individual words. Interestingly, most translations that are received well by oral audiences are translated via dynamic equivalence.

[69] Used carefully, Eugene Lowry's *The Homiletical Plot* can provide a schematic for developing a narrative-like flow out of a didactic letter. Lowry argues for constructing the sermon in a narrative form using a sermonic "plot." No matter the text being exposited, a sermon can thus be a "story." To develop this, Lowry suggests five stages: (1) upsetting the equilibrium, (2) analyzing the discrepancy, (3) disclosing the clue to resolution, (4) experiencing the gospel, and (5) anticipating the consequences. (Lowry, "Homiletical Plot," 26).

abundantly in Christ's sufferings, so through Christ we share abundantly in *comfort* too. If we are afflicted, it is for your *comfort* and salvation; and if we are *comforted*, it is for your *comfort*, which you experience when you patiently endure the same sufferings that we suffer. Our hope for you is unshaken, for we know that as you share in our sufferings, you will also share in our *comfort.*

It is almost impossible not to notice the repetition of the word "comfort," especially if the passage is read aloud. The apostle uses the term nine times. Notice also that other words are repeated: "Christ," "abundantly," "afflicted/affliction," and "suffering," among others. Since the use of repetition was covered when examining poetry, significant time and space will not be spent here investigating it. Suffice it to say that the preacher of New Testament letters should be ready to repeat himself. Paul, Peter, James, John, and the author of Hebrews all utilized repetition.

Audible and Complete

Scripture was originally meant to be experienced through a (usually public) oral reading. The words of Scripture, whether Old Testament law or New Testament letters, were intended to be experienced by oral learners. They were meant to be experienced audibly. They were meant to be heard.[70] Therefore, the preacher needs to read the Scriptures clearly and faithfully.[71]

Additionally, the New Testament letters are a single, complete unit. From the opening greeting to the conclusion, the letters have a flow to their argument that is complete and unified. For this reason, the public, audible reading of the complete text of New Testament letters should not be avoided in churches, especially those with oral learners. Paul expected first-century churches to read his letters publicly and audibly among the worshiping community. So too should we.[72]

---

[70] Of course, the Scriptures were written down. "And we are writing these things so that our joy may be complete" (1 Jn. 1:4). I would argue that John and the other biblical authors wrote "these things" down so that they could be read and heard.

[71] During the lockdowns necessitated by the Covid-19 pandemic in 2020, a group of men from our church met via video to read Scripture together. We took turns reading through and eventually read most of the New Testament letters to each other, each in a single setting. The effect was palpable and further convinced me of the necessity of verbal, audible New Testament reading.

[72] There are other genres not covered in this paper. Prophecy is the most noticeable omission, but much of prophecy is poetic or narrative. Other genres like apocalypse parables, proverbs, law, or even genealogy are less frequent in the pages of Scripture. A good introduction to the New Testament or Old Testament will provide details about the genres which are not covered here. For an Old Testament introduction, see Tremper Longman III and

Summary

Preaching (and the training of preachers) in an oral context must include an understanding of the stylistic, rhetorical differences of the literary genres of Scripture. This is necessary because the Bible—in its varied forms—was written to be read aloud to and with oral learners. Retaining some of this stylistic form in the sermon will allow the preacher to communicate the truths of Scripture more effectively among oral learning congregations.

The Bible is filled with diverse forms of literature. Understanding how these forms work and, in particular, how they work within an oral learning culture, allows the literary forms of the Bible to serve as a guide for a *narrative* expository sermon.

Bibliography

Ajibade, Ezekiel A. *Expository Preaching in Africa: Engaging Orality for Effective Proclamation.* Plateau State, Nigeria: Hippo Books, 2021.

Alter, Robert. *The Art of Biblical Narrative.* Revised & expanded edition. New York: Basic, 2011.

———. *The Art of Biblical Poetry.* Revised & expanded edition. New York: Basic, 2011.

Arthurs, Jeffrey D. *Preaching with Variety: How to Re-Create the Dynamics of Biblical Genres.* Grand Rapids, Kregel: 2007.

———. *Devote Yourself to the Public Reading of Scripture: The Transforming Power of the Well-Spoken Word.* Grand Rapids: Kregel, 2012.

Box, Harry. *Don't Throw the Book at Them: Communicating the Christian Message to People Who Don't Read.* Pasadena, CA: William Carey Library, 2014.

Brown, Rick. "Communicating God's Message in an Oral Culture." *International Journal of Frontier Missiology* 21.3 (2004): 122–28.

Corley, Bruce, Steve Lemke, and Grant Lovejoy, eds. *Biblical Hermeneutics: A Comprehensive Introduction to Interpreting Scripture.* Nashville: Broadman & Holman, 1996.

Raymond B. Dillard, *An Introduction to the Old Testament*, 2nd ed. (Grand Rapids: Zondervan Academic, 2006). D. A. Carson and Douglas Moo, *An Introduction to the New Testament*, 2nd ed. (Grand Rapids: Zondervan Academic, 2005) serves as a helpful tool for exploring New Testament genres.

Craddock, Fred B. *Preaching*. 25th anniversary ed. Nashville: Abingdon, 1985.

———. *As One without Authority*. St. Louis: Chalice, 2011.

Dempster, Stephen G. *Dominion and Dynasty: A Theology of the Hebrew Bible*. New Studies in Biblical Theology 15 (Downers Grove: IVP Academic, 2003).

Graves, Mike. *The Sermon as Symphony: Preaching the Literary Forms of the New Testament*. Valley Forge, PA: Judson Press, 1997.

Greidanus, Sidney. *The Modern Preacher and the Ancient Text: Interpreting and Preaching Biblical Literature*. Grand Rapids: Eerdmans, 1998.

Harvey, John D. *Listening to the Text: Oral Patterning in Paul's Letters*. Grand Rapids: Baker, 1998.

———. "Orality and Its Implications for Biblical Studies: Recapturing an Ancient Paradigm." *Journal of the Evangelical Theological Society* 45 (2002): 99–109.

Lewis, C. S. *Reflections on the Psalms*. New York: HarperCollins, 1958.

Long, Thomas G. *Preaching and the Literary Forms of the Bible*. Philadelphia: Fortress, 1989.

Lovejoy, Grant. "'But I Did Such Good Exposition': Literate Preachers Confront Orality." *Journal of the Evangelical Homiletics Society* 1.1 (2001): 22–32.

Lowry, Eugene L. *The Homiletical Plot: The Sermon as Narrative Art Form*. Exp. ed. Louisville: Westminster John Knox, 2001.

Miller, Calvin. *Preaching: The Art of Narrative Exposition*. Grand Rapids: Baker, 2006.

Moon, W. Jay. "Understanding Oral Learners." *Teaching Theology and Religion* 15.1 (2012): 29–39.

———. "Fad or Renaissance? Misconceptions of the Orality Movement." *International Bulletin of Mission Research* 40.1 (2016): 6–21.

Ong, Walter J. *Orality and Literacy*. 30th anniversary ed. New York: Routledge, 1982.

Peterson, Eugene H. *Eat This Book: A Conversation in the Art of Spiritual Reading*. Grand Rapids: Eerdmans, 2006.

Ryken, Leland. *How to Read the Bible as Literature...and Get More Out of It.* Grand Rapids: Zondervan Academic, 1985.

———. *Words of Delight: A Literary Introduction to the Bible.* Grand Rapids: Baker Academic, 1993.

———. *Words of Life: A Literary Introduction to the New Testament.* Eugene: Wipf & Stock, 2019.

Ryken, Leland, James C. Wilhoit, and Tremper Longman III. *Dictionary of Biblical Imagery.* Downers Grove: IVP Academic, 1998.

Ryken, Leland and Tremper Longman III. *A Complete Literary Guide to the Bible.* Grand Rapids: Zondervan Academic, 2010.

Sailhamer, John H. *The Pentateuch as Narrative: A Biblical-Theological Commentary.* Library of Biblical Interpretation. Grand Rapids: Zondervan Academic, 1992.

Steffen, Tom. "A Narrative Approach to Communicating the Bible, Parts 1 & 2." *Christian Education Journal* 14.3 (1992): 86–109.

Steffen, Tom and William Bjoraker. *The Return of Oral Hermeneutics: As Good Today as It Was for the Hebrew Bible and First-century Christianity.* Eugene: Wipf & Stock, 2020.

Walton, John H. and D. Brent Sandy. *The Lost World of Scripture: Ancient Literary Culture and Biblical Authority.* Downers Grove: IVP Academic, 2013.

Wardlaw, Don M., ed. *Preaching Biblically: Creating Sermons in the Shape of Scripture.* Philadelphia: Westminster, 1983.

Woodroof, Tim. *A Distant Presence: The Story Behind Paul's Letter to the Philippians.* Narrative Commentary Series. Colorado Springs: NavPress, 2001.

Chapter 13: A Relational Approach to Teaching and Training Oral Learners

David Crim

Abstract

The Philippines, like other majority-world cultures, has a rich oral tradition. And, despite a Western influence upon education (dating back to the early 1900s) and a high literacy, orality is still a sub-surface influence in the culture. Yet, the education system of the Philippines has been highly influenced by the country's colonial history. The most important and lasting contributions on education came during America's occupation of the country, which began in 1898. It was during that period that English was introduced as the primary language of instruction and a system of public education was first established—a system modeled after the United States school system and administered by the newly established Department of Instruction. Though Western educators had good intentions, they brought with them a Western approach to learning and teaching that does not connect with the way Filipinos, and most other Asian cultures receive, process, and communicate information. Considering orality, what is the most natural way to engage oral learners in transformational learning that equips them to relate the Scriptures to their lives and to their culture? What is the impact of orality upon learning environments, learner preferences, and teaching strategies? What can we learn from extant literature of the relationships between orality and hermeneutics? What recent learning theories in transformative education can be applied to theological education in an oral context? This chapter, drawn from the author's research in the Philippines, proposes interventions and teaching-learning strategies that will form a relational approach to education and training that best suit oral-preference learners.

Introduction

The Philippines has a rich oral tradition. However, the country's colonial history and modern Western influence (dating back to the early 1900s) has highly influenced the education system of the Philippines. The most important and lasting contributions to education came during America's occupation of the country, which began in 1898. During that period, English was introduced as the primary language of instruction, and a public education system was first established—modeled after the United States school system and administered by the newly established Department of Instruction. Though Western educators had good intentions, they brought an approach to learning and teaching that does not connect with how Filipinos and most other Asians learn. Recent research has revealed that after almost 100 years of evangelicalism in the Philippines, there are critical social issues that arouse questions regarding the influence of evangelical Christianity. Some scholars suggest that a Western approach to teaching and training in the Philippines has not adequately prepared pastors, church planters, and leaders to equip the church.[1]

My research pursued answers to such questions as: What is the most natural way of learning to engage Filipino oral learners in transformational learning that equips them to relate the Scriptures to their lives and their culture? What is the present learning context in education in the Philippines? How does orality impact learning environments, learner preferences, and teaching strategies? What can we learn from extant literature on the relationships between orality and hermeneutics? What recent learning theories in transformative education can be applied to theological education in an oral context? How can we thoroughly engage today's Filipinos in learning so that Filipino Christianity influences culture?

Answering these critical questions served as a guide to mixed-method research designed to pursue a needed shift to an oral paradigm for theological education, church-based discipleship, and missional training. Synthesizing and correlating findings from an integrated literature review in hermeneutics, orality, and education with two case studies and a focus group, the research proposed interventions that connect teachers to Filipino students' learning and classroom preferences. The research theorized that these interventions and teaching strategies will facilitate a more appropriate learning environment that engages Filipino students (and others with an oral learning preference) in a transformative theological education.

This chapter aims to report the findings of my grounded theory research discovered by analyzing participant responses in a focus group. The focus group consisted of randomly selected university and seminary graduates and students in the Philippines. A recent study among Bachelor of Science students in Electronics and Information Technology at the Cagayan State University in Lasam, Philippines, served to compare and verify the analysis of the focus group responses.

---

[1] Dan. "State of the Philippine Evangelical Church Today: A Positive Response," (https://waves.ca/2011/06/14/description-of-the-evangelical-churchtoday/, 2010).

The Focus Group

The focus group was conducted among participants in an iDisciple Philippines conference event. Twelve people agreed to participate in the focus group by responding to a questionnaire. All the participants in the focus group have at least a college education. Two were enrolled in a seminary. The participants were representative of various Filipino socio-economic cultures and languages: professionals, clergy, workers, urban dwellers, provincial villagers, and from all three of the major island groups—Luzon, the Visayas, and Mindanao. Nine of the participants were females, and three were males. The ages of the participants ranged from 25 years old to 40 years old.

Eight Directed, Open-Ended Statements

The focus group engaged the participants in responding to eight directed statements that sought to glean from their classroom experiences the types of teaching-learning methods their professors employed and their impact on their learning. The statements sought to discover the interpersonal relationships they experienced in the classroom and between the student and the professor. The statements allowed the participants to explain the practicality of their education.

The Statements

1. Describe your favorite teacher/professor and what made them your favorite.
2. Tell us about your most enjoyable classroom or learning experience and how it impacted your life.
3. Tell us about your least favorite subject and how you think it could have been better.
4. Share with us ways one or more of your professors reached out to you to hear your ideas about how educational experiences could be improved at your school.
5. Tell us about an experience in which a professor stretched your thinking, ideas, or worldview about a concept or subject.
6. Describe ways that a professor provided learning experiences other than reading or lecture and how this enhanced your learning.
7. Tell us about an experience when you struggled with an assignment, and your professor made adjustments to fit your needs better.
8. Tell us about an exciting classroom discussion you experienced and why it was meaningful to you.

Two Questions

As a follow-up, the participants were asked two questions to understand their professors' frequency of lecture, reading, and writing use. Their responses provide a simple data baseline reflecting their professors' sensitivity to the context of the learners.

The Questions

1. As best as you can remember, how often did most of your university or seminary professors use lectures as the primary teaching method?
   ☐ all the time
   ☐ most of the time
   ☐ some of the time
   ☐ seldom
2. As best as you can remember, how much of your classwork and homework assignments in your university or seminary were primarily reading and writing?
   ☐ all the time
   ☐ most of the time
   ☐ some of the time
   ☐ seldom

Research Analysis

The data analysis used grounded theory strategies to identify categories, patterns, and themes from the participants' responses. These findings were compared to the extant literature selected for this research. In the reading and analysis of the participant responses, followed by the correlation with the literature, three categories with corresponding patterns and themes were assigned: teacher, learning, and classroom preferences.

Teacher Preferences

A Teacher Who Is Present and Engaged

Participant responses to statements 1 and 4-7 exposed the participants' preferences about a professor's character, personality, style, and manner of teaching. Without exception, all participants prefer teachers who are engaged and available. One student, in describing how his class could have been better, related three insightful observations:

- Teachers need to understand the students: what they already know and what knowledge is lacking to complete a task.

- Teachers need to provide clarification so that students understand the information and the task at hand.
- Teachers must be present for assistance, helping students to understand concepts and master them.

The Lingenfelters support the desire for an engaged teacher. They suggest that "spending time with students in social situations" will allow students to "volunteer information that will inform the teacher's planning".[2]

A Teacher Who is Professional and Planned

The word *professional* appeared several times in the focus group responses. One student applauded a professor's strict code of classroom ethics and her demand for excellence. Participants noted that a professor's knowledge of and passion for the content and subject matter is another aspect of professionalism. Their confidence in the teacher is closely related to the teacher's theoretical knowledge. This confidence is strengthened when the teacher not only demonstrates expertise but also how to apply the body of knowledge. Students want teachers to demonstrate a balance between "knowing their stuff," as one participant reported, and knowing how to communicate it in a natural and applicable way.

A Teacher Who Facilitates and Challenges

One participant describes a teacher who "clarified the lesson, was willing to re-teach if needed, and was present to facilitate the understanding of concepts in practice." Another participant wrote, "We want teachers to facilitate rather than indoctrinate." Focus group responses revealed that teachers who facilitate are much preferred over those who present a lesson and expect the students to understand it. Participants expressed a sense of de-motivation when teachers could not connect the lesson to life. Students desire to know how what is being taught relates to future studies and careers in the real world. Most participants explained a willingness to be challenged and a desire for challenge.

The sentiments of the participants echo the Lingenfelters' observations. They write, "Teachers cannot possibly teach to all the potential differences, but they can become more culturally sensitive to the diversity of their students. One of the most important things they can do is explain the context of what they are doing and make their teaching techniques explicit."[3]

---

[2] Judith E. and Sherwood G. Lingenfelter. *Teaching Cross-Culturally: An Incarnational Model for Learning and Teaching* (Grand Rapids: Baker Academic, 2003), 104.

[3] Lingenfelter and Lingenfelter, *Teaching Cross-Culturally*, 104.

This type of teaching requires a commitment to presence, engagement, and communication beyond simply dispensing information. Wan and Hedinger write, "Teaching and learning that is focused on simple information transmission can take place with minimal interaction. On the other hand, when a joint project that requires achieving real-world goals is a part of the teaching environment, that environment readily fosters meaningful interaction."[4]

A Teacher Who Understands

Several students expressed frustration when teachers' expectations were not realistic. Again, the Lingenfelters speak to unrealistic expectations, writing, "Every teacher brings to the classroom expectations about curriculum that are rooted in his or her training and experience...We are the experts, and we assume our knowledge base is right for our assignment. In many situations, nothing can be farther from the truth."[5]

In recent research among senior high school students in Caloocan, Philippines, educators learned "that students enjoy learning when their preferred type of activities are performed—hence, having the attributes of an active learner."[6] The research demonstrated that a teacher's ability to recognize students' learning styles and plan learning activities motivates students to engage.

A Teacher Who Connects

Every participant preferred a teacher who could connect learning to life. In describing their least favorite classroom experience, their dislike often related to an inability to understand the value of what they were learning. For example, one participant complained that a chemistry teacher focused most of her energy on memorizing the chemical elements but failed to explain "the actual use of those elements in real life."

Participant responses show that students desire to learn what is needed for the future (even for the following classwork) and what is practical and helpful for life. James Plueddemann clarifies the teacher's and the curriculum's responsibility to engage students in connecting theory and practice. He writes, "in addition to teaching content, the educator's task in

---

[4] Enoch Wan and Mark Hedinger, *Relational Missionary Training: Theology, Theory & Practice (Urban Ministry in the 21st Century)*, (Portland: Urban Loft, 2020), 98.

[5] Lingenfelter and Lingenfelter, *Teaching Cross-Culturally*, 104.

[6] Karl Aventijado, Alessandra Ignacio, Tjay Ramos, Marc Tnerife, and Jose Noel Syguia. "The Journey to Learning: Through the Learning Styles of the Senior High School Academic Strand Students A.Y. 2019-2020," 2020.

any situation is to help students make connections between the subject matter and their experience."[7]

Plueddemann's reference to Ted Ward's metaphor of a rail fence describes the educational model that engages students in making these connections. He emphasizes that the "responsibility of the teacher doesn't end with teaching content and relating it to the life experience. It's also to help students build fence posts between the subject matter and their needs."[8]

Brookfield describes making education "coterminous with life."[9] Shaw states, "When it comes to planning an actual lesson, most students need to be guided through the process toward applying the message in a specific, measurable, attainable, relevant, and tangible way."[10] Plueddemann critiques, "Globally, formal education is becoming more and more divorced from the real world of the learner and is often just a means for passing exams in order to get into the best schools, in order to earn high salaries."[11]

These five preferences explain what the participants in the focus group expect and desire from their teachers and the type of teaching that has an impact on their lives. Further, the many congruencies found with the body of literature on hermeneutics and educational theory referenced here support the viability of the teacher preferences stated in composing such a theory.

Learning Preferences

Closely related to the five teaching preferences are four learning preferences that arise from the focus group responses.

Students Prefer Hands-On Experience

Regarding an impactful classroom experience, one participant remarked, "The professor did not spoon-feed us." The participants consistently echoed a resistance to knowledge as a commodity. Shaw has critiqued the pursuit of knowledge in today's classroom as an "external commodity to be digested like lunch."[12] Repeating a phrase from the preference for professionalism,

---

[7] James E. Plueddemann, *Teaching Across Cultures: Contextualizing Education for Global Mission* (Westmont: IVP Academic, 2018), 19.

[8] James E. Plueddemann, *Teaching Across Cultures*, 20.

[9] Stephen D. Brookfield, *Teaching for Critical Thinking: Tools and Techniques to Help Students Question Their Assumptions* (San Francisco: Jossey-Bass, 2012), 4.

[10] Perry Shaw, *Transforming Theological Education: A Practical Handbook for Integrative Learning* (Carlisle, Cumbria: Langham Global Library, 2014), 221.

[11] James E. Plueddemann, *Teaching Across Cultures*, 59.

[12] Perry Shaw, *Challenging Tradition: Innovation in Advanced Theological Education*, ICETE Series (London: Langham Creative Projects, 2018), 103.

students want to be facilitated rather than indoctrinated. Knowledge that is a commodity trains learners to conform to a teacher's expectations.

One participant said, "Computer labs and extra-curricular activities helped me develop personally." Students enjoyed interaction and collaboration with others. These hands-on, experiential, and out-of-the-classroom experiences allow students to practice, improve, and master the lessons.

This type of learning is what Mezirow means by transformational education. He sees education as a much deeper process than most other educational philosophies. Transformational learning engages students to learn facts, attitudes, and skills and opportunities to develop beliefs, values, and ways of thinking.

Students Prefer Collaboration

All but two participants noted the enjoyment and transformative impact of group learning. This is not surprising, given the collective nature of Filipino culture. Working together with peers is preferred and enjoyed by Filipinos. A participant noted the benefit of working with people with diverse skills and strengths. He enjoyed bonding with others in the project and liked the challenge of defending his ideas.

Thigpen's research in Cambodia identified the veracity of what she calls "collective learning." She writes, "In the emerging fields of study, social neuroscience and social physics, researchers Jones et al. chronicled 'how different probabilities of positive interaction from distinct peers rapidly influence social learning.'" Thigpen continues her case with evidence from economist Peyton Young, whose studies noted that neighbors are often considered the most influential in one's decision-making process. In addition, Maurice Taylor observed that successful adult classrooms involve "collaboration of peers, a distinct classroom socialization process, and social learning behaviors." Thigpen also notes the studies of Merrifield and Bingman in Appalachia and the West Coast in America, which recognized the "others-oriented learning strategies" of learners who participated.[13] These strategies included watching others, having someone model a skill, dialogue, and cooperative learning. Likewise, the Lingenfelters learned that students found it easy to learn in groups in Africa and on the island of Yap. They observed that Yapese "do not like to do anything by themselves. They prefer to answer questions, take tests, and write papers as a group."[14]

---

[13] Lynn Thigpen, *Connected Learning: How Adults with Limited Formal Education Learn* (Eugene: Pickwick Publications, 2020), 119-120.

[14] Lingenfelter and Lingenfelter, *Teaching Cross-Culturally*, 56.

Students Prefer Active, Creative Learning

Several students described being given the freedom to create as a favorite classroom experience. One student mentioned the creation of a storyboard for an advertising class. Another remembered the opportunity to work with others to present a video documentary on an assigned topic.

Shaw notes, "One of the most insidious outcomes of curricular control is the extent to which it undermines the creativity that is essential to our being created in God's image."[15] He agrees with Ivan Illich, who observed, "Once young people have allowed their imaginations to be formed by curricular instruction, they are conditioned to institutional planning of every sort. 'Instruction' smothers the horizon of their imaginations."[16] Shaw adds, "If we are to affirm the benefit from the various gifts that people bring to the learning context, we need to provide space for intuition, feeling, sensing, and imagination, alongside the traditional skills of analysis, reason and sequential problem-solving."[17]

Maggay, in exegeting her Filipino culture, draws from the former days when history and community events were preserved in songs learned by school children and sung by workers. She conjures visions of farmers singing while working in the field, sailors singing while hoisting the sails, and the many occasions of life—from feasts to funerals—during which singing expressed joy and mourning. This recalls the creative arts that have, for centuries, been a staple in education and cultural formation, especially in oral cultures. Maggay describes a continuous "oral cognitive orientation" that has survived the impact of print, even in places like Metro Manila, where "brilliant oral culture" still exists in universities.[18] This being the case, it makes sense that active and creative learning experiences resonated with the focus group participants. Thigpen refers to William Goold's insightful chapter on using creative arts with oral learners. He avowed, "For oral learners, art-making is not an optional aesthetic experience."[19]

---

[15] Shaw, *Challenging Tradition*, 107.

[16] Ivan Illich, *Deschooling Society* (London: Marion Boyars, 1970), 56.

[17] Shaw, *Challenging Tradition*, 282.

[18] Melba Padilla Maggay, *The Gospel in Culture: Implications for Communication and Education* (International Orality Network, 2016), Kindle Location 797.

[19] William C. Goold, "Envisioning a Model: Integrating Theological Education and Creative Arts in the Practice of Orality for Oral Preference Learners," in *Beyond Literate Western Practices: Continuing Conversations in Orality and Theological Education*, edited by Samuel Chiang and Grant Lovejoy (Hong Kong: International Orality Network, 2014), 109.

Students Prefer Critical Thinking

In statement 5, participants were asked to share experiences where a professor stretched their thinking, ideas, or worldview about a concept or subject. More than half the participants had little or no response to the statement, but those who did shared experiences that gave rise to two themes: the power of imagination and critical thinking. In describing their favorite professors (statement 1) and their favorite classroom experience (statement 3), participants often referred to teachers and learning environments that stretched their imagination, opened their minds to new perspectives, or more pointedly, engaged them in critical thinking. One participant related a history lesson during which the professor took the students on a field trip to learn about one of the Philippines's national heroes, Jose Rizal. She remembered, "My imagination ignited as to how I would live if I'd been born during Rizal's lifetime and how I would react toward the colonizers."

What is critical thinking? Ben Paris defines it as "the ability to evaluate the connection between evidence and potential conclusions. It is the ability to make logically sound judgments, identify assumptions and alternatives, ask relevant questions, and to be fair and open-minded when evaluating the strength of arguments."[20]

As Shaw identifies, "critical thinking" is often "limited to the comparison and analysis of academic texts." He suggests "a much more demanding and complex form of critical thinking." He insists that students be "practical Christian thinkers," as indicated by Hough[21] and Banks,[22] or "reflective practitioners" per Schön[23] and Carr.[24] This, Shaw suggests, can be accomplished by facilitating students to "analyse, synthesize and evaluate theoretical academic material in the light of practical life situations, and vice versa." Steffen reminds us that in an oral context, critical thinking is closely tied to story and community relationships, spawning his idea of "character thinking."[25]

---

[20] Ben Paris, "Failing to Improve Critical Thinking" (https:// www.insidehighered.com/views/2016/11/29/roadblocks-better-critical-thinking-skills-are-embeddedcollege-experience-essay), accessed April 28, 2022.

[21] Joseph Hough, "The Education of Practical Theologians" (Theological Education 20: 55-84, 1984).

[22] Robert J. Banks, *Reenvisioning Theological Education: Exploring a Missional Alternative to Current Models* (Grand Rapids: Eerdmans, 1999).

[23] Donald A. Schön, *The Reflective Practitioner: How Professionals Think in Action* (Aldershot: Ashgate, 1991).

[24] Wesley Carr, *Handbook of Pastoral Studies: Learning and Practising Christian Ministry* (London: SPCK, 1997).

[25] Shaw, *Challenging Tradition*, 125.

Brookfield writes that education should be "a quest of the mind which digs down to the roots of the preconceptions which formulate our conduct; a technique of learning for adults which makes education coterminous with life and hence elevates living itself to the level of adventurous experiment."[26] As complex and ambiguous as critical thinking in education might be, the research shows that it is essential to deep learning and is desired by students who are serious about learning and life.

Speaking to both themes, critical thinking and imagination, Mezirow describes critical thinking as

> helping a learner bring formerly unquestioned assumptions and premises into critical awareness in order to understand how he or she has come to possess certain conceptual categories, rules, tactics, and criteria and then to judge their validity enhances the learner's crucial sense of control over his or her life.[27]

Mezirow's point recalls Gadamer's and Thiselton's concept of personal horizons. Gadamer's discussion of the concepts of history and tradition includes an analysis of *Erfahrung* (experience), which, he states, "provides the basis in our actual lives for the specifically hermeneutic way we are related to other persons and to our cultural past."[28] The type of experience he means is dialogue: question-and-answer experiences that "provide an ongoing integrative process in which what we encounter widens our horizon."[29] The more significant impact happens when one is willing to overturn an existing perspective or discover it as too narrow. Gadamer describes the effect as doing more than cataloging knowledge or adding to our reservoir of information. Widening one's horizon deepens an implicit sense of broader perspectives of human life and culture. Seeing a new horizon (perspective) also allows us to see our limits and overcome some of our dogmatic opinions. In other words, applying Gadamer's philosophy of hermeneutics, learners need a teacher who will facilitate experiences through which they distance themselves from their horizon, see the horizons of others, and are given the opportunity to confirm, reform, or transform their view into a new horizon. This requires imagination and critical thinking. On critical thinking, Gadamer writes, "A person who thinks must ask himself questions."[30]

---

[26] Stephen D. Brookfield. *Teaching for Critical Learning*, 4.

[27] Jack Mezirow. *Transformative Dimensions of Adult Learning* (San Francisco: Jossey-Bass Publishers, 1991), Kindle Location 2285.

[28] Hans-Georg Gadamer, *Truth and Method* (London: Bloomsbury Revelations, Reprint Edition, 2013) Kindle Location 1090.

[29] Gadamer, *Truth and Method,* Kindle Location 109.

[30] Gadamer, *Truth and Method,* Kindle Location 18474.

Classroom Preferences

A key classroom component of deep or transformative learning is the educator's understanding of and promoting the natural creativity and imagination of the students. This explains Shaw's view of the "insidious" nature of education. Education, under the control of curricular constraints, tends to rob the learner's creativity. Shaw agrees with Illich's observations that education too often smothers students' imagination. An analysis of participants' responses to statements 2, 3, 6, and 8 give evidence of classroom preferences that motivate and nurture learning.

Classroom Freedom

As noted earlier, most of the participants in the focus group communicated a desire for creative freedom and an appreciation for classroom experiences in which professors provided opportunities to create presentations, videos, art forms, and other activities. Their favorite professors, their favorite classroom experiences, and, a few times, their suggestions for better learning experiences included creative and imaginative activities.

Shaw views the "schooling" model in the standard classroom layout, consisting of rows of chairs facing a lectern, prevalent in most theological institutions, as a deterrent to classroom freedom. "Even as we enter a class such as this," Shaw critiques, "we know the presumed role of the teacher: instructor, director, professional expert authority, an intellectual master in the field of study."[31] Shaw believes that this type of classroom setup creates an emotional distance, thus limiting the necessary freedom that stimulates students to share their opinions in an open classroom discussion. Instead, professors control everything—the syllabus, the seating, and the agenda— and create a classroom where they are the center of attention.

This traditional classroom makes the robust exchange of ideas almost impossible. Instead of seeing multiple faces, the students see one face and the backs of their learning peers. Most class time consists of a sage on a stage, the only person with anything essential to say. As Illich so accurately describes, this style of classroom and learning smothers not only imagination and creativity but the freedom students need to express their beliefs, ideas, and perspectives. Not only that, but it also exacerbates the distance felt in a high power distance culture like the Philippines.

---

[31] Shaw, *Challenging Tradition*, 103.

Classroom Discussion

Classroom freedom leads to stimulating classroom discussion. Unfortunately, only three participants reported meaningful classroom discussions (statement 8). Shaw explains that without classroom discussion, "students will be best served by listening." He writes, "The unspoken assumption in formal classroom settings such as these is that the students are ignorant 'open receptacles,' eagerly awaiting the answers to life's issues."[32]

Shaw references Edward Lindeman's description of this process as an "additive process."[33] The teacher—the academic expert—lectures to the students, who then echo back to the teacher what has been lectured. In this way, the teacher retains "total control over the goals, content and evaluative criteria of the educational activity."[34] What results is a system in which students incorrectly assign achievement to making good grades and receiving a diploma. Yet, what have they learned that will carry them through life?

Classroom Discretion

Mezirow warns against teachers' completely hiding their ideas, opinions, and perspectives. He writes that teachers "cannot be expected to hide their own ways of seeing and interpreting."[35] He suggests that the teacher's point of view is one of several points of view from which students may learn. After all, according to Gadamer, the power of hermeneutics is that one can step away from their horizon and view other horizons, critically examining their and others' perspectives. In this way, one's horizon is either confirmed, changed, or enhanced. According to Mezirow, "Advancing one's own perspective...from which a learner may gain insight is perfectly ethical, even though the status of the educator may tend to influence the learner inadvertently." However, Mezirow agrees with Shaw that what is not acceptable are deliberate efforts to "sell" one's point of view or "to manipulate learners into agreeing with it or acting upon it." He adds, "We assume that educators know the difference between education and indoctrination, and we should keep in mind that adult learners usually do, too."[36]

A significant challenge for educators in the Philippines is discretion: an awareness of their status in the classroom, the potential of subconsciously leading students to adapt their own views void of critical reflection and to

---

[32] Shaw, *Challenging Tradition*, 104.
[33] Shaw, *Challenging Tradition*, 104.
[34] Shaw, *Challenging Tradition*, 121.
[35] Jack Mezirow. *Transformative Dimensions of Adult Learning*, Kindle Location 2290.
[36] Mezirow, *Transformative Dimensions*, Kindle Location 2290.

lean over backward to avoid it. Most respondents communicated a desire and need to see the professor beyond the classroom; that is, not necessarily literally, but at least as a person in touch with the real world and conversant in the challenges and issues of the careers they are studying. They genuinely desire to hear from their teachers their first-hand experiences. At the same time, an appreciation for the teacher's authority, expertise, and professionalism is evident in their responses.

Theory from the Analysis

Drawn from the data analysis from the focus group, in correlation with extant literature and studies, the research proposed the theory that oral learning is relational, meaning that it is a pilgrimage on which students and teachers engage in a narrative, sequential, and problem-solving journey to transformation. In oral cultures, learning must be a relational experience. This includes appropriate interaction with the teacher, collaborative learning with peers, and practical learning experiences that relate (connect) what the student is learning to life.

Narrative

Oral learning must be narrative. This instructs the teacher to design lectures and other teaching moments that are less propositional and more story (narrative) and symbolic. A narrative approach in the classroom will include dialogue, discussion, debate, visuals, symbols, sounds, and other learning experiences that will draw the student into the conversation and an environment of shared learning with the teacher and their peers, rather than the traditional approach in which the teacher is the expert, the sage on the stage, and often the only real learner in the classroom.

Sequential and Continuous

Oral learning must be sequential and continuous. This means that students need to see a thread, or a learning plot, within the learning experiences. Rather than fragmented and siloed, curriculum design should be holistic, creating an apparent integrative path of learning in which one lesson builds to another, one skill leads to another, and one discipline grows from another. In this way, learning intertwines and connects the lives of students and teachers as co-learners in curricula that lead them down a path of discovery that continues throughout life.

Problem-based

Oral learning must be problem-based. As students work in collaborative groups to identify a problem and work together to solve it communally, they are provided opportunities, facilitated by the teacher, to put into practice and master learning objectives within real-life scenarios.

Pilgrimage

Learning must be a pilgrimage. Plueddemann's pilgrimage paradigm of education and learning—pilgrims teaching pilgrims—helps educators shape curriculum and learning experiences that provide a three-dimensional or holistic approach to education, where the students and teachers, together, engage in affective, behavioral, cognitive, and reflective learning that convinces students of the value of learning and the importance of what is being learned.[37]

A Correlating Study to Affirm Analysis and Theory

The research investigated a study designed to research the learning styles, study habits, and academic performance of Filipino university students in applied science at Cagayan State University. The investigation aimed to discover correlations between the focus group and an extant study of Filipino learners and to affirm or invalidate this research's theory. The study sought to "determine the relationship among the learning styles, study habits and academic performance of the students."[38]

The Findings

The findings regarding learning styles are most important and significant to this research. The analysis of the data revealed the primary learning preferences among the sample as follows:

Visual Learning Style

Visual learners absorb information best when they can visualize relationships and ideas. This may include reading a text, observing a chart or diagram, or watching someone perform a task. The study found that most of the sample "remembered and understood concepts and information better

---

[37] Plueddemann, *Teaching Across Cultures*, 14-18.

[38] G.C. Magulod, Jr. "Learning styles, study habits and academic performance of Filipino university students in applied science courses: Implications for instruction." (*Journal of Technology and Science Education,* 9(2) (2019):184-198. https://doi.org/10.3926/jotse.504), 186.

when they read."[39] Reading activities in the study included reading a text, seeing words on the board, completing activities in a workbook, receiving lecture notes, and viewing slides or handouts.

Group Learning Style

Another primary learning style among the sample students was group learning. The study revealed that most of the students valued group learning and collaboration. Most students had better recall of concepts and information when working with others. This analysis is confirmed and referenced by a study by Sertel Altun, which found that cooperative learning has a significant effect on students' academic achievements in science technology.[40]

Kinesthetic Learning Style

Kinesthetic learning was another primary learning style emerging from the data. The researcher described this as "experiential or with total physical involvement in the learning situations."[41] This learning preference includes hands-on activities, lab experiments, role-playing, field trips, and other active learning opportunities.

Minor Learning Preferences

Corresponding to the significant learning style preferences, the study revealed three minor intentions: tactile, auditory, and individual learning. The study showed that students learn well when engaged in tactile activities, such as making models or materials, hearing or listening to lectures or audio recordings, and can also learn through individual studies when built on active and group learning.

Summary of Findings and Correlation to Current Study

In summary, the study of applied science students' learning preferences "showed that the applied science courses of Cagayan State University manifest learning preferences with the appeal to graphical, contextualized, experiential and collaborative teaching strategies."[42] Furthermore, the study demonstrated a significant relationship between learning styles and

---

39 Magulod, "Learning Styles," 188.
40 Sertel Altun, "The Effect of Cooperative Learning on Students' Achievement and Views on the Science and Technology Course." (*International Journal of Medical Education*, 7 (3), 2015, 451-468), accessed May 1, 2022.
41 Magulod, "Learning styles," 188.
42 Magulod, "Learning styles," 188.

academic performance. The higher the exposure to visual, group, and kinesthetic learning and collaborative learning activities, the higher the students' academic achievement.

Though the study and the study sample were narrow in scope—students in applied sciences at Cagayan State University—the findings correlated with the results and the theory of this research. They represented students from a broader geographical location and courses of study. Not only the findings but the interventions in the study affirm the teacher preferences, learning preferences, classroom preferences, and the learning theory and components stated above.

Appropriate Shifts in Theological Education Among Oral Learners

The conclusion of my research synthesizes the findings and theory into strategical shifts in theological and missiological education and training in the Philippines and other oral contexts. These shifts will facilitate transformative learning that connects with students' hearts, heads, and hands, thus more appropriately preparing them for a world and lifetime of ministry and mission.

The shifts consider what the research reveals about how oral students learn. They are constructed from learning preferences and environments that grow from oral culture and worldview. Each shift follows the hermeneutical principles that lead to transformative education. When applied, four strategies synthesized from the research and the proposed theory will enable the shifts needed in theological education and missionary training among oral learners.

Multimodal Learning

The multimodal learning strategy will shift learning from text exclusively toward using text in partnership with multiple sensory and visual ensembles. These ensembles reflect the world in which students live and how they make sense of information.

Outside the walls of our institutions, students live in a multimodal world of images, actions, sounds, narratives, and other modes of communication and information acquisition. The multimodal world in which students and all of us live presents a variety of rich and textured modes and media of communication, dissemination, and interpretation. No longer is the classroom limited to print on paper or chalk on a board. As Serafini suggests, print or text is very seldom a monomodal environment today. Text is almost always ensembled with other semiotic modes.[43]

Modes could be described as channels by which information is communicated in a way that gives meaning. These modes could be written text, audible stories, symbols, signs, rituals, body language, sounds, and other media. These modes of receiving and synthesizing meaning are experienced in different ways by each of the human senses: visual, auditory, or tactile. When various modes are used in a learning activity, they create a dynamic learning experience. For instance, a lecture might be augmented by a video, images, music, and text, which can enhance a student's learning experience. Thus, two or more multimodal learning modes can provide a well-rounded educational experience. Since school environments have diverse student populations with various learning styles, a multimodal approach helps each student achieve academic success.

Semiotics is the study of how meaning is created and communicated. These systems of communicating meaning provide a diverse ensemble of texts that can be employed in the classroom as vehicles of transformative learning. In *Orality and Literacies*, Chong categorizes five semiotic systems: linguistic, visual, audio, gestural, and spatial.[44] Eubanks favors oralities that "feature spoken elements interlocked with other elements such as literature, sound, music, gestures, and performances."[45] Multimodal learning offers educators a vast repertoire of teaching strategies, bringing into the classroom multiple textures of learning experiences for the students. These various textures of education connect with the students' diverse learning styles in the classroom, empowering them to make meaning rather than merely accumulate information.

Multidimensional Learning

In his chapter on multidimensional learning, Perry Shaw theorizes a "holistic learning for effective theological education."[46] This holistic approach involves intentional strategies incorporating the three learning domains: affective, behavioral, and cognitive. Affective learning facilitates students to

---

[43] Frank Serafini, *Reading the Visual: An Introduction to Teaching Multimodal Literacy* (New York: Teachers College Press, 2014), 16.

[44] Calvin Chong, "Encountering Text as Multimodal Experience" in *Orality and Literacies: Implications for Communication and Education*, ed. Charles Madinger (International Orality Network, 2016), 23-24.

[45] Charlotte Eubanks. "Next: New Orality." State of the Discipline Report 2014-15. American Comparative Literature Association. https://stateofthediscipline.acla.org/ list-view/category?c=voice (accessed June 1, 2022).

[46] Shaw, *Challenging Tradition*, 85.

form values, attitudes, emotions, and motivations. This research has shown that students desire to understand the value of what they're learning, a connection between the lesson and life and are more satisfied with their teachers and the classroom when they feel enriched. Behavioral learning engages students in action and experience. This is what the focus group described as "hands-on" learning, employing action and experience. Cognitive learning stretches students to analyze and synthesize knowledge through complex thinking skills. The literature researched presented the necessity of critical thinking as a transformative tool. In addition, the students surveyed communicated their desire for critical thinking and the freedom to be creative and imaginative. These types of learning experiences require teachers to view teaching-learning as much more than mere transmission of knowledge. As Shaw states,

> Cognitive learning in our theological institutions is based on an understanding of knowledge rooted, not in the Scriptures, but in Greek philosophy and the Enlightenment, according to which, knowledge is some sort of object that needs to be acquired.[47]

Shaw asserts that when the Bible speaks of knowledge, "It is not speaking of some sort of objective knowledge, but of a relationship."[48] If theological institutions teach to possess knowledge as mastery in and of itself, to treat aspects of education as objects to be acquired, the changes inherent in transformative learning that leads to transformative actions in society will be minimal.

The three dimensions—affective, behavioral, and cognitive—operate in partnership with each other, not only in moving students through powerful holistic learning experiences but, as Shaw describes it, creating a learning disposition in the student. A balanced, holistic approach to learning initiates a strong internal motivation in the student to learn, question, and transform. Combining multimodal learning with multidimensional learning will help theological institutions, as well as church discipleship ministries, make the important necessary shifts toward a relational hermeneutic (approach to learning) that leads to transformative learning.[49]

---

[47] Shaw, *Challenging Tradition*, 85
[48] Shaw, *Challenging Tradition*, 86
[49] Examples of multidimensional teaching strategies can be explored in *Oralities & Literacies* (ION 2016), 32ff.

Narrative Learning

Walter Fisher stated a theory of human communication "based on a conception of persons as *homo narrans*".[50] He wrote that the symbolic interaction that narratives provide engages humans in both reasoning and valuing actions. The term *homo narrans* raises important questions regarding reason and logic. If narrative is a fundamental way of humans finding and making meaning, it can be said, as Fisher has stated, "that reasoning need not be bound to argumentative prose or be expressed in clear-cut inferential or implicative structures: Reasoning may be discovered in all sorts of symbolic action—nondiscursive as well as discursive."[51] Fisher argues that humans are not only valuing as well as reasoning but also that life is both symbolic and rhetorical and that humans infer as well as posit. This gives credence to the value of narrative in theological education. Vanhoozer writes, "In shaping the way we see the world and ourselves, stories sustain and enact social power."[52]

Thigpen defines narrative as "intentional-communicative artifacts, stylized communication patterns of symbols with pictures in the mind transferred to others so that awe and imagination take center stage, accenting cognition and volition."[53] Certainly, this definition of narrative presents a dynamic picture of the power of story. However, it also reveals that narrative goes beyond storying. While it is true that storytelling is a common feature in orality, as Thigpen observed, and as this research demonstrates, oral learners are also visual or kinesthetic. They are social and observational in their learning. There are other narrative approaches to learning besides story. Symbols, art, music, debate, case studies, and similar strategies to present and engage students in learning paint "pictures in the mind" that can inspire awe and imagination that lead to transformation. However, storying lies beneath these narrative strategies for learning.

Narratives are valuable educational tools for several reasons. They enable students to connect present learning experiences with prior knowledge and learning experiences. Narratives meet the learner at a profoundly human level, making learning close to life. Narratives offer opportunities for students to weave cognitive, affective, and behavioral actions into one

---

[50] Fisher, Walter R. "Narration as a human communication paradigm: The case of public moral argument." (*Communication Monographs,* 51:1, 1-22, (1984), DOI: 10.1080/03637758409390180), 1.

[51] Fisher, "Narration," 1.

[52] Kevin J. Vanhoozer. *Is There a Meaning in This Text?: The Bible, the Reader, and the Morality of Literary Knowledge (Landmarks in Christian Scholarship)* (Grand Rapids: Zondervan, 1998), 167.

[53] Thigpen, *Connected Learning,* 22.

learning experience. Narratives engage students in the kind of critical thinking that poses questions, not only about the characters and their actions in the story but about their own life experiences and ambitions. Narrative learning opens both teacher and student to explore new horizons that lead to transformative action.[54]

Relational Learning

The research demonstrated the value of relationships in Filipino culture (and other oral cultures), as well as the preference for relational learning among participants of a focus group of Filipino university and seminary students and graduates. The analysis of their responses and the review of extant literature in the research shows that education is not a business transaction and is more than the transmission of information. Education, if it is to be effective and transformative, must be an invitation to personal and communal growth.

Following Bordin's study on working alliances in psychotherapy, Daniel Rogers submits that

> Teaching and learning activities can be assumed to have embedded working alliances. This occurs solely as a result of a student seeking some type of change (e.g., learning, skill acquisition) and a teacher serving as the agent of that change (e.g., crafting learning outcomes, designing tasks to foster learning).[55]

By the phrase "working alliances," Rogers likely has in mind the type of collaborative learning environment described in this research, in which an atmosphere of freedom pervades the classroom and learning opportunities through the relationships of teacher and students, as well as student peer learning. Where Bordin and Rogers fall short is the relationship between the lesson and the real life of the teacher and student. Following Plueddemann's work, this research makes it clear that students need both fence rails (theory and practice) and fence posts (multimodal, multi-dimensional, and narrative learning experiences) to relate an education experience to the needed transformative actions in their lives.

---

[54] For an excellent resource for including case studies as a narrative teaching tool, see Paul G. and Frances Hiebert. "Case Studies in Missions" (www.GlobalMissiology.org, 1985). Steffen's and Neu's *Character Theology: Engaging God Through His Cast of Characters* (Eugene: Pickwick Publications, 2023) is an excellent resource for narrative learning.

[55] Daniel T Rogers, (2009) "The Working Alliance in Teaching and Learning: Theoretical Clarity and Research Implications," *International Journal for the Scholarship of Teaching and Learning*: Vol. 3: No. 2, Article 28. https://doi.org/10.20429/ijsotl.2009.030228 (accessed June 15, 2022).

The analysis of the focus group responses also shows that teachers serve as fenceposts when they build appropriate relationships with students and share their own stories of real-life learning and transformation. The commitment of institutions and their faculty to relational learning, accompanied by sound technique and andragogy, creates the type of learning environment that engages students in intentional, purposeful, inspiring, and transformative learning. Rapport, trust, and mutuality between students and teachers plow the deep and fertile soils of learning that produce transformation.

Conclusion

Multimodal learning provides a diversity of texts, voices, and images—sensory and visual ensembles—that reflect the world in which students live and how they make sense of information. Multidimensional learning engages students in a holistic approach to learning, creatively employing affective, behavioral, and cognitive learning experiences that provide multiple layers of integrative learning. Narrative learning uses the power of story and symbol, prominent features of oral cultures, leading students to make character assessments and come to new horizons of learning and living. These three strategies create a relational learning environment. They also resolve to the purpose of this research and the realization of the paradigm of theological education that will shape the minds, hearts, and hands of a future generation of pastors, church planters, missionaries, and church leaders who will finally make a Kingdom impact in Filipino culture: that is, a relational approach to learning and teaching.

Bibliography

Altun, Sertel. "The Effect of Cooperative Learning on Students' Achievement and Views on the Science and Technology Course." *International Journal of Medical Education*, 7 (3), 2015: 451-468.

Brookfield, Stephen D. *Teaching for Critical Thinking: Tools and Techniques to Help Students Question Their Assumptions.* San Francisco: Jossey-Bass 1st Edition, Kindle Edition, 2012.

Gadamer, Hans-Georg. *Truth and Method.* Bloomsbury Revelations. London: Bloomsbury Academic. Kindle Edition, 2013.

Illich, Ivan. *Deschooling Society.* London: Marion Boyars, 1970.

Lingenfelter, Judith E., and Sherwood G. Lingenfelter. *Teaching Cross-Culturally: An Incarnational Model for Learning and Teaching.* Illustrated edition. Grand Rapids: Baker Academic, 2003.

Magulod, Gilbert. "Learning Styles, Study Habits and Academic Performance of Filipino University Students in Applied Science Courses: Implications for Instruction." *Journal of Technology and Science Education* 9, no. 2 (March 1, 2019): 184. https://doi.org/10.3926/jotse.504.

Maggay, Melba Padilla, Editor. *The Gospel in Culture: Contextualization Issues Through Asian Eyes.* Grand Rapids: ISAAC (Institution for Studies in Asian Church and Culture) and Manila: OMF Literature, Inc., Kindle Edition, 2013.

Mezirow, Jack. *Learning as Transformation: Critical Perspectives on a Theory in Progress.* First Edition. San Francisco: Jossey-Bass, 2000.

———. *Transformative Dimensions of Adult Learning.* San Francisco: Jossey-Bass Publishers, Kindle Edition, 1991.

Pantoja, Dan. "State of the Philippine Evangelical Church Today: A Positive Response," https://waves.ca/2011/06/14/description-of-the-evangelical-church-today/.

Plueddemann, James E. *Teaching Across Cultures: Contextualizing Education for Global Mission.* Grand Rapids: IVP Academic, 2018.

Serafini, Frank. *Reading the Visual: An Introduction to Teaching Multimodal Literacy.* New York: Teachers College Press, 2014.

Shaw, Perry. *Challenging Tradition: Innovation in Advanced Theological Education.* ICETE Series. London: Langham Creative Projects. Kindle Edition, 2018.

———. Transforming Theological Education: A Practical Handbook for Integrative Learning. Kindle Edition. Carlisle, Cumbria: Langham Global Library, 2014.

Steffen, Tom. *Honor, Shame, and the Gospel: Reframing Our Message and Ministry.* Edited by Christopher Flanders and Werner Mischke. Littleton, CO: William Carey Library Publishers, 2020.

———. *Worldview-based Storying: The Integration of Symbol, Story, and Ritual in the Orality Movement.* 1st edition. Orality Resources International, Center for Oral Scriptures, 2018.

Steffen, Tom and William Bjoraker. *The Return of Oral Hermeneutics: As Good Today as It Was for the Hebrew Bible and First-century Christianity*. Eugene: Wipf and Stock, 2020.

Thigpen, L. Lynn. *Connected Learning: How Adults with Limited Formal Education Learn*. Eugene: Pickwick, 2021.

Thiselton, Anthony C. *The Two Horizons: New Testament Hermeneutics and Philosophical Description*. Illustrated edition. Carlisle, Cumbria; Grand Rapids: Wm. B. Eerdmans-Lightning Source, 1980.

University of East-Calooacan. "The Journey to Learning: Through the Learning Styles of the Senior High School Academic Strand Students A.Y. 2019-2020", Caloocan City, 2020. https://www.researchgate.net/publication/343976548_The_Journey_to_Learning_Through_the_Learning_Styles_of_the_Senior_High_School_Academic_Strand_Students_AY_2019-2020

Vanhoozer, Kevin J. *Is There Real Meaning in This Text?* Grand Rapids: Zondervan, 1998.

Wan, Enoch, and Mark Hedinger. *Relational Missionary Training: Theology, Theory & Practice*. Edited by Kendi Howells Douglas, Stephen Burris, and Jen Johnson. Portland: Urban Loft, 2020.

Waismann, Friedrich. *The Principles of Linguistic Philosophy*. Stuttgart: Macmillan, 1965.

Chapter 14:
Relational Training for Oral Bible Translators: A Case Study

John G. Ferch

Abstract

Bible translation has traditionally been a highly academic and mechanistic exercise requiring a high degree of literacy. Oral Bible Translation has recently emerged as an alternative approach to written translation, providing an end-product that is immediately useful in oral communities. However, the "back-end" processes that produce these oral translations can still depend on a literate translation team that can navigate printed Bible study resources and manage a software-driven translation workflow. This case study demonstrates how a relationally oriented approach to oral Bible translation can encourage locally-owned processes from the very beginning. This approach results in an accurate and natural collection of oral Scripture recordings that does not depend on a literate translation team. It traces how relational training and quality assurance methods were used to guide the translation of Mark's Gospel through an entirely oral process. The steps of exegesis, internalization, drafting, community testing, consultant checking, and final recording are discussed.

Introduction

"How oral can we go with Oral Bible Translation?"[1] John Stark raised this question when he introduced the idea of Oral Bible Translation (OBT) to the Evangelical Missiological Society during the 2020 conference. Importantly, Stark acknowledged that "every active Oral Bible Translation project has a literate starting point," since the basis of all Bible translation is the written Word of God.[2] Nevertheless, in his proposal for "incarnational mentoring," Stark encouraged trainers and consultants to employ oral training methods to the fullest extent possible when working with oral-preference translation teams.

Since making this proposal, Stark has continued to refine and model the paradigm of "incarnational mentoring" as he has led the development and implementation of global OBT strategy at Spoken Worldwide. To date,

---

[1] John Stark, "What Can We Expect from Oral Bible Translation?" in *New and Old Horizons in the Orality Movement*, eds. Tom Steffen & Cameron D. Armstrong (Eugene: Pickwick, 2022), 165.
[2] Stark, "What Can We Expect," 165.

Spoken has twenty-one active OBT projects in varying stages of completion across South America, Africa, and Asia. This case study examines one of these projects among the "Xomale"[3] people of central Ethiopia. Its goal is to more fully demonstrate Spoken's methodology of incarnational mentoring, showing how this relationally oriented approach to translation has allowed an oral-preference translation team with minimal formal education to successfully translate the Gospel of Mark using entirely oral processes.

The fundamental theoretical premise of this case study is that "primary orality" learners from collectivistic cultures learn more effectively in a relational context. Oral preference learning is not the same as auditory learning. Social interaction and genuine relationship are intrinsic to the learning process. My own prior research has explored this connection extensively in the North American Inuit context.[4] In that study, I found that orality, human relationships, personal experience, and the physical environment all converge to produce an ideal learning experience among the Inuit. Lynn Thigpen found the same in Cambodia, and cites findings from similar studies in Thailand, Somalia, Vietnam, and Appalachia.[5] For her, the connection between relationships and orality was so strong that she proposed "Connected Learning" as a replacement for the term "Oral Learning," which she considers a misnomer.[6] The present study maintains distinct nomenclature for "oral learning" (learning through spoken rather than printed words) and "relational learning" (learning through social relationships rather than independently), while acknowledging that in many contexts these function as two sides of the same coin.

Context and Project Design

Xomale is a semitic language of central Ethiopia spoken by the Xomale people, a Gurage tribe of approximately 126,000.[7] The language has no formal orthography, though speakers who are literate in Amharic are able to

---

[3] For security and safety purposes, pseudonyms are used for the names of the target language, locations, and key individuals throughout this paper. "Xomale" is an invented code name that seemed more reader-friendly than merely saying "Language X."

[4] John Ferch & Enoch Wan, *Relational Leadership Development: An Ethnological Study in Inuit Contexts* (Portland: Western Academic, 2022), 53-65.

[5] Lynn Thigpen, "Deconstructing Oral Learning: The Latest Research," in *New and Old Horizons in the Orality Movement: Expanding the Firm Foundations*, eds. Tom Steffen & Cameron D. Armstrong (Eugene: Pickwick, 2022), 28.

[6] Thigpen, "Deconstructing Oral Learning," 35.

[7] "Joshua Project," Frontier Ventures, accessed 5 October 2022, https://www.joshuaproject.net.

adapt the Ge'ez script to write in Xomale.[8] Language vitality is classified as "stable," and children generally learn to speak Xomale in the home before learning a language of wider communication in school.

The Xomale are identified as an unreached people group by Joshua Project, with 3.4% of the population identified as Christian and 0.1% Evangelical.[9] At the time of project start, no Scripture existed in the Xomale language.[10] The Xomale people are overwhelmingly Muslim, and there are no Xomale churches. Though churches are present in the Xomale district, these are only attended by Oromo speakers, which is the majority language of the broader region.

Though these demographics make the language a prime candidate for an oral Bible translation project, Spoken did not identify the project through a set of database statistics, but rather through their relational network. Though databases are helpful in identifying global translation needs, the fundamental question that Spoken asks when starting a new project is, "What relationships do we have in place that can make this project feasible?" Spoken's process depends on relationships from the very beginning.

The initial relationship for the Xomale project was found in-house, with Spoken's own staff member, Yohannes Faye. Now living in the US and serving in Spoken's pastoral development program, Yohannes was born and raised in Ethiopia. When Spoken began looking to expand into the field of OBT, Yohannes was a natural starting point. Yohannes had a long-time friend and former ministry colleague named Fekadu Mulugeta who had mentioned the Scripture needs of the Xomale people. Yohannes introduced John Stark to Fekadu's son Misikir, who was living in Addis Ababa and active in an orality-based ministry founded by his father, Harvest Mission Ethiopia (HME). HME had extensive experience in Oral Bible Storytelling (OBS) across Ethiopia, but not OBT. Stark began building a relationship with Misikir as they explored the concept of OBT, which eventually led to a formal partnership between Spoken Worldwide and HME.

Fekadu knew of a single Xomale believer named Mohammed, whom he had discipled years previously. Known with contempt as "Mohammed the Christian," he continued to witness about Christ in his community. Upon his conversion, his family had taken away his wife and married her to an uncle, and mobs approached his property several times with intention to kill him.

---

[8] David M. Eberhard, Gary F. Simons, and Charles D. Fennig (eds.), *Ethnologue: Languages of the World*, Twenty-third edition (Dallas: SIL International, 2020). Online version: https://www.ethnologue.com.

[9] "Joshua Project."

[10] "ProgressBible Database," SIL International, accessed 23 April 2021, https://progress.bible.

Together, Misikir, Fekadu, and Mohammed approached the three Evangelical Oromo-speaking churches (Baptist, Full Gospel, and Lutheran denominations) in a town adjacent to the Xomale district to determine if there was any interest in a Xomale OBT project. This meeting took place in December 2020. Though these Oromo ministry leaders were initially hesitant, the HME representatives reported that during the meeting, "the Holy Spirit really opened up their hearts" and they became eager to help address the needs of their Xomale neighbors. The churches expressed their support for the project, and one church agreed to provide meeting facilities and pastoral accountability for a local translation team.

With the support of the local churches, Spoken and HME established a formal Memorandum of Understanding in January of 2021. Spoken committed to provide funding, training, and ongoing consulting to translate the New Testament, Psalms, and Proverbs using oral methodologies. HME agreed to provide in-country management and staff for the project, including accounting, a project manager, and a local translation team. Through its donor relationships, Spoken secured a grant to fund the project over a course of five years.

Misikir was appointed as the local project manager, and Spoken appointed Tim Hunter as Consultant/Trainer to provide day-to-day consulting and training via Zoom, with periodic in-person visits. Spoken's Consultant/Trainers play a key role in the incarnational mentoring approach. In written translation projects, the consultant is often a third party who is not closely involved in the day-to-day activities of the translation team. The team often works independently of the consultant, who comes into the picture during the later stages of translation for quality assurance checks. At Spoken, a Consultant/Trainer is paired with the team at the very beginning of the project to guide the team through the entire translation process. In this role, Tim Hunter continued mentoring Misikir in OBT principles as he prepared to lead the translation team. I (John Ferch) joined Spoken Worldwide as OBT Consultant/Trainer in May 2021, and was assigned to the Xomale project alongside Hunter, with the goal that I would eventually take over full consulting duties on the project, freeing Hunter to take on additional projects in West Africa. True to Spoken's values, I was mentored in the role by working side-by-side with Hunter until December 2021, when I took on full consultant oversight of the project.

HME worked with the local association of churches to identify any additional Xomale-speaking believers who could become part of the translation team. The churches recruited a total of twenty-one believers who could speak some degree of Xomale and would be interested in joining the project. One of the churches hosted a meeting between these individuals and

HME in January 2021. Prior to this meeting, John Stark guided Misikir through a series of activities to introduce the churches to the concept of OBT. These followed the basic format outlined by Stark in his 2020 article.[11] Through these activities, it became clear that of the twenty-one potential translators, only twelve could speak Xomale fluently, and three of these could not commit to the time requirements of the project. Further discussion narrowed the list to six individuals, and after the first training sessions in February 2021, only four remained committed to the project.

By March 2021, the team was finalized: four Xomale translators would meet at the host church in the neighboring town, led by Misikir Fekadu as HME Project Coordinator (based in Addis Ababa). Tim Hunter (and later myself) would provide regular consulting and training from the US. Though smaller than originally envisioned, the team began meeting together regularly, and Hunter travelled to Ethiopia for the first in-person translation workshop from March 18-27, 2021. During this visit, Hunter provided further mentoring for Misikir and guided the translators through the translation of two initial passages they had begun processing: Mark 2 and John 6.

In the ensuing months, the translators continued learning experientially by translating introductory passages from different books and genres, including Luke 2, Hebrews 1, and Psalm 23. By May, the team had a good "feel" for the translation process, and the translators made the decision to focus on the Book of Mark as their first complete book.

Oral Exegesis

All four translators were Christians. Two had ministry experience in Oromo- and Amharic-speaking churches prior to joining the translation project, but none had any formal Bible training or translation experience. Formal education levels among the translators ranged from middle school to high school equivalency. All four were familiar with the general plotline of Scripture and its major characters to varying degrees, but none had training in exegesis, and they had limited knowledge regarding most individual stories or passages. Thus, the first step in translating any passage was to ensure that all team members developed an appropriate understanding of its meaning.

Exegesis is traditionally a highly literate and individualistic exercise. When working with oral learners, a different approach to exegesis is necessary. Though all the Xomale translators were able to read Amharic, their reading level was not sufficient to benefit from the advanced Bible study resources that an exegete might normally use, especially in Bible translation.

---

[11] Stark, "What Can We Expect," 159-163.

On an even deeper level, they were not accustomed to the idea of interpreting a text (or story) in isolation. For the Xomale, like many oral peoples, information is naturally processed in a group setting as it is told, retold, and examined from different angles by different individuals. For these reasons, the team used an oral approach to exegesis as the first step in translation.

Oral exegesis is an ancient practice that is currently in the process of being "rediscovered" by the missiological community. For a complete treatment of the practice, readers are referred to the recent work of Tom Steffen and Bill Bjoraker, *The Return of Oral Hermeneutics.*[12] Their model exemplifies the approach taken in the Xomale project.

The team would begin by listening to the passage to be translated read aloud multiple times from the Amharic and Oromo translations. Amharic was used as the main source text, and Oromo was frequently consulted as well. After hearing the passage several times, the four translators would discuss it as a group, led by Misikir. Their discussion would survey the logical argument or flow of the passage. For Mark's gospel, which is almost entirely narrative in genre, this argument was traced by analyzing four major features of each passage: people, places, events, and feelings. Misikir would guide the team through a discussion of each of these features, and in doing so would have opportunity to provide important background information orally as the need arose in the discussion. In many cases, the group's collective knowledge was sufficient to overcome areas of confusion.

To prepare for these exegetical discussions, Misikir would meet with the Spoken consultants, Tim Hunter and myself, via teleconference, usually a day or two before the team's meeting. This too was a predominantly oral discussion, as we would survey the key areas of understanding in the text and highlight any areas of potential confusion. Together we would develop the key talking points for the translators to consider. We would often review written resources in this meeting, including SIL Translator's Notes, lexicons, commentaries, maps, and textual variants. However, the goal was always to distill these insights from the relevant literature into an oral delivery that would be useful to the translators. After the exegetical discussion with the translators, Misikir would again meet with the consultants to pass along any unresolved questions that the team might have had and to clarify any areas of confusion.

Early in the process, most of the exegetical meetings took place in person. The consultants and the project coordinator would spend several days preparing a series of passages for exegesis, and then Misikir would travel to

---

[12] Tom Steffen and William Bjoraker, *The Return of Oral Hermeneutics: As Good Today as it Was for the Hebrew Bible and First-century Christianity* (Eugene: Wipf & Stock, 2020).

the translators and spend several days with them performing exegesis. He would then return to Addis and debrief with the consultants, since Internet access was unreliable at the project site. Other weeks, the translators would travel to Addis and meet together at a conference center. As the translators gained proficiency, Misikir began to conduct most of these exegetical discussions via telephone. Each translator was assigned a smartphone for use in the project, and he would call one of them and participate in the exegetical discussion via speakerphone.

Accurate exegesis, then, was ensured by involving the consultants early and often in the exegetical process, allowing them to mentor the project coordinator in his own understanding of the text and to guide the translators accordingly. Rather than relying on written texts, it was the relationships between the consultants, the coordinator, and the translators that became the locus of trusted authority in the exegetical process.[13]

Internalization

Though generally not part of a written translation project, the step of internalization is essential to oral Bible translation. In internalization, the translators become familiar enough to convey the entire passage naturally, without written notes or prompts. It is not to be confused with rote memorization, since the emphasis is on a natural yet accurate retelling of the entire passage. Kris Toler has provided a detailed survey of the process.[14]

Toler identifies a number of different activities that can be used to aid in internalization, including roleplay, storyboarding, and mnemonic devices. These can be used to varying degrees of effectiveness depending on the preferences and cultural expectations of the group. The internalization method that the Xomale translators found most comfortable and effective was to take turns telling the story (or passage) to one another. By listening to the passage repeatedly and comparing each telling to the source text for accuracy, the translators were able to critique one another in their understanding of the story and to learn it by heart quite effectively. Taking place in a group setting, internalization activities provided an embedded form of peer review as the stories were learned.

Internalization was usually completed immediately after the exegetical meeting, while the passage was still fresh in the translators' minds. The project coordinator would participate in this step when meeting with the translators in person, but more often it was completed independently. The

---

[13] Thigpen, "Deconstructing Oral Learning," 29.

[14] Kristofer Martin Toler, *Internalization: A Key Ingredient in Achieving Naturalness in an Oral Translation* (M.A. product, Dallas International University, 2020), 67-71.

consultants' role in the internalization process was minimal. Stark and Hunter provided some early guidance in the area during the project launch, but since Misikir was already familiar with the idea of internalization from his OBS experience, he was able to quickly adapt the same principles and experiences for OBT. The translators, coming from a storytelling culture themselves, were quick to learn and implement the process.

Oral Drafting

As the translators' internalization of the passage improved, they moved naturally into the drafting stage of the process. Since their goal was not rote memorization of the Amharic text, but rather learning the message of the passage by heart, they would naturally reach the point where it became easier to retell the story or passage in their own heart language, rather than in Amharic. Drafting and internalization, then, would often take place hand-in-hand, as with each telling of the story the translators gradually moved from Amharic to Xomale with increasing accuracy.

Early in the project, Misikir demonstrated to the translators how to create an audio recording using an app on their smartphones. Since the translators were already familiar with smartphones, the learning curve was minimal, and they quickly became familiar with the process of making recordings and sharing them among the team using the Telegram social network. As the internalization of a story advanced to the point where the translators became satisfied, they would begin to record one another while telling the passage. Multiple recordings would often be made until the translators agreed on a version which represented the most mature translation of the passage. This would then be sent to Misikir via Telegram as the official first draft of the passage.

Since Xomale and Amharic are both Semitic languages with many similarities, much of the drafting was straightforward. As they retold the passage to one another, they would consider different ways of conveying the same message in Xomale, weighing different synonyms and colloquial expressions to achieve the most natural wording. The most difficult words to translate were technical religious or cultural expressions for which no parallel concept existed in the Xomale language. Since the Amharic people have an ancient Christian tradition which they trace back to the Ethiopian eunuch of Acts 8, and an association with Judaism attributed to the Queen of Sheba's visit to Solomon, the Amharic scriptures contain plenty of Greek and Hebrew terms which have been transliterated, more or less, directly into Amharic. The Xomale, however, have no such connection, and their Islamic orientation renders many of these expressions meaningless. In these cases, they relied heavily on the consultants to develop a clear understanding of the terms, and then discussed different translation options. The consultant and project coordinator maintained a Key Terms list to ensure these words were translated consistently.

One of the earliest examples of these discussions dealt with how to translate the name of God. The Xomale have thoroughly adopted the Arabic term "Allah" to speak of God, and it is considered the true "Xomale" way to speak (even though it is technically Arabic). The Amharic scriptures use a different term. The team held much discussion over which term to use. Some favored importing the Amharic term into the Xomale scriptures, to differentiate between the Christian and Muslim concepts of God. Others argued that in order to be accepted as a true Xomale translation, it was essential to use the name Allah…otherwise the translation would always be viewed as a foreign import. When the translators learned that in many Arabic-speaking countries, Christians and Muslims alike use the term Allah to speak of God, even in the Arabic Bible, the team decided that this was the preferred option. This was a difficult decision made with much trepidation, and it was not unanimous—in fact, it contributed to the departure of one of the six initial team members.

This early decision set an important precedent for the project: as much as possible, they would attempt to use natural language that the Xomale people were familiar with rather than importing terms from the Amharic Bible. For well-known characters, the team adopted the Arabic names rather than importing "Christian" names from Amharic (e.g. *Issa* for Jesus, *Dawood* for David, *Merima* for Mary, *Musa* for Moses). Technical cultural terms were often translated using a descriptive phrase (e.g., "synagogue" became "the Jewish place of worship," "priests" became "those who sacrifice before *Allah*," and "apostles" became "those ordained and sent by *Issa*"). Place names, particularly those with no commonly known Arabic cognate, were generally imported from Amharic.

Oral Consultant Checking

In most of Spoken's OBT projects, once the translators establish a working draft of a passage, they take it into their community to test it for naturalness and clarity. Unfortunately, given their community's hostility towards Christians, the Xomale translators were very nervous about this step, and the consultants agreed to delay it as the team considered their options and developed an appropriate approach. Hunter and I began planning a trip to guide the translators through this process in person. In the meantime, we began checking the first drafts for accuracy. This flexibility was a natural outworking of Spoken's relational approach. Rather than forcing a "best practice" pattern that the translators were not ready for, we (the consultants)

231

were able to listen to their concerns and adapt our approach to the translators' level of readiness. Since we as consultants were already involved in the project on a day-by-day basis, we were easily able to move directly into the Consultant Checking stage of the project. This could have caused significant delays in a more "hands-off" project following a software-driven workflow.

The team experimented with several different approaches to consultant checking to determine which worked best. There were no English-speaking Xomale people to be found, so the team resorted to a two-step backtranslation via Amharic, supplied by Misikir. Though not fluent in Xomale, Misikir was familiar enough with the language to provide an English backtranslation with assistance from the translators.

Early in the project, he attempted to provide a written backtranslation. He transcribed the recordings and then translated them into English in an interlinear format. We consultants reviewed these and then discussed our findings with Misikir via live teleconference. Though functional, we found this process to be cumbersome and counterintuitive. The written transcription and backtranslation process was very time consuming for Misikir, and the written document was a poor representation of the oral product that was our goal.

The team soon moved to a process of live oral backtranslation. During daily teleconference meetings, we would listen to the Xomale audio recordings and Misikir would provide an oral backtranslation, phrase by phrase. We consultants would compare this to the major English translations, noting points of divergence, omission, or addition. In this relational environment, we could easily ask questions and receive clarifications, and immediately identify issues requiring follow-up. Misikir would then pass along this feedback to the translators, which the team would implement by recording a revised draft.

The process was still less-than-ideal, since Misikir's understanding of Xomale was limited and subject to the translators' own influence. However, the relational nature of the project helped counteract these shortcomings. Since the consultants took a daily role in the project from the very beginning, instead of waiting until the end to review the "finished product," we were able identify problem areas quickly and to offer advice on an as-needed basis as soon as questions arose. This helped prevent major issues from becoming "embedded" in the translation, which would have required significant revision (and re-internalization) later on down the line.

Oral Community Testing

After four months, the entire book of Mark had been drafted, checked, and revised. The translators and consultants were confident in the accuracy of their work, but how would it be received by the community? Having become comfortable with exegesis, internalization, and drafting, the team was eager to move on to another book of the Bible, but the consultants advised the team that before moving on, it was necessary to answer this question and make any necessary revisions. Unfortunately, the consultants' in-person visit had been postponed several times, first due to civil unrest in the country, and then due to delayed visa processing caused by the ongoing COVID pandemic. With no good opportunities for a visit on the horizon, the team began to tackle the challenge of community testing in earnest.

The team weighed several approaches to community testing. They considered digitally altering their voices to disguise them from listeners, testing with non-native Xomale speakers in the Christian community, and limiting their testing to the two Xomale individuals who had dropped off the team shortly after the project launched. After much discussion, the team agreed that each person would choose one trusted individual with whom to share a few recordings. They would do this while at home over the weekend, and then report back. Bathed in much prayer, the translators took the Word of God to the Xomale people in their own language for the first time.

In preparation for testing, the consultants coached the translators how to gauge comprehension and solicit helpful feedback from the listeners. In a written translation project, this step is often conducted by "interviewing" the community members after they read or listen to the text. Translators will gauge comprehension through a series of predetermined questions designed to reveal areas of confusion or misunderstanding in the passage. Responses would be recorded in detail for later analysis. The Xomale translators were uncomfortable with the idea of interviewing their friends and neighbors regarding such controversial recordings. Taking written notes would be even more threatening in their oral culture, and would undoubtably cause people to refuse participation or give dishonest feedback. Instead, they decided to hold simple conversations with the listeners, asking them to summarize what they heard and exploring their response to the recordings in a natural way. This approach closely resembles what Bryan Harmelink calls "Conversational Testing," which he finds "less inhibition-producing, and the guided conversation provides an opportunity for teasing out connections of the

Scripture with daily life."[15] This relational approach to community testing, the translators felt, would yield more useful results and be acceptable to the community.

The consultants proposed basic talking points, but importantly, these were flexible and not pre-written. Nor were the translators required to keep written transcripts of their conversations. Though some did choose to make notes after their conversations, their goal was to conduct their testing orally as much as possible. After a day of testing, they would discuss their findings with one another, and Misikir would debrief them each individually about each passage that was listened to, taking written notes for the consultants to review.

For the most part, the translators were surprised and encouraged by the response of their listeners. Most of the people who listened were excited and pleased to hear stories about God in their own language. Many of the listeners were so interested that they asked to hear the stories multiple times. The translators had expected to be insulted or treated badly for sharing Christian scripture, as they had come to expect after the community's response to the Amharic scriptures. But since this was not written and was shared orally, like an everyday story, people were open to listening and discussing. For the first time, Mohammed felt that he could share the Word of God with someone without having to argue and depart with harsh words.

Encouraged and emboldened after their initial experiment, the translators gradually expanded the circles of friends with whom they would share their recordings. One translator, who had been rejected by her father upon conversion, took a big step in sharing with her own sister, who quickly became a regular source of helpful feedback. Mohammed began sharing with his mother, a devout Muslim. He recounted his experience in detail, as transcribed by Misikir:

My mother was visiting at my house along with my brother-in-law and his wife. As we were having coffee, I played for them our recording of Mark 3:2-30 from my phone. When my mother got to the part where it says "I tell you the truth, people will be forgiven for all sins, even all the blasphemies they utter. But whoever blasphemes against the Holy Spirit will never be forgiven," my mother came closer to my phone and she asked, "What was it that he just said? Forgive? Is he saying that sins can just be canceled? I do *Salat* [Islamic prayer rituals] five times a day and crimes are just cancelable?" Then my brother-in-law laughed. I didn't get

---

[15] Bryan Harmelink, "Questions about Questions: Exploring the Impact of Cognitive Linguistics on Testing for Translation Quality" (paper presented at the Bible Translation Conference, Dallas, TX, October 2005), 36.

to talk more about it, but I realized that the word "forgive" had captured my mother's ears. I have spoken with my mother about the gospel so many times and this is the longest that I have seen her hear God's word.

That is not to say that all experiences were positive. Several days later, Mohammed was detained by a police officer and five mosque officials and questioned about his activities. Another translator was forcibly removed from his friend's house by a family member and pushed to the ground. These were the most extreme instances of persecution encountered, but plenty of people refused to listen or argued with the translators when the translations conflicted with Islamic doctrine. Nevertheless, the translators pressed on, and eventually shared portions of Scripture with over 100 individuals, all through organic connections in their existing relational networks. Five people professed faith in Christ after listening and discussing the recordings of Mark, and the translators reported instances of healing and exorcism as the Spirit validated their message in the eyes of their neighbors.

The feedback they received confirmed many of the early decisions they had made, particularly regarding the use of *Allah* and *Issa* for God and Jesus. These terms were accepted so naturally by the Xomale people that when they heard Mohammed using them, people often asked Mohammed whether he had finally decided to return to *Allah*. Mohammed's reply was that he never left *Allah*, he simply came to know Him more fully. One woman said that "all her life, she had never heard anyone talk about *Allah* in her language like this." Even the translator who had disagreed with this decision early on and left the project changed his mind when he saw the final results.

In other cases, the community testing caused the translators to reverse decisions they had made. Originally, they had decided to introduce a new term for "sin," borrowing from Amharic. The Xomale term *wenjel*, which means something closer to "crime" in Amharic, is more commonly used to discuss wrongdoing in religious contexts, but the translators felt uncomfortable with this term. Listeners repeatedly asked why they chose to say something unfamiliar instead of simply saying *wenjel*, since this word was easily understood not only by the Xomale but the greater Gurage Islamic community as well. After receiving this feedback and discussing with the consultants, the translators updated their drafts to use the familiar word.

By taking a relational approach to community testing, then, the translators were able to ease into this crucial step at a pace with which they were comfortable. Even though they could not be present in person, the consultants coached them one step at a time, helping them to "learn by doing" and giving constructive feedback along the way. The translators used simple oral conversations about the recordings within their existing relational networks to gain feedback that improved the recordings significantly. More

235

importantly, through this organic approach the Word of God began to take root and bear fruit in the Xomale community.

Final Performance

After the community testing, the translators and consultants talked through the findings and made necessary revisions, and the translators recorded their "final draft" of Mark's gospel in December 2021. Their final task was to use this draft to create a production-quality recording that could be approved for public distribution. Following best practices in Oral Bible Translation, the consultants asked the translators to select one translator to perform the entire book in a single voice. To eliminate frequent background noise from birds, livestock, and vehicle traffic that characterized their draft recordings, the translators decided that these final recordings should be made in a Christian recording studio operated by SIL in Addis Ababa.

It took the translators many months to overcome this final step. Each month, a different issue seemed to arise that prevented them from doing so. The group-task orientation of the Xomale culture also contributed to this delay. The translators began drafting and community testing the book of Luke, bringing these steps to completion before finally sending someone to Addis to make the final recording in August 2022. A nineteen-year-old woman who was recognized as the most natural-sounding storyteller of the group spent three weeks in Addis, accompanied by her twenty-one-year-old roommate who had joined the translation project in May of 2022. The rest of the team joined them in Addis for the third week of recording, provided a final round of peer review, and selected a few recordings for further revision.

After the recordings were completed, the consultant and project coordinator provided one final check via backtranslation. This was especially necessary because of the changes that had been introduced to the translation after the community testing. By this time, another Xomale believer (one of those who had left the original team of six) had been hired as an independent backtranslator. She listened to the Xomale recordings and translated them into Amharic recordings for Misikir to review. Misikir then translated these into English recordings for the US-based consultant, and together we reviewed their findings in September 2022. Through this process, out of forty-eight recordings, eleven were identified as having minor errors that required revision. These were made in December 2022, and the Xomale translation of Mark is now available to the community using SD cards and social media.

Conclusion

By building its OBT projects around relationships, rather than a software program or a literacy-based training process, Spoken Worldwide has found the flexibility needed to empower oral-preference translation teams with limited formal education to take ownership of their own Bible translation activities. By pairing each translation team with a highly involved consultant from the very beginning of the project, Spoken's translators are able to take a "learn by doing" approach in which the consultant speaks into the process at each step of the way. The relationship between Spoken's consultant and the local project coordinator is central to the process. Through the resulting relational network, which has indigenous ministry leaders in the center, supported by funders and trainers in the west, local mother-tongue translators on the field, and surrounded by the entire local community that participates in the testing and distribution process, an accurate and natural collection of oral Scripture recordings can emerge through locally owned processes.

The relational orientation of this OBT process has the added benefit of promoting relational reconciliation in the Xomale community. The power of stories, shared relationally between friends, has begun to break down perceived barriers that written texts have created. Mohammed finds that when listening to these stories in their own language, his neighbors receive him differently. He says, "I have never felt more loved and understood by my community. They sit and talk with me, and I never have to go through arguments. I have been asked for the audio recordings by many. They want to keep it with them and hear it while they're alone." In particular, Mohammed's relationship with his mother has been restored, as she has developed a greater understanding of his new faith by listening to the stories. Moreover, she herself has been drawing closer to a personal reconciliation with *Allah* through the stories of *Issa*.

Another story from the community testing of the Gospel of Luke illustrates the power of relationships to bring about this reconciliation. One of the translators encountered a blind man and shared with him recordings from Luke 1-2. The man was in a field with his daughter who was cutting grass, and the translator offered to help them with the work while they listened to the stories of Jesus. After listening, the man replied,

> "I know the Quran very well, and we have never been told about *Issa* very much at all. This is very great, especially in the language that we can understand. I can't refuse listening to this because it is in my mother language.

"We have been told that the Christians have changed the Bible and we always fear hearing what they have to say. But here [in Luke 1:1-4], it says that it was written carefully. I felt like my heart is melting, the stories themselves sound very powerful. I felt satisfied in my heart while hearing it. I normally hated talking with Christians, but this message is different.

"How come they never told us about *Issa* in the mosque? Why were we forbidden to hear these stories? We need to know these stories. I can feel my heart being excited about the stories that I will be hearing in the future. I want to hear more about the child that was born in the barn. Even though we will never be like you, we would like to listen to these stories and decide for ourselves."

This case study surveys how Spoken's approach of incarnational mentoring has played out in one local project. The same principles applied in different cultural contexts have taken many different shapes. Team sizes, financial investments, and production rates all vary widely depending on the relational dynamics at play. However, by prioritizing personal relationships over process, objectives, or training content, oral preference translation teams can be formed, trained, and guided through the translation process with minimal formal literacy requirements.

Bibliography

Eberhard, David M., Gary F. Simons, and Charles D. Fennig (eds.). *Ethnologue: Languages of the World.* Twenty-third edition. Dallas: SIL International, 2020. Accessed 30 May 2022. http://www.ethnologue.com.

Ferch, John & Enoch Wan. *Relational Leadership Development: An Ethnological Study in Inuit Contexts.* Portland: Western Academic, 2022.

Frontier Ventures. "Joshua Project." Accessed 5 October 2022. https://www.joshuaproject.net.

Harmelink, Bryan. "Questions about Questions: Exploring the Impact of Cognitive Linguistics on Testing for Translation Quality." Paper presented at Bible Translation Conference, Dallas, TX, October 2005.

SIL International. "ProgressBible Database." Accessed 23 April 2021. https://progress.bible.

Stark, John E. "What Can We Expect from Oral Bible Translation?" in *New and Old Horizons in the Orality Movement: Expanding the Firm Foundations.* Eugene: Pickwick, 2022. 151-170.

Steffen, Tom & William Bjoraker. *The Return of Oral Hermeneutics: As Good Today as it Was for the Hebrew Bible and First-Century Christianity*. Eugene: Wipf & Stock, 2020.

Thigpen, Lynn. "Deconstructing Oral Learning: The Latest Research" in *New and Old Horizons in the Orality Movement: Expanding the Firm Foundations*. Eugene: Pickwick, 2022. 15-45.

Toler, Kristofer Martin. *Internalization: A Key Ingredient in Achieving Naturalness in an Oral Translation*. M.A. product, Dallas International University, 2020.

Chapter 15:
Will You Disciple My Wife?

Tara Rye

Abstract

In this chapter, you will hear how a male leader in Southeast Asia contacted a female leader in North America to disciple his wife in Bible storytelling. Both leaders were praying for God's provision. Neither anticipated what God would do, but both knew they were seeking God's will. From those prayers, God has forged a team that encourages and strengthens each other to learn, share, and teach Bible stories so that discipleship multiplies. You will hear how an indigenous Bible translator and a North American Bible storyteller partner to spread the gospel using storytelling and stick figure drawings to help with recall. You will be encouraged in prayer, learning, practice, encouragement, accountability, strategy, and mobilization.

Why and How the Partnership Began

When I received a friend request from a man wearing a *topi*, I was intrigued. I thought, "Why would he be contacting me on social media?" Unknown to Abel,[1] I had prayed that morning asking God for a divine appointment for new disciples. Unknown to me, Abel was praying to reach his nation. God had convicted him that this would not happen unless the women were discipled. In his culture, the men and women always sit separately and never mix company except within families. It was not common for the men to share with the women what they were learning. Abel recognized that as a fourth generation Christian, women and children were not being reached because those groups were not being evangelized or discipled.

The day after I accepted his friend request, Abel wrote on one of my posts to pray for his country. I asked for the name of his country, and he shared it with me. I wrote it down in my prayer journal and started praying. That night I received a long message from Abel telling me about his people group.

---

[1] All names have been changed for security purposes.

The Joshua Project calls this people group "unreached." This means that it is less than 0.1 percent Christian.[2] There is zero percent literacy among the women, and the men have less than 2 percent literacy. Sadly, with unreached people groups, political and religious beliefs threaten to divide the family and community culturally when someone chooses to follow Jesus.[3]

Abel shared that his people typically take care of cattle and cotton crops. They do not have TVs, radios, or Wi-Fi, and the women are not allowed to use cell phones. They are truly an oral culture.

He then asked, "Will you disciple my wife?"

I found myself asking God, "God is this my person of peace? Am I to do this?"

Immediately, I heard in my heart a resounding, "Yes!"

My response was, "Here I am, LORD!"

We set up a time to meet. I knew that because of the culture and nation Abel was from, I would have to make sure that my husband was present whenever we met. For our first meeting, we met late at night for us and early morning for Abel and his wife, Senda. We introduced ourselves and chatted about what the possibilities might be for our time together. We took time to get to know each other and to pray. We discovered that because of our different lifestyles, this was not a good rhythm for our meetings. They have children and we are empty nesters.

We spent a little over two hours in that first session. One of the first things we shared with them was the "Learn, Share and Teach" infographic on how to use an audio Bible. The infographic was created by the Audio Scripture Ministries Graphic Design Storyteller, Allison Wilcox, to emphasize the process we would encourage listeners and tellers to use with their people group. The process was created by the ASM team based on my years of learning from experts in the field such as Dr. John Dent at Lifeway Publishing, Dr. Darrel Eldridge of Southwestern Baptist Theological Seminary, J.O. Terry of Journal of Bible Storying, John Walsh of Bibletelling International, Nancy Wilson of StoryRunners, Dr. Ray Neu of Spoken Worldwide, and Dr. Mark Getz of Simply the Story. The principles in this infographic would provide a basic structure for the process of using a Bible story to make disciples. Abel and Senda really liked the infographic but said that they would need it to be reversed because they read from right to left and not left to right. I had created the storyboards from my North American mindset of how we read,

_____

[2] "Mawari Bhil," *Joshua Project*, Frontier Ventures, joshuaproject.net/people_groups/16414/PK.

[3] Tara Rye, *Program Analysis: Marwari Bhil Bible Translation Project* (Dallas International University, 2021).

and not theirs. It was in this moment that I knew we were developing a safe and healthy bond because they were willing to correct me and speak their specific needs to me.

Figure 21. Learn, Share, Teach Infographic[4]

To meet their needs, we provided an infographic in reverse that also had empty text boxes so they could insert their language for the training they lead:

Figure 22. Learn, Share, Teach Infographic (Revised)

---

[4] Allison Wilcox, "Learn, Share, Teach Infographic," Talking Bibles International.

The First Training

Our first training with a group of women was on a Saturday afternoon, which meant we had to be ready to teach at seven o'clock in the morning, our time. They gathered eight women plus children in one room in their house with a male interpreter, while there were six men in the other room with a male interpreter. I was so nervous the night before because I had never discipled or trained someone from their area, and I wondered if what I would share would be beneficial in their context. I found myself repeating to myself, "Trust the story and the simplicity of the process. It is God's Word. It does not return void."

When the video call opened, they had two video call sessions going because the women and men could not be mixed. It was called a training for the women, but all the husbands were present to observe. Initially, we were not able to see the women's faces because they wore head coverings and had their bodies turned away from the screen. Babies were crying while older children were moving around the room playing. The men sat quietly in their room with little to no movement and listened in on the training.

Our goal was to tell the story at least five times during our session so that they would internalize the Bible story and be able to tell it to others. We wanted the story to become a part of their story DNA. My mentor, John Walsh of BibleTelling, reminded me often when he was training me that the power of five is a gift to the storyteller. The power of five has proven beneficial in numerous contexts. As a storyteller trainer, I have learned that patient endurance in listening to the same story over and over helps the story confidence birth inside the storyteller. The goal is to be able to internalize a story in such a way that they might be able to say, like my other mentor J.O. Terry, "It is as if I am telling about my best friends."

I typically open my training with 2 Kings 4:1-7, "The Widow's Oil." This story is relevant to me and my ministry because God used it when my university closed 2018, and I no longer had a classroom to teach my Introduction to Orality course. God put it in my heart that I am like the widow. My little jar of oil is the Bible stories that I know, and I am never to stop pouring out His stories until I have no more vessels to tell them to. My university may have closed, but what God called me to do will never end because I can always tell His story. Yet I still wondered how this story would work since they did not have the Bible translated in their native language. When I asked if anyone knew the Bible story of "The Widow's Oil," I discovered that no one knew this story and it was the first time they had heard it. The gift of a virgin storytelling moment is inspirational and motivational. It is as wonderful as the moment of salvation!

Figure 23. "The Widow's Oil" Storyboard[5]

"There was a widow who was married to a prophet of God who was devoted to God, but when he died, he had a debt..."

It was a slow process. I would say a few short sentences and then the two men would translate for the two rooms. As I told the story something beautiful began to happen. The women began to turn slowly toward the screen and allow us to see their profiles. And by the time I was done telling the story and invited one of them to retell it, they were sitting with their faces toward the screen. We were no longer looking at the back of their heads or their profiles, but their beautiful, lovely faces. I was so excited when Senda, Abel's wife who I was discipling, volunteered to be the first to tell the story. She stood up and walked right up to the screen and told the story perfectly! To my surprise, the interpreter then said, "Wait! Another lady wants to share!" Another lady stood up and walked right up to the screen so we could see her face clearly and told us the story. This happened until every single woman in the room told the story. Instead of one volunteer we had eight volunteers. They were so excited to hear the Word of God and know His story that they wanted to honor the LORD by telling it. I praised them profusely.

I wondered if I might have been a little over the top for them because I could not contain my excitement and I celebrated loudly after each one of them finished telling their story. But then Abel, Senda's husband, said, "Tara,

---

[5] Tara Rye, *Stick Figure Bible Stories*, 2021. All Stick Figure images are used with permission.

the men want to tell the story, too! They see that this is easy and want to share." We then listened as every single man told the story as well. In total, there were fourteen people that told the story that day and the interpreters had to translate it for us each time.

The story of "The Widow's Oil" was literally spoken thirty times that day! Something powerful happens when we hear God's Word over and over, even if it is in another language. Suddenly, the women's training became a community training of both men and women! Barriers fell away and hearts rejoiced in receiving the truth. Everyone told the Bible story! I was amazed as the simple seven-verse story broke down social barriers. Abel's prayers were being answered. Women were being discipled while husbands discovered they were being discipled, too. But the real test would come in whether they would go and tell others in their villages.

We taught two stories in the training that day. I told "The Widow's Oil" and my husband, Greg, told the story "Jesus Honors His Mother," which is more commonly known as "Jesus Turns Water to Wine" (John 2:1-11). The second story was chosen based on the felt need of Abel and Senda. It was determined that if we chose a story that illustrated how Jesus honored his mother, then men would begin to see the value of honoring women through communication and meeting their personal needs. The story also illustrates the importance of obedience to what Jesus asks us to do. The two servants did exactly as Jesus asked and poured water into sacred jars intended for wine. Their obedience allowed them to experience the miraculous in the moment. At first, I was concerned about introducing a story that included drinking wine in their culture, but Abel and Senda assured me that it would not cause offense and the focus would be more on the relationships rather than on the wine. Sure enough, the discussion focused more on the way Jesus honored his mother, the servants, the hosts, and the bride and groom. I was surprised to discover that no one brought up the issue of whether or not we should drink wine. This typically happens in the North American culture where I live when this story is told.

The Blessing of Simplicity

There were five villages represented that day. Some of them traveled long distances to hear the Bible story. In our follow up session with Abel and Senda, we discussed that it was important to listen to the story, tell the story, and retell the story until you know it is accurate among the group. Then it is important to challenge the group to go and tell the story to others. We suggested that when the group regathers the next week, Abel and Senda should ask how the storytelling went and to see if anyone would volunteer to tell the story. We reminded them of the infographic we had discussed previously. We emphasized the challenge to tell the story five times because that is what will cause God's story to be multiplied in the villages. Because God's Word does not return void, we can trust that when these stories go out with good follow up discussion, the group members will begin to see transformation take place.

To our delight, Abel and Senda shared that the method was so simple that it was easy to replicate in their context. It really was not necessary for their people to travel to have a video call with us. After one session they said, "We can do this! If you teach us stories, then we will gather people and tell them. We will travel to remote villages to tell them." After one lesson, we were no longer needed because the Learn, Share and Teach method is so simple. Literally, we were already seeing the power of story multiplying. Story confidence was born. Story confidence energizes organic going and sharing with others. Story confidence grows the storyteller and the community. We immediately started receiving updates of them going and sharing. They even found another people group that was hungry for more Bible stories. No one had been out to visit them and share Bible stories in a long time. They asked for Abel to find a way for a Bible translation to be made in their native language, too.

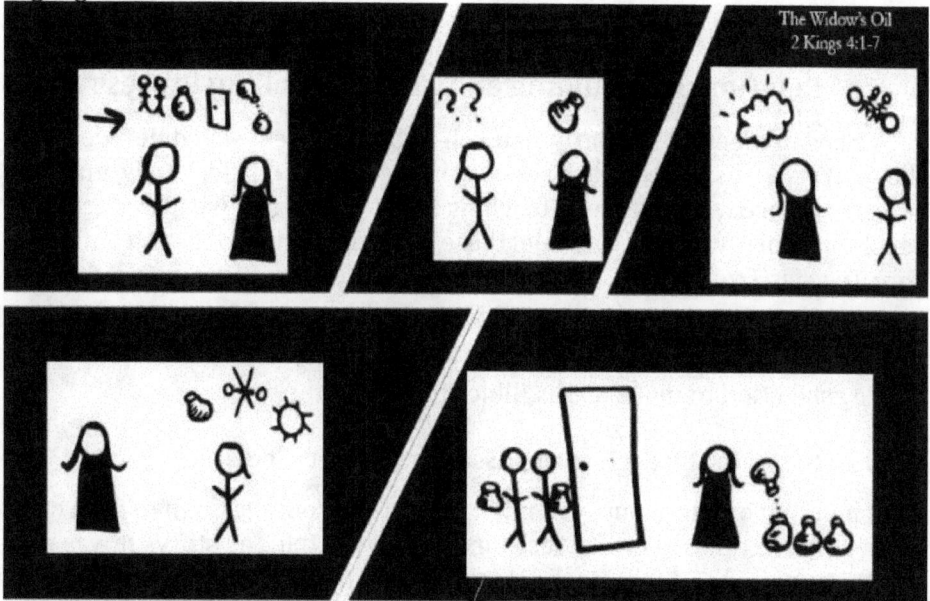

Figure 24. "The Widow's Oil" Storyboard written from right to left

In our first conversation with Abel and Senda, they shared that their people liked to use art or visual aids to help them recall the stories. When Abel found me on the internet, he noticed that I used stick figures to train people in story recall. They asked me to use the stick figure drawings with them in training and they asked if they could print them to use when they go out into their villages. These drawings are just one more tool to encourage story recall. They were not intended to be the only tool used. The main focus is on hearing and telling the story.

Every time we met, I would invite them to tell me anything that I might be doing wrong or that I might need to change in order to better serve them. I recognized that I did not know how to serve in their context, so I needed them to disciple me as well. So as I created the storyboards for each story, I would create one storyboard that would work in the North American context and then another storyboard in reverse for the Greater South Asia context. There were several incidents when they would suggest an alternative image for greater clarification, but for the most part my rudimentary drawings were acceptable to them. I also began to tell the stories using a reversed storyboard. I confess I had to make sure that I did not look at the storyboard while I told the story because it really caused me moments of confusion because it was out of order for me! I began to understand a little of their frustration and confusion with North American material.

Relationship Building and The Storytelling Process

We began meeting regularly as much as our different schedules would allow. We always started each session off by discussing life, family, and ministry before we went into a teaching focus. Each time we introduced a new Bible story, we tried to model these basic elements adapted from *Tiny Tara Teaches Truth*.[6]

Pray:

We asked God to make us His Bible storytellers.

Read or listen to the Scripture passage at least twice:

Depending on the group, you might need to encourage them to read or listen to it five times. For our sessions, we always told the story. It was rare that they would need to hear the story twice. Their gift of hearing and telling

---

[6] Tara Rye, *Tiny Tara Teaches Truth: A Story-centric Approach to Internalizing the Bible* (independently published, 2018).

never ceased to amaze me. It was humbling and challenging because I often need to hear it, see it, and use various strategies for accurate recall. The irony of this reality often causes me to pause before the LORD in amazement. Truly, we are experiencing the reality that His ways are not our ways.

Basic recall tips that use different learning styles:

At the very beginning, we discussed these methods of learning. Once we recognized that they only needed to hear and see the board, we used the storyboard division to illustrate the story division but did not create a word outline or word phrase. It was not necessary for their oral community to use the one-word outline or word phrases.

Create Story Divisions

This was modeled with each session. It was modeled both verbally and with images. We explained that it is creating a memory map in your mind of the story, like watching a movie in your mind.

Create a Storyboard

This was modeled with each session. Neither of them was comfortable in trying to create their own images for story recall. We explained that the goal is to get the listener to be the creator of the recall image so that it is culturally relevant.

Create a Word Outline for Each Division

This was only explained once in case they were to use the training in a literate setting. This was a possibility since Abel was attending seminary and met regularly with other language specialists in the region.

Create Short Word Phrase for Recall

This was only explained once in case they were to use the training in a literate setting.

How to begin and end a story:

This was explained once and modeled with each story to prevent syncretism. We emphasized this is a critical element to storytelling because we must guard the sacred oral text. We did not want to imply that any information spoken of before or after a story might be a part of the Biblical narrative.

Good beginnings might be…

- Everything in the Bible is true.
- In the Bible…

Good endings might be…

- You can learn more about Peter in Acts 1-12.
- Thank you, God for the telling of Your Word.

Share your story five times:

We pointed out that we do not add to the story, use side notes, commentary, or extra thoughts as we tell the Bible story. We simply tell the story. We reminded them of the importance of encouraging others to go and tell the Bible stories themselves. It was quite beautiful when the women realized that the God of the Bible trusted them with His Word! Abel shared that he noticed the women were more confident and less shy. The privilege of telling God's story gave them a sense of inner pride and value that was observed in their demeanor.

Group Setting

The process we used for introducing the story in a group setting is as follows. This can be adjusted from group to group and week to week based on the need.

Listen to the Story

Before we simply tell the story and allow the group to listen, we will tell them they will be asked to retell the story after. This causes a shift in the hearer. We tend to focus more when we realize that we will be asked to retell something.

Group-tell the Story

The second telling happens as we get the group engaged in telling the story back to us. Depending on the group, we may need to use questions as story prompts. It is always important that you start the story off for the group with the opening line. Consistently, groups tend to freeze the moment we invite them to tell the story back to us. So, we start by saying something like "In the Bible we are told this true story… There was a widow… ." Make sure to allow the group to finish the sentence. Only use the story prompt if the group needs it.

Tell it Incorrectly

For the third telling of the story, if a group is not willing to retell the story, then the teacher will tell the story incorrectly, so the group can correct it. This breaks down barriers and allows the hearers to know that they can correct the teacher to protect the sacred text of the Bible. This also gives people permission to become the lead storyteller. It reminds everyone that the Bible is to be told by all people and not just the person up front or with a title.

Tell a Partner

For the fourth telling invite the hearers to tell the story to a partner twice. Remind them to correct the storytelling if needed and retell to check for accuracy.

Tell the Story to the Group

For the fifth telling, invite someone to tell the story to the group. At this point, it is fun to see if someone in the group will tell the story to the whole group. If necessary, correct the storytelling and retell the story to check for accuracy. It was pure joy to see how everyone was willing to tell when we did the training. However, there might be circumstances where people are not willing to tell in a group. Encourage them that this is a safe place and that if we practice with one another then we are better equipped to tell people when it might not be safe, but very necessary to tell.

What do you do if the person tells the story inaccurately and needs to be corrected? It is always important to make sure that we do not shame a storyteller. There was one time that when Senda told the story with a few discrepancies that mattered. Instead of asking questions, I simply said, "Let me retell the story," and I did. I never corrected her, but the story did. When she retold it, she caught the discrepancies and self-corrected. After this happened, I noticed that they were more likely to ask me to retell the story if they were not as secure in their recall. A storyteller must be willing to retell the story as many times as necessary for the hearer to feel secure in communicating the story accurately.

251

Conclusion

We are now a full year and a half into our discipleship and training with Abel and Senda. Our story list comprises of thirty stories or story sets. This couple became like family to my husband and me. We cannot wait for our video calls and regularly the children are brought into the calls. One time, we carried the computer down to my parent's living area and the children sang, "Happy Birthday to Grandma!" We pray for each other often and message each other almost weekly, if not daily. Honestly, Abel and Senda do not need us, but we encourage one another and hold each other accountable in our walk with the LORD and in making disciples. God has used this unlikely partnership to make us all better disciple makers.

Somehow God, in His sovereign will, chose us to go to a place we never thought possible to make disciples, through video calls of all things. We use several different methods as we train, including stories, questions, art, stick figure drawing, graphs, audio recordings, video, and PowerPoint slides, and we are open to doing what is necessary to encourage one another.

Abel has been faithful in sending us messages about different women that are out telling the Bible stories. One time, he sent us a video of him standing beside a shrine while Mrs. R taught in the school attached to the shrine, teaching the story of Creation. Mrs. R proved to be a passionate storyteller that was faithful in finding ways to go and tell. A year or so after we started the training, Mrs. R's husband was relocated to another city because of a job. We reminded Abel that she was a faithful storyteller and that she will now take it to an even further village that would have heard if she did not move and go there. They have now reported that there are thirty new believers in their area. Abel and Senda will travel there to baptize them.

Abel provided a generational list of the women storytellers that have been trained through their ministry. These are the names they know and have recorded. It is beautiful to watch.

GSA Generational List of Women Storytellers

Trainer	Tara Rve						
Trainer	Senda* (First training March 6, 2021)						
Trainer	Ra	Ki	Ja	Sa	Ma	Sa	Su
Learner (Some of them became a trainer, see below)	1. Su 2. Po 3. Sa 4. Mrs. A 5. 17 schoolgirls 6. 21 schoolboys 7. 7 women in different villages	1. 28 women in 4 different villages	1. Jh 2. Ku 3. Si 4. Ma 5. Ta 6. Ma	1. So 2. Sa 3. Li 4. Mu	1. Ma 2. Ze 3. Ru 4. Ma 5. Mrs. Ro 6. 8 House children	1. Dh 2. Sa 3. Ja 4. Pa 5. Sa	1. Fa 2. Na 3. Ba 4. Sa 5. Ja 6. Mu 7. Sh 8. Fa 9. Ku 10. Wa 11. Ru
Info	GSA people Women of rural area Age between 18-45	GSA people Women of remote area Age between 18-50	GSA people Women of rural area Age between 18-50	GSA people Women of rural area Age between 16-55	GSA people Women of urban area Age between 25-50	GSA people Women of rural area Age between 25-55	GSA people Women of remote area Age between 18-50
Trainer			Ku	So	Ri	Pa	
Learner (Rural children, Age between 4-14 Years)			1. Su 2. Sa 3. As 4. Ai 5. Ni 6. Ko 7. Sa	1. Sa 2. Ki 3. Ro 4. Ru 5. Mu	1. 55 children in 5 different villages	1. An 2. Sh 3. Sh 4. Ki 5. Ka 6. Su 7. Sa 8. De 9. Ro 10. Ma 11. Ri	

*ALL NAMES changed for security. 7/19/22

Figure 25. Greater South Asia Generational List of Women Storytellers

Abel said, "Often it takes five to ten years to reach someone with a Hindu background, but we discovered that with the women it is easier through the women. We men are not as effective with reaching the women." God is answering his humble prayer to reach His nation. Abel heard God say to his heart, "You will not reach the nation if you do not reach the women!" Thank God for a man that was willing to lift up his wife so that his nation may hear.

> "How, then, can they call on the one they have not believed in? And how can they believe in the one whom they have not heard? And how can they hear without someone preaching to them? And how can anyone preach unless they are sent? As it is written: "How beautiful are the feet of those who bring good news!" (Romans 10:14-15)

Senda recently taught herself the entire story of the Flood, and she has trained leaders to tell the story. They are out telling it now in a region that is wrecked with floods. Abel sent a recording recently of Mrs. S telling the story of the Flood. She is from the unreached people group Abel and Senda discovered in their travels. Mrs. S and her people have no Bible and will only hear if someone tells them. The simplicity of "Learn, Share, and Teach" replicates easily. Just like Mrs. S, Mrs. R is now storytelling in her region and Mrs. K is telling in hers. Senda is a trainer's trainer and is building the kingdom through the women of this region telling Bible stories. All to the glory and praise of God!

Bibliography

Frontier Ventures. "Marwari Bhil." *Joshua Project.* https://joshuaproject.net/people_groups/16414/PK.

Rye, Tara. *Program Analysis: Marwari Bhil Bible Translation Project.* Dallas International University, 2021.

———. *Stick Figure Bible Stories.* Independently published, 2021.

———. *Tiny Tara Teaches Truth: A Story-centric Approach to Internalizing the Bible.* Independently published, 2018.

Conclusion: Orality in 21st Century Missiology

John G. Ferch

The contributors in this volume collectively make the case that a shift towards oral methodology is a needed correction for missiological discipleship and leadership development in the 21st century. In the latter half of the 20th century, orality (specifically, chronological Bible teaching/storying) was pioneered as a necessary and effective *evangelistic* strategy by New Tribes Mission and the International Mission Board, and subsequently embraced by organizations worldwide.[1] It became clear that people groups with no heritage of biblical knowledge or Western logic are not won to faith through propositional discourse, analytical reasoning, or systematic theology, but through narrative engagement with the gospel story. Discussing the biblical metanarrative from creation to Christ to final consummation became a preferred means of introducing those from different worldviews to Christianity.[2]

Nevertheless, orality as a *training* strategy remains largely underdeveloped. Mission agencies and denominations remain entrenched in variations of Western academia as effective means of training leaders and ministry practitioners, even among those groups originally evangelized through orality. The assumption tends to be that in order to grow into maturity and to "teach others also" (2 Timothy 2:2), a transition to literacy is necessary.

It is worth noting that both Jesus' and Paul's models for personal discipleship and leadership development presume oral methodology. In Acts 1:8, Jesus' mandate for the expansion of the Church is fundamentally *relational* and *oral*. His followers were sent not to be scholars, academics, or authors, but to be *witnesses*. Moreover, the basis for this ministry of witness was not abstract thought or study, but divine relationship with the third Person of the Trinity. In casting this same vision for the next generation in his own disciple Timothy, Paul points Timothy toward "what you have heard from me in the presence of many witnesses." Timothy had learned by listening to Paul in the context of relationship with the local community, and Paul instructs him to pass this body of truth on to third and fourth generations of believers. The source of Timothy's own strength in this endeavor? "Be strong in the grace that is in Christ Jesus" (2 Timothy 2:1). In

---

[1] Chapters 4 and 5 by Henderson and Dinkins are testament to this history.
[2] As demonstrated by Griffin in Chapter 8.

both cases, the expansion of the church is sourced in a "vertical" relationship with the Triune God that overflows into "horizontal" relationships with fellow human beings, carried along by that age-old vehicle of interpersonal relationship: oral conversation.[3]

The following reflections draw upon the arguments and observations that have been made throughout the preceding chapters, demonstrating why orality-based principles are necessary for contemporary missiological training and practice. These concluding propositions may serve as avenues for future research, but more importantly, can guide mission leaders in adapting their methodology for oral-preference leaders and disciples.

Orality capitalizes upon contemporary advances in technology.

Entirely oral transmission of the Gospel was, arguably, not possible prior to the present age. To preserve His message without corruption or change for future generations, God used the technology of literacy. Though ancient communities depended on public oral readings and group discussion to engage that truth, reading and writing were fundamental to the revelatory process. As Henderson aptly warns, without some means of anchoring truth to a form of publicly recognized and acknowledged measure (which is the Latin origin of our word "canon"), transmission of the Word of God quickly devolves into a game of Telephone, where each subsequent messenger has opportunity to introduce his or her own "spin" on the biblical message.

Guttenberg's invention of the printing press in the fifteenth century took Scripture engagement out of the public sphere of listening and group discussion and transformed it into a matter of private reading and introspective reflection. Exegesis moved out of auditoriums and discussion halls and became relegated to private offices and libraries. Technological advance fundamentally altered the way God's people interacted with His message.

Today, technologies such as YouTube, mobile phones, and portable MP3 players (which are already fading from mainstream relevance!) open the door for people to engage God's truth orally. Apart from a written "anchor" text, such avenues for engagement were impossible only one hundred years ago, and impractical even twenty-five years ago!

Henderson warns about the insufficiency of human memory alone to safeguard the Word of God against corruption or redaction.[4] His arguments

---

[3] Refer to chapter 9 for further discussion of this "Paradigm of Relational Interactionism" and its implications for the gospel.

[4] See chapter 4.

are well-taken. Thankfully, with the advent of modern audio recording and playback devices, the written word is no longer the only way to accurately preserve a message for future generations. Such technological advances have allowed the field of Oral Bible Translation to emerge. Today, God's Word can be effectively translated, preserved, shared, and engaged just as accurately in audio format as in print—subject to all the same testing and validation steps that a written Bible must pass.[5]

Orality is well-suited to polycentric leadership structures.

As the church moves into the era of missions "from everywhere to everywhere," polycentric forms of leadership become essential to the task. "Top-down" hierarchies centered in a single global headquarters become ineffective and inefficient when managing a diverse array of teams around the world, each influenced in different ways by local cultural contexts, logistical realities, and strategic priorities. Under polycentric leadership structures, decision-making is moved out of the Western boardroom and onto the field. Human relationships are essential to this shift in leadership structure. In his study of the topic, Joseph Handley identifies six themes that characterize effective polycentric leadership. Of those, "Relationality" itself is one of the six, and three others, Charisma, Collaboration, and Communal, are heavily relational in nature (Entrepreneurism and Diversity are the only two that are not directly relational).[6]

Multiple contributors have made the link between orality and relationality. Miller has demonstrated the important role of relational epistemology in oral societies, Wan and Hanuk have examined the cultural role of relationship in oral Tajik communication, Montague has argued for the importance of reading the Epistles relationally when working from an oral hermeneutic framework, and Crim and myself have demonstrated the importance of relational pedagogical methods when teaching and training in oral cultures.[7] All this to reemphasize the point that relationality and orality go hand-in-hand. They are two sides of the same coin. It follows that for effective polycentric leadership structures to take root, global ministries will need to shift their priorities from programmatic entrepreneurism to oral and relational organizational values. People must take precedence over policies, faster will not always be better, and face-to-face communication that enables

---

[5] See chapter 13.
[6] Joseph Handley, *Polycentric Mission Leadership* (Oxford: Regnum, 2022).
[7] See chapters 3, 9, 11, 12, and 13, respectively.

collaborative, discussion-based decision-making will need to take precedence over written documentation.

Orality is necessary for the era of global missiological partnership.

Tom Steffen has argued that the modern missionary movement has entered its fourth major historical epoch: "the Facilitator Era."[8] In this era, the Western Church moves out of the driver's seat and allows indigenous congregations to take the wheel, so to speak. Though the missionary mandate remains the same, the role of the Western missionary is rapidly becoming that of empowering, training, and equipping—indeed, *facilitating*— global Kingdom workers as they take the baton of ministry leadership in their own contexts. More and more, the task of proclaiming God's Kingdom is undertaken through partnership between various individuals, agencies, and entities working at many different levels and with different sets of expertise, as opposed to a single monolithic, vertically integrated mission organization.

The theme of partnership in oral discipleship is highlighted by both Rye and Neu from an informal perspective, and by Armstrong from a more formal academic viewpoint. All three demonstrate how different individuals and organizations have been able to work together across cultural, denominational, and geographic barriers for greater Kingdom impact than any one of them would be able to effect individually.[9] In each case, orality was a central player in bridging these gaps and enabling effective ministry partnership. Relationship is foundational to effective partnership, and orality is the "heart language" of relationship.

Orality breaks down barriers in contexts of hostility towards the "literate" gospel.

Literate missionary approaches have left a bad taste in the mouth of certain subsections of the world's population. Qalb and Angeles discuss the "Folk Religion Orality Gap" that emerges when ministries prioritize literate approaches to discipleship in oral contexts.[10] They argue that oral approaches can effectively bridge this gap, particularly in their Muslim context of Southeast Asia. In a similar way, I have described how the Islamic Xolame of central Ethiopia, historically so resistant and hostile to the gospel

---

[8] Tom Steffen, *The Facilitator Era: Beyond Pioneer Church Multiplication* (Eugene: Wipf & Stock, 2011).

[9] See chapters 1, 10, and 14.

[10] See chapter 2.

message, have embraced Gospel of Mark when presented to them orally in their own language.[11]

Another context where we see this dynamic at work is in the North American Indigenous setting. Griffin and Miller have both discussed how literacy was abused to subjugate and subdue indigenous culture.[12] Griffin offers an Anishinaabe retelling of the gospel story as a means of helping them to engage the message from an insider cultural perspective, rather than in the trappings of Western literacy.

Orality breaks down barriers and lowers people's guard. To people who are used to engaging in discussion and processing information orally, an oral Bible will often be welcomed in the same places where a literate text will be perceived as a foreign threat. Yuk found chronological Bible storying to be effective in engaging Atheist, Buddhist, and Muslim ESL students with the Christian message.[13] In an age where many of the remaining unreached peoples of the world are actively hostile to the Christian message, the development of scripturally accurate and culturally appropriate oral methodologies for training and discipleship is of paramount importance.

Orality encourages the emergence of non-Western homiletics and liturgy.

In the age of colonial missions, Western liturgical structures were exported around the world as the assumed means by which people "do church." Even in remote African villages, people often encounter the Word of God in a large, rectangular auditorium-type structure with rows of seats arranged facing a platform at the front of the room. Homiletics is typically a one-way affair in which the Word of God is first read, and then explained or expounded upon by a preacher who can easily speak for over an hour. Worship often features the same electric guitars, electronic keyboards, and subwoofers that characterize any western megachurch—never mind the dirt floors and lack of a fog machine!

Oral discipleship methodologies allow people to encounter the Word of God not in the exported trappings of the West, but using systems and structures that are natural and comfortable vehicles for local truth. Montague's chapter on training for homiletics does much to advance this cause.[14] He challenges pastors in oral contexts to reconsider how the Word of

---

[11] See chapter 14.
[12] See chapters 4 and 8.
[13] See chapter 6.
[14] See chapter 11.

God is preached. He reminds us that the Word was experienced through group listening and oral discussion long before it was preached to a literate audience. Ray Neu pushes the envelope even further, casting the vision for an entirely oral paradigm of church planting by illiterate pastors.[15] Hanuk and Wan envision the emergence of a thoroughly Tajik liturgy centered around biblical Tajik poetry.[16]

Imagine a group of African believers gathering under a shade tree or a group of Inuit believers circled up in a community hall—both natural and culturally-relevant gathering places for community meetings—to hear and discuss the Word of God under the leadership of an experienced storytelling pastor. These are perfectly valid expressions of church life, and quite possibly much closer to the experiences of Jesus and Paul in the synagogues and house churches of the first century, where people also preferred to sit in circles and engage the Word through group discussion rather than one-way lecture (cf. Luke 4:16-30, Acts 20:7-12).

Orality enables and empowers the transition to indigenous ministry leadership.

If literacy is a requirement for Christian maturity, then the transition to indigenous church leadership in oral communities may be contingent upon a significant cultural shift that can sometimes take generations. If literacy is imposed as a requirement for the office of "elder" or "pastor," then the pool of potential church leaders is artificially skewed towards the younger generation who can attend school, learn to read, and possibly even attend seminary to develop a literate hermeneutic and homiletic. Trevor McIlwain made this same observation in the *Building on Firm Foundations* curriculum that is credited with launching the contemporary Orality Movement over forty years ago, observing that these younger men quite often tend to be weaker in the areas of moral character that are the true criteria for church leadership according to 2 Timothy 3 and Titus 1.[17] Nevertheless, contemporary missions agencies and institutions of theological education continue to insist that pastors be able to read in order to study and teach the Word of God. Ironically, this position was the central point of a promotional

---

[15] See chapter 1.

[16] See chapter 9.

[17] Trevor McIlwain, *Building on Firm Foundations: Guidelines for Evangelism & Teaching Believers*, Revised Edition (Sanford: New Tribes Mission, 2005), 68.

video produced by McIlwain's own organization, New Tribes Mission, in 2021![18]

It is certainly true that an elder must be able to teach (2 Timothy 3:2). But it does not follow that a person must read in order to teach. Stahl & Stahl have demonstrated how oral pedagogy can be combined with oral hermeneutical principles to equip indigenous ministry leaders to teach the Word of God completely orally.[19] Ray Neu and myself have discussed how Spoken Worldwide uses similar methodology train Bible translators and to mobilize entire denominational structures for oral pastoral leadership without relying on printed study resources or written documents.[20] Rye's experience, too, demonstrates how oral teaching methods have been used to train multiple generations of indigenous leaders in Southeast Asia.[21]

Orality complements the rise of Zoom in educational contexts.

For many years, distance education was an individualistic, literacy-driven exercise. Before the Internet, correspondence courses depended on the exchange of textbooks, exams, and written assignments between instructors and students via the postal service. Generally accepted best practices for online learning in higher education, including Bible colleges and seminaries, prescribed asynchronous learning activities centered around textbook reading, written assignments, and the occasional supplemental video or audio track.[22] Even in those courses employing a high degree of multimedia content, community interaction and group learning was limited to text-based Internet discussion boards built into the Learning Management System. Similar principles also informed curriculum-based models for church-based, non-academic leadership training, such as BEE and TEE.[23] These principles worked well for self-directed, independent Western learners, but left oral and relational learners at a disadvantage—a truth I quickly learned when assigned to develop a distance education-based Bible college curriculum for indigenous students living in remote Alaska Native villages![24]

---

[18] Jack Crabtree & Chris Walker, *Orality vs. Literacy* (2021; Papua New Guinea: New Tribes Mission PNG), Vimeo. https://vimeo.com/570472322.

[19] See chapter 7.

[20] See chapters 1 and 14.

[21] See chapter 14.

[22] Marjorie Vai & Kristen Sosulski, *Essentials of Online Course Design: A Standards-based Guide* (New York: Routledge, 2011); Robin M. Smith, *Conquering the Content: A Step-by-step Guide to Online Course Design* (San Francisco: Jossey-Bass, 2008).

[23] Dinkins recounts this experience with TEE in chapter 5.

[24] John Ferch & Enoch Wan, *Relational Leadership Development: An Ethnological Study in Inuit Contexts* (Portland: Western Academic, 2022).

All this changed nearly overnight when COVID closed college campuses around the world. Suddenly, every class became an online course, and in-person instructors had little opportunity to adapt their content to fit online course design standards. Arguably, such standards may have failed many traditional college students depending on synchronous learning and face-to-face interaction with an instructor. Videoconferencing technologies such as Zoom, Google Meet, and Microsoft Teams were quickly adopted to meet this need.

These were not brand-new technologies, and many colleges had already begun experimenting with live online course delivery prior to COVID.[25] Nevertheless, it was COVID that brought live, face-to-face online education into the mainstream. At Western Seminary, where I now teach on a part-time basis, intercultural courses in the doctoral programs now meet entirely online. Students and instructors meet face-to-face from around the world via Zoom for oral discussion.

Importantly, with this change in delivery methodology, the learning content itself has shifted as well. No longer must learning center around pre-recorded lecture and written materials. Even live oral lecture is falling out of favor, as instructors discover the challenge in keeping students engaged through lecture when separated by computer screens. In the "Zoom Classroom," discussion, collaboration, and group learning become paramount, facilitated by tools such as virtual whiteboards, breakout rooms, and screen sharing. For the first time, oral learners separated by great distances can easily benefit from online learning in their own native learning style. Moreover, traditional training curricula are being reshaped by oral and relational learning principles as they adopt live group teleconferencing via the Internet.

Case studies in this book have demonstrated the effectiveness of oral teaching and learning via Zoom (and similar technologies) across the spectrum of educational contexts, including formal, informal, and nonformal learning environments. From the *formal* perspective, Armstrong's chapter discussed the role of Zoom in the formation of a graduate-level program in Orality Missiology.[26] Tara Rye and Ray Neu both addressed the central role of Zoom in their *informal* oral discipleship and training programs, and Neu also mentioned the use of Zoom to deliver a more formal Old Testament Survey class.[27] My own chapter demonstrated how Spoken Worldwide has used

---

[25] Alaska Bible College, where I served as Vice President for Academic Affairs, began using Google Meet on a limited basis for distance education in 2016.

[26] See chapter 10.

[27] See chapters 1 and 14.

Zoom to train Bible translators and consultants using completely oral methodologies—a decidedly *nonformal* alternative to the traditional training paradigms used in the field of Bible translation.[28]

Zoom is here to stay. It opens the door for oral learners to learn remotely without leaving their preferred learning style behind. Moreover, it implores those institutions that are historically more literacy-based to engage oral pedagogy if they wish to use Zoom effectively.

These summary observations are but a few of the implications that can be drawn from the research represented in this volume. Taken as a whole, the case is clear: for effective missiological engagement in the 21st century, churches and ministries must engage orality as a legitimate and effective tool not only for evangelism, but also for discipleship and leadership training.

Bibliography

Ferch, John & Enoch Wan. *Relational Leadership Development: An Ethnological Study in Inuit Contexts.* Portland: Western Academic, 2022.

Handley, Joseph. *Polycentric Mission Leadership.* Oxford: Regnum, 2022.

McIlwain, Trevor. *Building on Firm Foundations: Guidelines for Evangelism & Teaching Believers.* Revised Edition. Sanford: New Tribes Mission, 2005.

Smith, Robin M. *Conquering the Content: A Step-by-step Guide to Online Course Design.* San Francisco: Jossey-Bass, 2008.

Steffen, Tom. *The Facilitator Era: Beyond Pioneer Church Multiplication.* Eugene: Wipf & Stock, 2011.

Vai, Marjorie & Kristen Sosulski. *Essentials of Online Course Design: A Standards-based Guide.* New York: Routledge, 2011.

---

[28] See chapter 13.

About the Contributors

Jay Angeles (M.A. in Intercultural Studies, Asia Pacific Theological Seminary) and his wife have been serving in Indonesia since 2011 through pioneering student ministry, community development, and teaching missions in a local theological college. He is currently enrolled in the Asia Graduate School of Theology - Philippines Ph.D. Program in Orality. He is also director of the School for Missionary Service of the World Missions Department of the Philippine General Council of the Assemblies of God. He can be reached at angeles0813@gmail.com.

Cameron D. Armstrong, Ph.D., serves with the International Mission Board in Manila, Philippines. He is Program Director of the ThM/PhD in Orality Studies at Asia Graduate School of Theology – Philippines. Cameron and his family previously served for ten years in Bucharest, Romania.

David Crim, D.Miss., and Cindy, his wife of 46 years, returned from the mission field in the Philippines last March, where they served for more than 11 years. Prior to the Philippines, the Crims worked among Filipino people on the island of Lanai in Hawaii. David also served as a church planter in Wyoming and Missouri and worked as a curriculum editor at LifeWay Christian Resources for 7 years. In total, the Crims have been in ministry and missions for the entirety of their marriage. David earned his bachelor's degree from Oklahoma Baptist University, his Master of Divinity from Midwestern Baptist Theological Seminary, and his Doctor of Missiology from Malaysia Baptist Theological Seminary. Presently, David serves as the Program Lead for Intercultural Leadership in the Mission Point Graduate School of Ministry at Williamson College and as pastor of the Calvary Baptist Church in Petal, Mississippi. The Crims have two married daughters and four grandchildren.

Larry Dinkins finished his ThM at Dallas Theological Seminary in 1979 and then went with his wife Paula to Thailand through OMF International and began a church planting ministry with leprosy patients. In 1987 the Dinkins transitioned into a Bible teaching ministry at the Bangkok Bible College. In 1995 Larry finished classwork for a Ph.D. at Biola University, allowing him to return to Thailand to start a TEE program in North Thailand. Larry acted as a founding director of the newly formed Chiang Mai Theological Seminary in 2000 before the family evacuated Thailand in 2002 due to a diagnosis of cancer in Paula's bone marrow. After nine years of treatment, Paula's struggle with cancer ended and she went into the Lord's presence. In 2012 Larry returned to Thailand to resume his ministry of Bible teaching. Dr. Dinkins is the coordinator for both Walk Thru the Bible and Simply the Story in Thailand.

John Ferch serves as Oral Bible Translation Consultant/Trainer with Spoken Worldwide. In this role, he mentors indigenous translation teams in oral preference cultures around the world. This is an intensely relational process as translation principles are developed entirely through oral exegesis and experiential learning. Prior to joining Spoken, John served for six years at Alaska Bible College, where he learned the importance of orality while training indigenous Alaskan ministry leaders in the formal academic context. John holds a Doctor of Intercultural Studies from Western Seminary, as well as M.Div. and BA degrees from Moody Bible Institute. He lives in St. Louis, MO with his wife Katie and their three children.

Mackenzie Griffin is a Cree-Saulteaux woman from Sunchild First Nations in Alberta, Canada. She grew up off-reserve, in a small hamlet called Fort Assiniboine, an hour and half north of Edmonton, Alberta. Currently, she lives in Kelowna, British Columbia, where she completed her undergrad in Creative Writing and Cultural Studies. Now she is studying at NAIITS – an Indigenous Learning Community taking her Master of Theology. Her thesis surrounds Indigenous concepts of harmony and wholeness and the harmful language around sin within the Western church for marginalized peoples. Mackenzie is a poet and author and has published articles and chapbooks with the University of British Columbia and Faith Today.

Timothy Hanuk (a pseudonym) serves Jesus in a Central Asian country. With a US-based sending organization, he and his family have lived rurally in Central Asia for the past 20 years actively engaged in church planting ministry. These 20 years living alongside farmers, teachers, and lay-pastors in oral preference cultures, as well as studies at Western Seminary, have given insight into employing cultural patterns into Bible education. He holds an M.A. and Th.M., and is currently in the Ed.D. program at Western Seminary. He is married, with 4 children, 2 daughters-in-laws, and 2 grandchildren.

Phil Henderson was born and raised in Papua New Guinea. He became a missionary with Ethnos360 (then known as New Tribes Mission) in 2002. He is married to Elin and they have 2 children. Phil and Elin have worked among the Makhuwa-Mwinika (Moniga) people group in Mozambique since 2004. The Moniga are a Muslim people group numbering around 200,000. He spends half the year working amongst the Moniga in Bible translation, lesson development, and discipling church leaders. The other half of the year is spent travelling as the International Director of Church Development, visiting different fields, training church planting consultants, and discipling ministry leaders. For the past few years, he has been working on a Ph.D. in Intercultural Studies at Columbia International University, investigating how metanarratives are used to support religious legitimacy, with a specific focus on the Islamic metanarrative.

James Miller has been a missionary pilot in Alaska since 2012. His ministry has included church revitalization in off-the-road villages with his wife, Shannon, and five children, and he trains Native leaders alongside an Alaska Native pastor. God has used James' varied ministry and vocational experiences to shape his missiology. His experience as a pastor, Marine Corps officer and pilot, police officer, missionary, and student of missions and philosophy have helped James develop both a practical and an academic perspective on missions. He has earned a B.A. in Pastoral Studies, M.A. in Israeli Studies, and M.Div. degrees. James is a PhD candidate at the Southern Baptist Theological Seminary and is writing his dissertation, "Native Knowing, Western Knowing, and Biblical Knowing: Developing an Integrated Epistemology for Missions."

Josh Montague serves with Training Leaders International, seeking to equip global pastors with theological education and pastoral training. Josh serves as the Director of Non-Formal Training and has degrees from Michigan State University and Multnomah Biblical Seminary. He is just shy of finishing his Doctorate of Intercultural Studies from Western Seminary, focusing on expository preaching among oral learners. Josh and his wife, Mary Ann, live in the Minneapolis area and are the parents of four children. Before joining TLI, Josh pastored in Michigan and Wisconsin for 15 years. If Josh isn't teaching overseas, you'll most likely find him camped out in the woods of northern Minnesota.

Ray Neu is a graduate of Moody Bible Institute, Northwest Nazarene University and George Fox Evangelical Friends Seminary. Lifelong learning runs deep for Ray. While teaching pastors for 5 years while serving in Belize, Central America he began to apply story-based methodology. In each case, the content became much easier to receive, retain and retell. By paying attention to oral communication styles, adult learning systems and memory capacities, Ray has designed oral and visual learning systems for several global partners, which are actively used on every continent. His passion for empowering those who deserve God's Word in a way in which they can relate drives innovative approaches to creating sustainable, culturally reproducible theological training. It has also earned him the moniker of "The Story Doctor." Ray's current role is as Director of Orality Coaching at Spoken Worldwide.

Danyal Qalb (M.A. Intercultural Studies, Columbia International University) is a pseudonym. He and his wife have been serving among unreached people in the southern Philippines since 2007. He is currently enrolled in the Asia Graduate School of Theology - Philippines Ph.D. Program in Orality Studies. Danyal teaches missions at a local seminary in the Philippines, and is currently the Director of Research at the Institutes for Orality Strategies. He can be reached at email@dqalb.de.

Tara Rye, D.Ed.Min., is the Bible Engagement Director for Audio Scripture Ministries. A long time ago as a passionate teacher, she gave her students every single detail of information she would learn, but she soon discovered that many were overwhelmed and did not understand what she was teaching. At first, she thought something was wrong with her and then she thought something was wrong with her students. Tara felt frustrated and really struggled because she wanted to teach in a way her students would understand. Out of frustration and resignation one day she simply told a story. To her surprise, her students were excited and were able to recall what she taught. Tara caught the truth that a story enables people to engage the Bible and encounter Jesus so that life change happens. She began to use oral strategies in Bible studies, speaking engagements, shelters, mission trips, on the radio, and as a college professor. She is passionate about helping others to be in the Word, be with Jesus, and be transformed.

Jim and Janet Stahl have been working with the Seed Company since 2007, partnering with organizations training people to tell Bible stories in their own languages, especially those languages without a Bible. Bible storytelling creates community ownership and builds capacity within the community in local ministries, and sparks interest to translate the Bible. They have trained people from over 80 language groups in the S Pacific, SE Asia, E Asia, S Asia, Africa, and the Americas in vernacular Bible storytelling. Jim has an M.A. in linguistics from the UT-Arlington, having researched sociolinguistic issues in South and Southeast Asia. Janet has an M.A. in Bilingual and Multicultural Education from S.I.T in Brattleboro, VT. She also has a background in chemical engineering. Prior to joining the SC, Janet and Jim served in Vanuatu with SIL for 15 years.

Enoch Wan, Ph.D., is a research professor of Intercultural Studies, the Director of Doctor of Intercultural Studies & Director of Doctor of Education Program, Western Seminary, Portland, Oregon, former President of Evangelical Missiological Society.

Yiyoung Yuk is originally from South Korea and met her husband while attending Disciple Training School in Switzerland. They both completed biblical counseling training with YWAM (Youth With A Mission) in Switzerland and later served in Brazil for three months before relocating to the United States. With a passion for spreading the word of Christ to people from all over the globe, Yiyoung served in various roles in Korean churches in North Carolina while also pioneering a Chinese ministry and volunteering to lead a Bible Storying group for international students and their spouses at Southeastern Baptist Theological Seminary for over four years. She holds a B.A. in English Literature and English Education from Dongduk Women's University in Seoul, South Korea. She also obtained an M.Div from Southeastern Baptist Theological Seminary and earned an Ed.D. from the same institution with a focus on ESL/Bible education. Yiyoung developed and illustrated a curriculum called "Chronological Bible Storying for ESL Learners" and focuses on teaching English through Bible stories from the Old Testament to the New Testament while emphasizing theology and English proficiency. Currently, she teaches at Emmaus Bible College. She is a K-12 ESL education director in teacher education program. Additionally, she leads a Bridge ESL ministry with Emmaus Bible College students, sharing the gospel wherever God leads her.

www.ingramcontent.com/pod-product-compliance
Lightning Source LLC
LaVergne TN
LVHW052017080426
835513LV00018B/2063